Stories to Be Told

March 2020
To Dick & Ellyn,
Thanks for making lots
of happy family memories
with the Wrenns
Marie

Stories to Be Told

Tales about the pioneer people and places in little Santa Clara River valley, Southern California

Marie Wren

Fillmore/Piru, California, history with a few
Oklahoma yarns thrown in for good measure

Library of Congress Control Number:		2020903139
ISBN:	Hardcover	978-1-7960-8829-8
	Softcover	978-1-7960-8831-1
	eBook	978-1-7960-8830-4

Print information available on the last page.

Rev. date: 02/22/2020

To order additional copies of this book, contact:
Xlibris
1-888-795-4274
www.Xlibris.com
Orders@Xlibris.com
796039

CONTENTS

INTRODUCTION

My full name is EARLE MARIE JOHNSTON WREN—Marie Wren for short! Before WWII, my husband, Eugene Wren, and I attended the same rural Oklahoma school with two rooms and about twenty-five country kids from grades 1 to 8. I graduated high school from Ardmore, Oklahoma, in 1945 and attended two years of college at Phillips University in Enid while Gene was serving his time in the army for WWII. When the war was over in 1945, we soon married, and I moved to Fillmore.

My grandparents were among the last Indian Territory pioneers, and I loved hearing their stories when we lived with them for three years when I was ten and twelve. In later years, I enjoyed hearing more details about those pioneer times and started writing my Rudd story for the family in Oklahoma. I self-published that family history in 2000 and soon needed a new project.

I started writing a weekly column for the *Fillmore Herald* and, later, the *Sespe Sun* as "Facts Fun and Fiction" and "FLY-By." This required more research and reading about our community. I am still only giving you facts, fun, and probably fiction in some of the stories; so please forgive me if you find errors. There is still so much to be put into print about churches and events and families in Fillmore and Piru. Long ago, I asked for families to send me their stories so I could use them, but few had the time or inclination to do it, so maybe I can tackle that task in the future.

I apologize to the many other churches, families, and organizations that I have not included—time just ran out on me. I still have an interest and might get the rest of our valley history on paper. It would fill a thick book as the Fillmore-Piru area has so many wonderful stories.

Each time a story is retold, it changes a bit, so I am sure you will disagree with some of the things I put into my columns—and that is okay too. They are still fun stories about the early days in our valley. I ran out of time and got old too quickly to cover everything. Now I am putting many of those columns together into this book, and I hope you will enjoy these stories about the good old days. The collections have come from a million sources, so there is no bibliography—just lots of reading, talking, and listening added to memories. My idea of a fun day is an afternoon at the Fillmore library reading old *Fillmore Heralds*. I hope you enjoy this collection.

ACKNOWLEDGMENT

These stories have been accumulating for many years from many sources. My husband, GENE WREN, often brought home new stories after his morning coffee break with other farmers and half the people who were living in Fillmore and Piru from 1950 to 2000—their stories were often repeated until one of us heard them and I put them into print. Many facts were probably fiction with the retelling or slightly changed, but they were all fun and interesting to repeat by storytelling or printing for the newspaper.

Historical info and other stories also came from many printed sources, including the following:

History of Ventura County by Sol Sheridan
This Land Was Ours by Wally Smith
As I Remember or Was Told by Claire Holley Bonar
A Family of Farmers by Ynez Haase
Old-Times' Tales of Fillmore by Edith Jarrett
An Anecdotal History of Fillmore, California, by Kenneth Fine
FILLMORE HERALD

All pictures were made available by the Fillmore Historical Museum. Martha Gentry, museum executive director, and docents Joleen Stethem and Susan Zeider helped me find the photos and sort them for this book. KSSP STUDIO, Charles Morris did the cover pictures. Ernie and Becky Morales, Julia Preciado, Michele Ybarra Gibson, and Betty Bishop also added facts for family details. My daughter, Kathryn Gavlak, came up with the title. Grandson Patrick Beekman helped me with my computer. This has truly been a family and community effort, and a special THANK YOU to everyone!

Chapter 1

HISTORY

MAP of the Mexican ranchos in Ventura County

Occasionally, adults wonder about the history of Fillmore. Once in a while, kids in school will get an assignment to learn about the place where we are living. Often I get into the mood to find out more about our town—Fillmore, Piru, Bardsdale, Grand Avenue, Sespe, and all the space in between.

In 1732, Cabrillo sailed along our coast and claimed all this area for Spain. It is my understanding that the men went on land and did a rather formal proclamation, declaring that Spain took ownership of the land and then went back to their ship and continued on their journey. Cabrillo's life was interesting, and someday perhaps, I will do more research about this part of our history.

Although Spain "claimed" this part of our nation, there were no Spanish settlers, so it was actually just vacant land with the native population of Chumash in the Ventura section and Tataviam east of Piru Creek.

By 1769, with England and Russia starting to explore these new lands, Spain decided they needed to actually take possession of it. Spanish explorer Portolá started from the San Diego area with twenty-seven soldiers, six volunteers, two priests (Crespi and Gomez), seven muleteers, fifteen Christian Indians, and two servants. Their job was to look at this new land and get ready to start colonies to hold it against other countries who might make a claim.

These sixty-four men had quite a journey ahead of them, starting from Mexico City to San Francisco. As with most exploring parties, scouts were sent out each day to find the route and a camping place for the following day. Sergeant Ortega and six or eight men were in this advance group to find good camping places with water and be sure any hostile Indians were cleared out. The Indians in Ventura County were rather placid and did not threaten these strange new men marching through their land.

If all went well, the group made about eighteen miles a day and rested every four days so both men and animals could recoup. Their route from Mexico City was later called CAMINO REAL—the King's Highway, as missions were soon established along this road. (The Spanish had already made a camino real from Mexico City into the New Mexico and Arizona sections from earlier explorations and missions.) All roads leading from Mexico City to a mission were called camino real.

Father Crespi kept a diary of their journey and listed what they saw, the Indians they encountered, and the general lay of the land. From his description, the group may have crossed from San Fernando Valley through Tapo Canyon and the Santa Susana Mountains to the Santa Clara River near Castaic/Camulos along Sepulveda Pass.

The diary for Saturday, August 12, 1769, states, "We started at three in the afternoon on this day of Santa Clara from her place, and following the same valley in the direction of west-southwest, over a road broken by arroyos and gullies formed by the floods from the mountain ridges which empty through them in the rainy season, we stopped on the bank of one of them which carried plenty of water [probably Piru Creek]. After traveling about three leagues, near the camping place we came to a village of heathen, as friendly as the preceding, and as soon as we arrived they came with their baskets of pinole and pine-nuts. Beads were given them in return. We called this village San Pedro Amoliano [near Fillmore], hoping that this saint may be patrol of these people and bring them to baptism."

Later, Fray Junípero Serra established a string of missions along the route taken by Portolá. The land from the coast to about Santa Paula became controlled by the Mission San Buenaventura, established in 1782. From Piru Creek to way over east, the land belonged to the San Fernando mission and was later called the San Francisco land grant, which became Rancho Camulos.

The missions forced the Indians to come work for them and become Christians. This split up families and generally changed the way of life enjoyed by the Chumash and Tataviam until then.

As missions were established, the Spanish government usually left a small group of soldiers to guard them, and that became the presidio. As families of the soldiers needed housing and supplies, a pueblo grew up too. Spain was encouraging settlers to live in their new land and hold it against any intruders.

The missions were sort of supported by the king of Spain, but in return as payment, he also expected them to provide hides and tallow from their cattle industry. Mission fields and gardens supplied most of the food and wine for everyone.

The king often could not, or did not, pay the soldiers and others in the government. It became common occurrence for those debts to be paid off with huge land grants. About the time Spain got the system working well, Mexico decided they would become an independent nation and did in 1821!

Sespe o San Cayetano was granted to Carlos Carrillo in 1833 from the San Buenaventura mission lands. His land was mostly on both sides of Santa Clara River between Santa Paula Creek and Piru Creek. This became Rancho Sespe as we know it. In 1839, Lieutenant Antonio del Valle received the allowable eleven leagues of land (48,000 acres) from the holdings of the San Fernando mission, where the del Valle land started. Natural barriers were often used for boundary lines. Eventually, the last 1,800 acres were called Rancho Camulos. These two Mexican land grants covered our part of the valley.

Rancho Sespe was a Mexican land grant to Carlos Carrillo in 1833. Land grants required the new owners to do several things, very similar to later homesteads in the United States. The owner was supposed to build a house, put at least five hundred head of cattle on it, and take care of things. The original Rancho Sespe ranch house was located between the old sycamore tree on Highway 126 and the river and used when they had their annual rodeo to slaughter cattle for their hides and tallow. It was never a big hacienda for the family, who lived in Santa Barbara almost fifty miles away. Later, pioneers living in the area after California became a state located remains of the old adobe house.

Eventually, Tom More bought Rancho Sespe. This is a long story since he thought he had purchased a lot more land than the courts awarded him, and he always felt cheated over that deal.

As American homesteaders flooded into the valley after the gold rush, they settled anywhere they saw water and good land and no one was living there. This caused major problems for the landowners, and Tom More did not escape the same fate. He wanted the settlers to move off his land; they wanted to stay. Water from the creek was involved, and Tom was gunned down after they set fire to his barn and he ran out to rescue his horses.

Later, the land became the property of Mr. McNab, who was eager to develop it. He laid out a town on the east side of Sespe Creek, but it was all on paper. Well, lots of ideas start that way.

Pole Creek cut through the middle of his new town, so he just relocated that creek. It flowed from Pole Canyon, where the Arundells lived, and came down the east end of Fourth Street past the big two-story house built by the Fairbanks family. The creek went southwest toward First Street, where there were two big sycamores in the yard of the big home on the corner of First and Saratoga. (These were cut down ten years ago.) Those shade trees had lots of apricots pitted under them later. The creek went on toward Kensington Street, and in the early days, a big sycamore there sheltered sheep in a pen near a small house. From there, it flowed into Sespe Creek near the railroad bridge. As you can see, it sure cut through the middle of town for Mr. McNab, so the whole creek was soon rerouted. Before it got to the end of Fourth Street, he put it into a new ditch with a ninety-degree turn and headed it straight south to the Santa Clara River. And it still flows that way. (I am still seeking a map showing this original creek, so if anyone knows where one is located, please give me a call.) One story says he changed the direction of the creek so he could use the water for irrigation, so who knows WHY; we just know he relocated the creek bed!

Once Mr. McNab got the creek out of his way, he was ready to plat his new town and look for people who wanted to live here. Southern Pacific was starting the railroad down the valley and buying rights-of-way for the tracks. When they talked to Mr. Ealy about two miles east of here, he told the railroad people, in no uncertain words, he was not selling. He had the stage stop on the top of that little hill and a good spring of water, and he was not interested in moving away from the ciénega.

So the railroad men kept going toward the west. They passed the ciénega with rising water and, occasionally, a sort of artesian water shooting out of the ground in a wet year. According to Paul Haase, the local school was located near there almost where the railroad tracks are now laid. By the time the railroad men found Mr. McNab, they also found their depot site. McNab was eager to sell and get his town started and on the map. And he did!

Once McNab knew Southern Pacific was bringing the track down the valley and they would have a depot, he was ready to develop the town all the way. He got Mulholland to lay out open channels and water lines and design the first system for water from Sespe Creek to town so every home and business could have running water. (This was the same Mulholland who was involved in the St. Francis Dam tragedy and the Los Angeles water system.)

The depot was designed and built by Harry Peyton, and that family still has descendants here. Southern Pacific named the depot FILLMORE in honor of their superintendent. The MAIN STREET ran parallel to the tracks like most towns in that day. The main cross street was CENTRAL AVENUE. The first businesses were along Main Street and the corner of Central Avenue. Peppertrees were planted along both these modern streets so horses and wagons and buggies had shade in the summertime. The Fillmore Historical Museum has a copy of the old plat map showing who bought the lots in the early days.

For a while, mail came from the Bardsdale post office that opened in 1887, but the government soon moved the post office to Fillmore, where the town was flourishing—Bardsdale was at a standstill on population. When the Santa Clara River had lots of water, it made crossing difficult to get mail. The railroad was on the north side of the river, so Fillmore got the post office.

Chinese laborers laid the rails. They had a camp for these men along the line and moved it as the rails were extended. There had been a camp near Rancho Camulos, and then it was moved to Fillmore. A few of these men stayed in Piru and Fillmore and lived here for many years. When the rails to Ventura were finished, the trains took over and started down the Santa Clara Valley in 1887—this soon signaled the end of stagecoach travel. Stops at San Martinez Grande Canyon, Camulos, and Ealy's near the ciénega were not needed. All had been stage stops sometime during the past seventy-five years.

Times were changing.

The trains from Los Angeles to Ventura and north to Santa Barbara improved transportation quickly for the county. Ventura County changed from cattle raising to mostly agriculture after the terrible drought in 1861. Most of the cattle died in those two years. The Americans arrived, and California became a state with taxes. The old rancho owners needed to prove land ownership, and this involved huge bills for lawyers and expenses to get to Santa Barbara and San Francisco courts. Most of the huge ranchos were divided into small plots and sold off to pay the Californio's debts. The new trains provided faster transportation and an easier way to ship farm products. (First generation born in California were known as Californios.)

From Fillmore, the fare to Los Angeles was $1.70; to Santa Barbara, it costs $1.65, and you could go to Ventura for $0.80 early in the 1900s. Before Fillmore had a high school, the kids rode the train to Santa Paula for $0.30 each way. Soon the Piru kids were coming to Fillmore for high school on train. Oh, the trains were great.

Southern Pacific had six freight trains daily along the line with stops in Piru and Fillmore and flag stops at Brownstone (end of Grand Avenue), Sespe, and Keith before getting to Santa Paula. It was not unusual for families to go to Los Angeles shopping, spend the night, and come home the next day. To read more about those interesting days, look at some of the early day *Fillmore Herald*s at the local library.

Southern Pacific kept passenger service on the line until the late 1930s or early in the '40s, I think. Roads had improved, more people had cars, and the speed limit was higher. As more people traveled by auto, there were fewer passengers on the trains. It was not long until the railroad started talking about getting rid of their passenger service entirely. Frank Erskine, and a group of Fillmore's finest citizens, made an appointment in Los Angeles to try and persuade SP to continue the service. They made an appointment with the highest official of the railroad available and went to make their appeal. After they made their speeches, the rail man asked them, "How did you gentlemen come to Los Angeles today?" Of course, they had driven the sixty miles from Fillmore to the Southern Pacific office and had no good answer to his question. Yes, Fillmore soon lost the passenger service.

The trains brought more settlers into our area and a need for good mail service. When Bardsdale got a head start on their subdivisions, their post office opened on May 18, 1876, with Surdam as postmaster. By 1897, William Dorman was the postmaster. Their tiny building was located between the church and the current LeBard property. It now sits at the Fillmore Historical Museum to remind each of us about the mail service before the turn of the century.

Elbert Turner was the first postmaster when the Fillmore post office opened October 24, 1887, and he just used a box for the mail.

The Sespe post office did not start operations until March 23, 1894, for those fifty families near the brownstone spur. When mining for Sespe brownstone rock started, those boulders were hauled down the canyon and shipped across the country by rail. That all took manpower, and those families also needed mail. Lee Phillips became the postmaster in 1908 and held that position for the next twenty-four years. When that little post office closed in 1932, the Sespe mail was transferred to Fillmore.

In 1887, Fillmore had a Southern Pacific depot, and there were four buildings along Main Street. One of these buildings was a rooming house run by the Turners. When the telephone came to Fillmore in 1892, the depot was number 1 for the operator. Christmas 1887 saw the arrival of Judge Elkins and his family. He built a two-story building on the northeast corner of Main Street and Central and opened a store on the ground floor with living quarters for his family upstairs. It wasn't long until Fillmore really started to grow.

When Richard Stevens arrived, he built a grocery store just across on the other side of Center. You can still see the original tile entry of that establishment. Other early pioneers were S. A. Guiberson, the Wileman family, George Barnes, and C. A. Harmonson. The Arundells and Hawthorns came to town about the same time. George Barnes opened a theater to show silent movies that were very popular. Often he had piano music played during the film but also used a large music box to accompany the action. If you visit the Fillmore Historical Museum, they will show you this music box. The Harmonson family was well-known for their musical ability, and several played instruments for an orchestra. The early citizens knew how to entertain themselves, and all loved music, which was mostly a do-yourself form of entertainment.

The northeast corner of Central and Sespe Avenue had a big oak tree on it while waiting for development. Many community band concerts were held there before the Masonic temple was constructed on the site.

Lots of families took a picnic lunch with them after church on Sunday and went to swim at Swallows Nest on Sespe. It was the perfect way to cool off when Fillmore had a hot spell. Most of the men enjoyed hunting in the back country. Some even had permanent deer camps they packed to in the fall and stayed a week at a time.

The trout fishing was legendary. Locals knew they could get a limit at that big hole near Jap Creek just before Sespe joined Santa Clara. One old-timer told me he often caught fifty in an afternoon. Fishermen from Los Angeles flooded Fillmore for the May 1 opening of trout season. They almost needed a reservation to stand on a rock. Local men and boys were not to be outdone, so schools and many businesses closed in town so they could all GO FISHING. Yes, Sespe had quite a reputation for fishing.

Everyone enjoyed going to Barnes Theater for a silent movie if it wasn't too hot (before air-conditioning). The skating rink in a vacant store building was just what they wanted for a change too. The school always had a play to do, and everyone participated in something for the May Festival. Where could the younger girls wear their mothers' latest creation if they did not wind the Maypole?

Fourth of July was celebrated under the oaks at Kenney Grove. Often they ran a train from town to the picnic site to shorten the walk. They had games and beer and lots of patriotic speeches all day. By the next weekend, they were ready to go to the dance held in the ballroom over the drugstore. It was a short walk down the block for ice cream at the Orange Leaf Café. Fillmore had plenty of ways to have fun when anyone had the time.

The first "crop" around here was cattle, but after the drought in 1861, things turned to agriculture. There were enough olives planted here that Fillmore had their own olive press at the end of Fillmore Street near the depot. Several families made their fortune with bees and honey of the best quality. Fields of grain were planted and did well. Every family knew their extra money would come from pitting apricots when the big orchards were harvested and the fruit dried. Picking up English walnuts gave kids work in the fall and, boy, did they hate getting that black stain on their hands after school started. As oranges became the best crop of all, the olives, apricots, and walnut orchards were turned into citrus. Fillmore had twelve packinghouses through the years, and they provided work in packing and shipping for lots of folks. Fillmore navel oranges were known throughout the United States.

Well, times change!

In less than ten years after the railroad arrived, the oil boom started in Sespe. There are still several little companies up the canyon that originated from the first wildcat oil wells. Union Oil drilled their first wells near Santa Paula and became known all over the world. The Montebello field was discovered on the Shiells's ranch along Guiberson Road on the south side of the river. Both Shiells Canyon and Calumet Canyon had oil-worker housing on both sides of the roads and even a school. (This school building is still standing on a little bluff overlooking Guiberson Road. The William Shiells Company used it as their office for many years with very few changes to the original building.) About 1911, Fillmore got their own oil refinery. All this brought more jobs to town for teamsters and oil workers during a time when the citrus orchards were being planted fast and furiously. Yes, oil and citrus went hand in hand for many years.

Fillmore was founded in 1888, and peppertrees planted for shade along Main Street and Central Avenue. Squire Tietsort planted the first ones around his house and probably encouraged using them along our main streets. By 1914, Fillmore incorporated into a real town with a mayor and city council. Sidewalks were soon planned. Old pictures show horses and wagons going down an unpaved street or tied under peppertrees. Soon the new city fathers wanted to remove the big peppertrees to make way for modern improvements and sidewalks.

Owen Miller owned and ran the Central Hotel and wanted those trees left alone. He sat on his porch with a shotgun to save the peppertrees near his business. Owen was also the local constable. Owen had access to his own moonshine so there seemed to be a slight conflict of interest with his job as constable, but he tended to duty when called. Mayor Everett Pyle sent Owen to Lockwood Valley on an official errand, and while he was gone, the trees near his hotel were cut down and the sidewalks soon completed. Later, R. A. Fremlin talked the city council into planting palm trees. (I can understand Owen's feeling since I often have been very vocal at chamber of commerce meetings when others wanted to cut down the palm trees before they became so popular. Now palms are the thing for every downtown.) Fillmore is often ahead of the curve!

Every town or community had a baseball team, and Fillmore was no exception. When there was a really wild game coming up, the town would be buzzing when supporters of the other team arrived. Jack Casner and his livery stable were kept busy on weekends. There might have been some extra one hundred rigs in town, and many of those wanted the livery stable to take care of their teams. During the week, Jack hauled gypsum from Grimes Grade to the local plaster mill near Sespe Creek on the west side of town.

Constable Owen Miller was a man with many talents. Besides his hotel, he also ran pack trains to Sespe Hot Springs for tourists who wanted to go and camp for a few days or a week. His livery stable provided many of the rigs and horses needed to keep things going around town. As times changed and transportation improved, more people in the growing Los Angeles area wanted to hunt and fish and explore Sespe. The hot springs became a real attraction for them.

In May 1927, the Sespe Development Corporation arrived in Fillmore and organized a business to install a monorail from Fillmore to the hot springs. There was a big sign (yes, the museum has a picture of it) and an official dedication, and lots of local folks bought stock to get in on the ground floor and complete this wonderful project. It made good sense to think that tourists and health seekers would come to Fillmore, take the monorail up Sespe Canyon to the hot springs, and soak in the mineral water all day or perhaps arrange for overnight accommodations in the adjacent hotel to be built near the springs. They would also have a sanitarium and lots sold for summer homes nearby. W. E. McCampbell was the local real estate agent who sold the sites. Chamber of commerce members had their names printed on the new letterhead stationery for this grandiose project. Work was started, and Fillmore was READY.

John McNab still owned some of this land, and he was right in the middle of everything. He had laid out Fillmore and wanted to promote the town further. He presided over the official dedication and celebration near the sign with the corporation representatives by his elbow. At that time, one of the speakers mentioned the monorail might even push through to San Francisco. People almost stood in line to buy stock at $100 a share to be a part of this vision. Four months later, the chamber had a meeting to get the first report on progress and how things stood. It soon became apparent that the corporation representatives were either very late for the meeting or something had happened. Those attending acknowledged none of them remembered seeing any of those men the last week or heard from any of their executives. It took a few minutes for it to sink in. Yep, Fillmore HAD BEEN HAD! Local people had bought stock in gold mines, bad oil companies, and now, the Sespe monorail with no return on their money.

The people in Fillmore had more than baseball to make them happy on weekends. Even after errands and chores were done, young people had lots of energy left, and parents were ready for some fun too.

McNab's town of Fillmore looked great on the map when he platted it, but as late as 1940, most of it was still just orchards, and the population was less than five thousand. Many of the city fathers lived in town in the middle of an orchard. They saw no reason to let perfectly good land not be used to make a living for them. Even as late as 1955, when the Los Serenos Tract was developed (from McNab-owned land), our kids walked through orchards all the way to Sespe School each day. We were really in town but out in the country. It was a safe neighborhood, and the mile of orchards gave the kids good exercise.

When citrus prices fell a few years back, many rural groves were pulled out and used for nurseries or row crops. Horses and corrals have invaded the old orchards with a few roping steers scattered around. There is very little work in the oil fields, and the refinery is gone.

Well, times change.

The town has developed all that city orchard land. Now I look forward to a drive through Bardsdale when the oranges are in full bloom, hoping to find one big orchard where I can park and just enjoy the fragrance. There is nothing like the fragrance of an orange grove in full bloom! Oh, the memories!

Do any of you remember the Fillmore airport? Probably not! Fillmore's first airfield was the Basolo alfalfa field just across the Bardsdale Bridge near the river. The Foster brothers came to town in 1919 with a surplus WWI Jenny and took people for a ride for $10 for ten minutes. You could see the whole valley and town during that open-air ride. Edith Moore Jarrett and Bill McHenry's wife were the only two women brave enough to give it a try.

After St. Francis Dam broke in 1928, some of McNab's property just east of town was covered with sand. The flood washed out the willow trees and covered everything with sand, and they were persuaded to let that acreage be used for a landing strip. It was oiled with throwaway stuff from the refinery and packed until there was a very nice and usable surface for small planes.

Don Shaw and Eddie Wileman made a glider—what fun for them! Marion McKeen was in charge of the airport and kept things going at Ventura County's first airstrip. About the time they got things really started, the Depression hit! There was no money for luxuries like flying, and soon the little airstrip was planted with citrus and flying was left to other parts of the county. (Shortly before Gerald Howard passed away, he showed me a picture he took on a short ride; it showed the town of Fillmore as seen through the lens of his little Brownie box camera. It was taken with Red Burk as pilot, and they took off from the Fillmore field.)

After WWII, a nearby area was again put to use for landings. A little building was installed for an office and a complete aircraft and engine service. At one time, they had fourteen planes there. It closed about 1949 when the county would not give them official permission for buildings and development. Basolo Field became Basolo Orchards once again. It is still Fillmore history.

1888

I seem to be drawn to the year 1888 (or within a few years of that date)! When you read about our whole country, during that time, people were really moving around, settling in new areas, and developing the country.

My own great-grandfather moved his whole family from Kentucky to southeast Colorado to homestead. The older boys and their wives were included and made that trek. They lasted about ten years. They did file homesteads, and I have those records. But a drought drove them out, and they headed back to Kentucky about 1893 with one team of horses and a wagon. They stopped to rest in Indian Territory and stayed. But they left four family members buried in unmarked graves in Colorado. Regardless of how the railroads promoted the land for homesteading, it was not a good place for dry-land farming, and few were able to survive.

In Sandra Day O'Connor's book about growing up on an isolated spread in New Mexico and Arizona, I discovered her grandfather got his start in 1880 when he moved to public lands and started the Lazy B Ranch. The Gadsden Purchase of 1853 firmly established the line between the United States and Mexico, and this no-good, desolate land was just waiting for someone to use it. H. C. Day bought small tracts of land around springs and natural water and drilled wells where needed to provide water for people and cattle. Then he put cattle on the government pasture. Twenty or thirty years later, when more people came to this area, the government determined grazing rights would go to those who had water near enough for a cow to walk to water. There were many disputes, but it was settled eventually.

The ranch was taken over by Sandra's father, who passed it down to her brother Alan to run. The next generation had no takers for the isolated lifestyle, and the property was sold in 1993. Thus ended three generations of the Day family who loved ranching, adapted to the isolation, and thought it was the best place in the world to raise a family. Times change. Sandra Day O'Connor's parent lived to see her sworn in as Supreme Court justice, and as you all know, this year she resigned from that body to spend time with her ill husband. It is quite a story if you enjoy current history.

The year of 1888 brought the Southern Pacific railroad down our own valley. Although Rancho Camulos was founded in 1839, it was a tourist attraction for the railroad after the book *Ramona* was published.

People came on the train and just took over the ranch site. Eventually, the del Valle family closed off the ranch to get rid of them. It was one thing to be hospitable; it was another thing to have tourists act like they owned the place.

Camulos planted the first seedling oranges in Ventura County and grew everything that would produce a cash crop for them. They even sold olive oil and dried chili peppers by the ton and made great wine and brandy. Peppers were planted again two years ago, so they have come full circle.

David Cook arrived in Piru in 1886 and started his own Garden of Eden on the Rancho Temescal property. He organized the town of Piru, laid out streets, built the Methodist Church, and had his own depot. It was quite a development for the little cluster of homes along Piru Creek. His many acres of fruit trees have been replanted and are now starting into full production. The remnants of his original olive orchards can be seen on the road to the dam. Many, many families in Piru can track their ancestries back to these original settlers.

Tom More's ranch house and a few shanties with a boarding house and saloon were the center of Fillmore. After Sespe Land and Water Company sold land to SP for a depot, things started to really grow. When C. C. Elkins arrived in 1887, he built a house and store to anchor the improvements. The land around town was sheep range, and Mr. Agoure had over six thousand on pasture here. The big sycamores on Kensington Drive were reported to be adjacent to one of his pens on Pole Creek. (Yes, Pole Creek used to come through town before the streambed was changed to accommodate development.) The railroad company had a gravel pit at the edge of town, and the section boss, Sam Robertson, kept over one hundred Chinese loading cars of gravel for over a year. These workers lived in a tent city nearby.

The same year, R. G. Surdam started a settlement across the river with a store and post office to accommodate the settlers on the south side of the river and the folks living in Fillmore. When the railroad came through, Surdam collected the mail sack from the train in Fillmore, took it across to Bardsdale to sort, and then often brought it back to the Fillmore people if he was going that way. Without a bridge across the Santa Clara, it was no easy task to ford the river, which had water most of the time. Quicksand was notorious, so crossing the Santa Clara was not easy.

Yes, 1888 is an interesting time. From homesteaders in Colorado, ranchers in New Mexico, and new development in our part of the state, our nation was on the move!

After Portolá

Soon after the Portolá expedition traveled down our valley, soldiers were sent to build presidios near the coast to protect Spanish claims to the land. By the time these forts were established, the missions were being built. Our end of the valley was located about halfway between Mission San Buenaventura (1782) and Mission San Fernando (1797).

Both these missions controlled huge land areas. The Buenaventura mission land extended inland almost to Piru Creek on both sides of the Santa Clara River. San Fernando mission land went from the same creek east into Castaic and to the top of Tejon Grade. Every mission impressed local Indians to Christianize and construct buildings, till the fields, and tend cattle and sheep. You cannot develop the land without lots of labor, and that was provided by the Indians, often under protest. The church thought it knew what was best for these uneducated aboriginals and insisted upon full cooperation from them. Often it was not a happy life for the Indians, but the Indians at San Buenaventura seemed to have fared better than most.

After the initial hard years, as herds of cattle and sheep grew, income became something that the priests could boast about. Spain contributed necessary items for the missions, but the majority of items needed to feed and clothe church personnel and workers were grown at home. The Indian men tended the cows and sheep and took care of making adobe bricks for constructing buildings. The women were taught to cook and weave cloth and take care of the usual household duties. Everyone worked whether they wanted to work or not.

Outlaying Indian rancherias continued to survive. Most of those were built near Santa Clara River, Piru Creek, Sespe Creek, or Lords Creek. People always seek nearby water to make life easier, and the local Indians were no exception. The Indians near Castaic and Camulos were in the Tataviam section of the country. Their tribe extended into the Antelope Valley and Tehachapi Mountains. A map by John Johnson at the Santa Barbara Museum shows rancherias at Piru, Camulos, and Castaic. Research on the family of Juan Fustero, the last local full-blood Indian, says he was born at the Camulos rancheria, where both Tataviam and Chumash people lived. This village was near Piru Creek, and both groups seemed to occupy the same overlapping territory. They got along together and shared dwelling and hunting areas.

On the west side of Piru Creek, the Ventureño Chumash group had rancherias along the Santa Clara, Sespe, Lords Creek, and all the way to the coast. Since most of the creeks ran year-round, many native people lived in the mountains too. The Portolá diary tells about the difference in shelter, but both groups lived off the land with similar habits.

When Alta California and Mexico became independent from Spain, the king no longer subsidized the missions. Mexico quickly decided to secularize the missions in 1834 and use all their wonderful land and improvements for the good of the public instead of the good of the church. Spain had granted large land holdings as Rancho Simi and Rancho Conejo in the county, but the rest of the land was up for grabs. Mexico sent in civilian administrators to close down church operations and free up land for the use of the citizens. It had been agreed with the church that half the land would go to the Indians, who now needed homes and fields to support their families after the missions were closed. The other half would go to the government of Mexico. The Indian lands would be near the mission churches, as that was where they were used to living. Guess what? It didn't happen!

Very few of the Indian families received any land. Squatters, who wanted their fields and homes near the old missions, quickly moved out the Indian families. Towns were starting to develop near the missions, and that land was valuable. Mexican citizens were not to be denied this opportunity. The Indians were pushed and shoved and soon had to live wherever they could find a spot. Some of them moved back to be near their original home rancherias.

Antonio del Valle petitioned twice for most the land that belonged to Mission San Fernando. The Mexican government awarded him title to eleven leagues of the land in 1839 (48,000 acres). Antonio died two years later before the legal work was completed. The 1,800 acres, which now comprise Rancho Camulos, were left to his son, Ygnacio del Valle. His widow and the children from this second marriage inherited the balance. The legal mess was horrendous, and eventually, all that land was divided and sold. Only Rancho Camulos remains intact with ten acres operating as a historical site, with tours to see the original abode buildings, chapel, and winery. The rest is still being farmed.

The vast area of Buenaventura mission lands between Santa Paula Creek and Piru Creek were awarded by land grant to Don Carlos Carrillo, who lived in Santa Barbara. Twice before, men in Santa Barbara had petitioned for grazing rights to the land called Sespe, but they had been denied through the efforts of Father Jose Senan at the mission. After Senan died, the new priest allowed Carrillo to put some of his cattle in the mission pastures. Four years later, at the start of secularization, six square leagues of land, known as Sespe o San Cayetano, was granted to Carrillo in 1833. Ventura County was divided into nineteen land grants within a few years. A new chapter began for our end of the Santa Clara Valley.

El Camino Real

About the time I've run out of ideas for writing this column, a friend comes to my rescue with a request or idea. This week, the request was for more about El Camino Real. When I did some research on this old road, my greatest surprise was to find that New Mexico had a camino real also! I will try to put together the story chronically.

Soon after Christopher Columbus discovered the New World in 1492, Spain invaded and conquered the Indians in Mexico and set up a capital in Tenochtitlan, or Mexico City. From there, they extended their territory north as each new silver lode was discovered. By 1535, Coronado and Vaca were exploring Arizona, New Mexico, and west Texas. In 1598, King Philip of Spain gave orders for Don Juan de Oñate to do further exploration, and he brought settlers to New Mexico. They established the first formal European town west of the Mississippi River to be the capital of the Spanish territory. The 1,500-mile trail from Mexico City to Santa Fe was known as El Camino Real de Tierra Adentro. This name was used for all main government roads in the New World colonies. By 1720, there were about thirty missions in that area connected by El Camino Real.

While Coronado and Vaca were exploring inland, Cabrillo was sailing along the Pacific Coast and checking out California from his ship. It was not until 1595 that king Philip II of Spaine sent Cermeno in a ship really looked over the land and do some mapping to lay claim. The English were getting active with exploration, and Spain did not want to lose the rights to Alta California. When the Russians started to drift south from their Alaskan foothold, King Carlos of Spain decided it was time to secure the land with presidios, missions, and pueblos.

Fray Juan Crespi was with one of the land parties traveling from the first mission in San Diego in 1769. He was along to record the journey, and his diary described all they saw. Gaspar de Portolá was the captain with Father Junípero Serra leading the group. The land groups were to be supplied along the way by two ships. The whole thing was a disaster, with huge misfortunes, starvation, and major problems. In the following fifteen years, Father Serra established nine missions between Monterrey and San Diego. San Diego was the first, and Buenaventura was the last. The padres who followed after Father Serra's death completed his work until there were twenty-one missions as far north as Sonoma.

Many of the missions were located near the coast, but a few were inland. All were connected by a trail that soon became a road for carts to haul supplies back and forth to the Spanish ships. This road connecting all the missions was called the King's Highway, El Camino Real. The most direct route from San Diego went north six hundred miles along the coast and ended at the mission at Sonoma. Side roads took travelers off the main road to the missions located more inland. Missions San Gabriel and San Fernando had a road connecting both together.

The trails between the missions gradually became roads used by most travelers. They stuck to the Royal Road to find a place for food and rest at the missions. They felt safer with other travelers on the road in this lonely country. One story says Anza and Serra once met on the trail between Pismo and Santa Barbara. Father Serra pleaded with the busy Anza to linger awhile to talk. Anza delayed his expedition a day, and he and Father Serra caught up on all the news of the continuing settlement of Alta California.

Father Crespi's diary clearly described the first journey from San Diego. You can recognize San Fernando, Castaic, Camulos, Piru, and Fillmore as they traveled to the coast in 1769. Yes, WE are on the original El Camino Real.

Camino reals crisscrossed Mexico. The one from Baja California joined the trail at the mission in San Diego and extended along our coast. As early as 1770, the mission path went through Pismo Beach to the mission in San Luis Obispo by way of Edna Valley. There is still a pristine piece of the footpath of the padres on a county road behind locked gates near Price Road. Most of El Camino Real is now known as Highway 101 or state roads. It was the beginning of our California highway system.

I have discovered El Camino Real is much more than our forty miles from Highway 5 to the coast.

Early Explorers

Most of us live our lives doing ordinary and extraordinary things along the way without realizing how we are affecting others. I am sure that Christopher Columbus dreamed of going around the world, but he only got partway when he stopped in the Caribbean and discovered the New World in 1492. He claimed this new land for the king of Spain.

Cortés came over and explored our southwest looking for gold after he had consolidated Spain's claim in Mexico. Spain started settling Mexico so they could hold that land; after all, France, England, and Russia all wanted a toehold in America too.

In 1542, Juan Rodríguez Cabrillo sailed up the Pacific coast looking over harbors and land so settlers could be brought north. He was Portuguese but sailed under the flag of Spain. He was sent by the viceroy of Mexico and had a priest on board to record all the things they found along the way. The little ship landed on Santa Cruz Island. Cabrillo died before the journey was completed, but his exploration added to the information about this part of the New World.

Sebastián Vizcaíno sailed the coast in 1602 and landed at Santa Cruz Island too. He secured information about the coastal Indians, rivers, and harbors.

Scouting the land by sea was needed, but it was also necessary to get soldiers and settlers on the land to hold Alta California. A large expedition was organized to explore by land from Mexico to Monterey and to find suitable spots for forts and missions. This Portolá expedition is the one most history students remember.

Fray Juan Crespi was part of this large group and kept a diary about all the things they saw, the condition of the land, and the Indians they met along the way. This is a portion of his report when they reached the Santa Clara Valley in the summer of 1769:

> We stopped on the bank of the arroyo, where we found a populous village in which the people lived without any cover. As soon as we arrived they gave us many baskets of different kinds of seeds and a sort of sweet preserve like little raisins, and another resembling honeycomb made of the dew, which sticks to the reed grass. It is very suitable site for a mission with much good land, many palisades, two very large arroyos of water and five large villages close together [near Castaic].
>
> Thursday, August 10. We set out at eight in the morning, following the valley west-southwest, and also the arroyo, which runs with a good stream of water, and has banks well grown with cottonwoods, live oaks and willows. The land continues good, with plenty of grass and is of large extent. After three leagues' march [about

7.2 miles] we stopped and found ourselves here without
any village. On arriving we found that the arroyo was
flowing with plenty of water, but soon observed that it
had dried up with the heat of the sun, sinking into the
sand of which it has a great deal in the large bed, which
resembles a river [between Castaic and Rancho Camulos].
This peculiarity struck us, and we observed afterwards
that other arroyos ran at night and dried up by day.

Friday, August 11. At half-past six in the morning
we set out from this arroyo following the valley. We
traveled about three leagues by the same valley, stopped
in the neighborhood of a very populous village on the
bank of another arroyo with much running water which
comes out of the mountains through a narrow canyon
and empties into this valley of Santa Clara [Piru Creek].

In the afternoon seven chiefs came to visit us with a
numerous following of Indians with bows and arrows,
but carrying the bow-strings loose, which is a sign of
peace. They brought us an abundant present of seeds,
acorns, walnuts and pine-nuts, which they spread out
before us. The chiefs offered to the commander several
necklaces of little stones, white, black, and red, whose
texture and material was similar to coral. There must
have been more than five hundred of the heathen;
the governor gave them some beads. This place is a
very suitable site for a good mission, for it has all the
requisites for it. With the sage that the heathen gave
us, a mule was loaded with a good pack; the rest was
divided among all the others.

Saturday, August 12. We started at three in the
afternoon on this day, following the same valley in
the direction of west-southwest, over a road broken
by arroyos and gullies formed by the floods from the
mountain ridges which empty through them in the rainy
season, we stopped on the bank of one of them which

carried plenty of water [Sespe Creek]. After traveling about three leagues, near the camping place we came to a village of heathen, as friendly as the preceding, and as soon as we arrived they came with their baskets of pinole and pine-nuts. Beads were given them in return.

Sunday, August 13. After we two said Mass, attended by the men, we left the place about eight in the morning through the same valley, which continues to the southwest and is now widening out. We traveled two hours during which we must have made two leagues, and stopped near a village of heathen a short distance from an arroyo which we would call at this point a river, as it is very wide and has a great deal of water running through it. The village is composed of twenty houses made of grass, in a spherical form, like a half orange, with a vent at the top by which the light enters and the smoke goes out. [Santa Paula.] It seemed to us that the bed must have a width of fifty varas of sand and about eighteen varas of running water [a vara is about thirty-one inches], very shallow and on a level with the land of this great plain, which we saw extending far to the south; indeed, it seemed to us that the level land might reach as far as the shore. In the afternoon we felt two earthquakes.

As we read this diary from 1769, we can still recognize many features of our valley that have not changed in over two hundred years—steep arroyos to carry winter rains to the river; wide, sandy stream beds; and the Piru and Sespe Creek, which used to run all year before modern man took the water for other use. Some things remain the same!

Early Days in the County

When Ventura County was formed, there were three townships. They were Ventura, Saticoy, and Hueneme. The Channel Islands were included in Hueneme Township. Fillmore and Piru were part of the Saticoy Township, so it covered a wide area.

Election precincts were Ventura, La Canada, Mountain View, Sespe, Saticoy, Pleasant Valley, San Pedro, and Hueneme. This end of the valley voted in the Sespe Precinct. The Sespe election was held at the house of F. A. Sprague, who was a judge, with J. C. Conaway. The inspector was S. M. Easley. Sprague was also justice of the peace.

In 1873, when the county was formed, the large landowners were Jose Arnaz, with 6,000 acres; Juan Camarillo, 4,055 acres; Edwards and Company, 17,000 acres; Williams and Company, 23,344 acres; T. W. More, 8,000 acres; Philadelphia and California Petroleum, 131.083 acres; and Ygnacio del Valle, 10,390 acres. This was a tax base of assessed land for the county with many small parcels thrown in for good measure. The following year, Tom More was assessed on land valued at $82,079 (Rancho Sespe) and Ygnacio del Valle (Rancho Camulos) at $57,290.

The prosperous year of 1874 saw the Bank of Ventura opening in September with a capital stock of $250,000. Shipments from the wharf included wheat, barley, corn, beans, wool, hogs, sheep, and oil. Goods were shipped for $1.50 per ton. Steamers advertised a $4.00 fare to San Diego or $3.00 to San Francisco. Yes, there was a price war between Pacific Coast Steamship Company and Pacific Mail, but locals enjoyed the rock-bottom prices for a short time.

In 1874, the voters approved of allowing liquor by an overwhelming majority. In 1898, the voters voted on an advisory proposition to make the county dry, and it barely passed—1,289 to 1,272. The supervisors were not ready to tackle that problem until 1900. They eventually passed an ordinance to make the county dry, and in 1902 the legislature passed an enabling act that the county was made entirely dry outside incorporated towns.

Santa Paula held several elections to get rid of their saloons and finally did it. Oxnard also voted on the subject and decided by an emphatic majority to retain its saloons. Ventura really couldn't make up its mind. They voted to be dry, then went wet and then voted out the saloons again. The last election to go dry was after women were given the ballot, so I guess the ladies had the final say in that matter.

By 1917, the county of Ventura was dry except for the city of Oxnard. (I have not found anything on Fillmore after it became incorporated, but it was dry before it incorporated.)

Brice Grimes was marshal in 1868. By 1914, Merton Barnes was the local justice of the peace, and John Galvin had arrived to defend those who needed legal counsel. Both J. P. Hinckley and Harold Osborne were "doctoring" in town by 1917, so the people had everything they needed.

This end of the county voted Hugh Warring supervisor in 1902 and William Shiells in 1914 and 1917. John Casner was constable. H. G. Comfort started the *Fillmore Herald* in 1907 and the *Daily Sun* in 1916. The Farm Bureau was organized in 1914 by the University of California with William Parker as the first farm advisor. The Fillmore unit had George D. Reid as director with Tom Robertson running the Bardsdale branch.

People were interested and active in community things. As transportation became easier, the east end of the Santa Clara Valley got to Ventura to participate even more. We are still at the edge of things, but we are still in the middle of county business and politics. Some things never change.

Fillmore in the early days

Genealogy: Chaffee

When I joined the Ventura County Genealogical Society, I did not realize they would be a source of information for several columns. Last month's quarterly was another good one for me. The following stuff comes from there:

Walter Chaffee came to Ventura in 1861, and the next year, he started farming on Tom More's grant near Fillmore. Later, he opened a general store in Ventura and became prominent in affairs there. The state legislature appointed him to the first board of trustees when Ventura incorporated, and he is known as the first unofficial mayor. The county of Ventura was born on March 10, 1873, when it officially separated from Santa Barbara County. (Imagine how hard it was for people in Piru and Simi to get to the courthouse located in Santa Barbara. On horseback, it was a long two-day ride. Now people fuss about having to drive their cars from Thousand Oaks to Ventura to do county business.)

During the Civil War, Walter Chaffee kept the American flag flying in front of his business. His flag was the only one south of San Jose lowered to half-mast when President Lincoln was killed. (Southern California was Confederate territory, so many were not concerned when Lincoln was assassinated.) Walter Chaffee and Thomas Arundell were charter members of the newly organized Lincoln Council of Freedom's Defenders with a chapter in Ventura in 1868.

This journal also included some good stuff about WWI. It stated that local draft boards were given broad discretion to decide deferments and exemptions—one reason to grant a deferment was having dependents. An Oxnard paper in September 1917 had several public lists. Among those deferred because of dependents included men in Piru: M. W. DeFever, Martin R. Dominguez, and A. J. Hillhoit. The Fillmore and Sespe men were Raymond de la Riva, Herbert S. Faris, Chris Firebaugh, Fred Lincoln, Charles Teeters, Ernest E. Thompson, and Edison Young. W. J. Galvin, J. J. Huddison and George Wietrick were found physically unfit. They also listed seventeen men that were leaving Ventura on the train to American Lake, Washington. Two men from this end of the county left with that group. They were Alexander Saltmarsh and Arthur W. Taylor. (I do not know anything about Alex Saltmarsh, but Art Taylor returned to Fillmore and raised a family here while practicing law. He was highly respected by everyone. They lived in the house with the big tree on the corner of Mountain View and Sespe.)

I hope I can find this kind of listing for WWII. When I do, I will pass it along to you.

Ciénega

During the summer of 1769, Fray Juan Crespi kept a diary and recorded all the things the early explorers saw as they traveled down the Santa Clara Valley. He talked about the land and Indians they met along the way. They camped near Piru Creek and must have passed the ciénega before they arrived to camp at Sespe Creek. Often Crespi spoke about the little streams that ran in the morning but soaked into the ground and disappeared before the sun went down. This diary is a very interesting read.

Ciénega is Spanish for "rising water." You will find this marshy place mentioned in many histories of our valley. It was located about two or three miles east of Fillmore, between the mountains on the north and the river. In wet years, the rising water became an artesian well that bubbled above the ground several feet high before finding its way to the Santa Clara River, but it was always a marsh.

According to Mr. Harper, an early day worker at the fish hatchery and later manager, one of his first jobs there was to keep the ditch clean and open from the artesian well to the trout breeding ponds. That water was good for raising trout, which were then planted all over the state. After a few years, the hatchery put in a well so the water could be pumped directly into the ponds, and they no longer relied upon the ciénega to provide their water. This pumping probably prevented the artesian flow, and soon the wetlands disappeared, but the groundwater was still high.

When the state decided to improve the hatchery with cement ponds instead of the old dug-out holes with wire screening at each end to connect them, they ran into a major problem. The groundwater was so high and the pressure so strong it floated the cement before it set. Now if you make a trip to the hatchery, you will see the cement ponds are set almost at ground level.

Not far from this marsh, an early day school was built and named Ciénega School. It served kids within walking distance for several years. It was not far from Mr. Ealy's stage stop and store at the top of a hill that we now call Adams Hill. This was the location Southern Pacific wanted for their depot, but Mr. Ealy was not inclined to sell, so the railroad went two miles west and made an agreement with Mr. McNab, thus the town of Fillmore was born.

The Fillmore area bordering the river, and east for several miles, still has a high groundwater level. About thirty years ago, one ranch company tiled an orchard in order to get the orange trees to grow properly. They produced little fruit when their roots were in water all the time. The tile pipes drained the groundwater away from the orchard to the river. Their orange production was vastly improved.

The very DRY Santa Clara River still has a high water table. When the Riverwalk houses were constructed, a major problem developed when they built the little dike. The contractor found getting the water table low enough to pour the footing another challenge. As Fray Crespi reported in 1769, the water disappeared during the day. It went underground, but it was still there. The hydraulics of both the seen and unseen water of the Santa Clara is very interesting. Even in drought years, irrigation wells along the Santa Clara maintain a high water table. Often it will be only fifteen to twenty feet of water.

Through the eons, sand, gravel, and dirt have washed down the creeks and arroyos to be dropped near the river channel. Our town sits on an alluvial plain. All the mountain water drains to the river one way or another. This puts water back into the underground basins for future use.

Tiling the orchards and putting in French drains for homes can usually control the water table to an acceptable level. The biggest natural problem will be liquefaction during a severe earthquake. Shallow drains will not prevent that. I hope the new home buyers are told about these possibilities. It is better to know and decide to take chances than it is to not know and have a big surprise someday. The city had a lawsuit after the Los Serenos flood when Sespe Creek decided to straighten out that big bend below the lookout and come pouring into town. They should avoid a second recurrence from bad planning. The city is responsible for making good decisions, protecting the citizens, and requiring contractors to take every precaution to protect homes. Building houses anywhere a subdivider can buy land may not be a good decision. Let's hope the little dike really works as planned.

Bardsdale

Real estate development started in California when the missions claimed immense sections of land to support their activities. When the missions were secularized by Mexico, their land was used to pay some of the Mexican soldiers after years of service. Many of them were granted up to eleven leagues of land, and the ranchos were formed. After this land became a state, the railroads wanted their share of the profits and started laying down rails for better transportation and a way to get produce to market.

Southern Pacific started talking about the railroad coming down the Santa Clara Valley, and by 1887, everyone got into the act. David Cook secured fourteen thousand acres on Piru Creek and up the canyon to start Piru. John McNab and his Sespe Land and Water Company had eyes on starting a town on the north side of the river, near Sespe Creek, where he had water rights for the future Fillmore and R. G. Surdam hoped to be ahead of all of them when he purchased a big chunk of the old Rancho Sespe property to lay out his own town on the south side of the Santa Clara River.

Surdam's new venture was called Bardsdale after Senator Bard, who was a Ventura County politician. Senator Bard was not pleased about this, but the name stuck regardless. Bardsdale was about 1,500 to 2,000 acres. This new town was marked out in ten-acre blocks, if measured from the middle of each street, and was really a great plan. Each street was named and had a good road. The map had a place for a church, a school, and businesses. It was very well done. For a time, the railroad ran cheap excursions from Los Angeles to Fillmore and brought prospective buyers in to eat barbecue, view home sites, and envision planting oranges. It was a beautiful place to live with railroad transportation near and had everything a family needed. Most of the sales were for the full ten acres with just one large house to accommodate big families. Soon the show was on the road, and Bardsdale was on the map.

The new community was strongly Methodist, and they soon built a beautiful little church to serve the people. The German Methodist Episcopal Church was firmly established. It still has a very active congregation and is the center of the small community. While many churches have dissolved in the valley in the past few years, the Bardsdale Methodist Church continues as a reminder of the way life and Sunday was celebrated so long ago.

The large school building had a tennis court and was very modern for that time. Eventually, the small school district was incorporated into the Fillmore Unified School District. After the kids were bussed to the larger schools in Fillmore, the building was sold, and it has been used for many things since then.

When Bardsdale started growing, there was a need for good mail service. Bardsdale got a head start with their development and their post office opened May 18, 1876, with Surdam as postmaster. By 1897, William Dorman was the postmaster. Their tiny building was located between the church and the current LeBard property. It now sits at the Fillmore Historical Museum to remind each of us about the mail service before the turn of the century. The postmaster went to Fillmore each day to pick up the mail for the whole area, and people then got it from the Bardsdale post office. Eventually, that got to be too much trouble for the larger population of Fillmore, and the Bardsdale post office was closed, and everything moved to a post office in Fillmore. Without a bridge across the Santa Clara River, that was a problem in the winter when it was a wet year.

With all the great planning for Bardsdale, Mr. Surdam failed to consider that the railroad was coming down the valley on the other side of the river! Yep! More people wanted to live in town near the railroad than across the river in Bardsdale, so Fillmore grew, and the new town of Bardsdale did not. Bardsdale is still mostly ten-acre blocks with one house and the ideal place for wonderful country-living.

Residents of Bardsdale still enjoy the rural ambiance as it is a great place to raise oranges and kids—just ask the descendants of several of the original families who still live there over one hundred years later.

Bardsdale Cemetery

Fillmore had their first "cemetery working" several years ago. I bet long ago, local people went to Bardsdale at least once a year to cut grass and trim around tombstones so graves could be located. In Oklahoma, we did this on Decoration Day, but I suppose in Southern California, it could have been done at any time. With the renewed interest in our cemetery, I thought you might like to know a little bit about it. I am sure you will recognize some of the names of the original shareholders.

The Bardsdale Cemetery Association was formed in Jun 1, 1895 by these shareholders:

R. F. Robertson
Mary Phillips
Robert P. Strathearn
Martin Stoll
R. J. Ealy
A. S. Strobridge
J. D. LeBard
C. C. Elkins
Edward Meser
B. S. Clayton
C. J. Michel
F. G. Hutchinson
E. Robert Dunn

The oldest grave we've been able to find is one for J. B. Randolph. Do any of my readers know anything about that family? (Please call me if you do.)

One of the earliest graves in Bardsdale was Lillian Elkins. She was the daughter of C. C. and Annie Elkins. Lillian was born April 14, 1893, and died November 2, 1895, from unknown causes. She was the baby of the family, and I have not found anyone who knows the cause of death. It seems to have been a very hush-hush situation. Perhaps it was an unfortunate accident, but even family members had no explanation when inquiry was made.

After Mr. Randolph was buried there in 1876, nearby you will find the five Stone children's graves. According to information from the Methodist Church, four of these children died within three days of each other, probably from diphtheria, in May 1878. Were these old graves just located on public ground, or were they moved to the cemetery after it was officially incorporated? We don't know, but I would sure love to find answers.

The cemetery was operated by this association until July 20, 1914, when it became the Bardsdale Cemetery District, operating under the Health and Safety Code of the state of California.

The original land was 11.20 acres and about a mile from the Bardsdale church. Another three acres were purchased about 1997 from Stewart Smithwick.

On November 3, 1981, the district appealed to the voters to approve a five-dollars-per-parcel tax to make it possible to continue operating and maintaining the cemetery. The measure was approved. At that time, the board was composed of William Dorman, Delfino Mendez, and Margaret LeBard. The campaign to get the measure passed was headed by Imogene Vest and Lloyd Emmert and one other helper that I cannot recall. They helped get out the information about the need for this parcel tax, printed out the reasons, and talked to everyone in town to get out the vote.

An endowment was started in 1985, with each burial charged one hundred dollars, and the money was put into the endowment fund with the interest used to provide everlasting maintenance of the graves.

The 1996 board was Margaret LeBard, Gene Wren, and Monty Winkler. Within a couple of years, the board was expanded to a five-member board. With frugal management, the board has been able to purchase the acreage for expansion, keep equipment well maintained, and install a sprinkler system for better irrigation.

The current board (2011) is composed of Monty Winkler, Rita Rudkin, Lynda Edmonds, Scott Lee, and Gabe Asenas. With a new manager, Doug Basolo, new ideas about maintenance and cleanup are floating around and being implemented.

Before 1932, gravesites were selected but not platted in the map book. Families just have to know where these old graves are located, so the board has a new project to find them and add to the map of the cemetery. It is slow work but has been started. Records are being put on the computer so things are going modern at Bardsdale.

This year, Sean Chandler's Eagle Scout project, Walk of Honor, was completed to honor the veterans in our area. If you wish to acknowledge someone, get your fifty dollars to Doug Basolo at the cemetery so a brick with the veteran's name can be ordered soon. I think we will see some great changes in the general appearance of the cemetery by Memorial Day in 2012. (Jay Woods sent me most of this information.)

Bears

Every couple of years, someone will report a bear in their avocado orchard or one will be hit by a car on the highway near the fish hatchery. A few years ago, they often helped themselves to honey up near Sespe or Piru Creek. These incidents always remind me of some of the stories about grizzlies in this end of the county in the 1800s.

According to Sol Sheridan, the most renowned bear hunter in Ventura County was Ramon Ortega. He was born in Santa Barbara but came to the county when he was a small boy. Much of his adult life was spent in the mountains, so he had lots of encounters with the grizzlies. Ramon was brawny, hale, and strong and unafraid to tackle any bear that came along. Of course, he also had some very close calls!

He recounted that he and another man killed forty bears in thirty-five days with just their reatas. During this time, he worked for T. Wallace More on the Sespe ranch. He used his lariat and lassoed seventy bears in five years before he owned a gun. In 1846, he rode horseback from Sespe to Santa Paula and counted 150 bears along the way. There were plenty of the bruins in this end of the valley.

Bull and bear fights were often used as local entertainment, and Ramon sometimes provided the bear. On one occasion, he lassoed the bear around the neck and his friend caught a back foot. The two vaqueros, on beautifully trained roping horses, started the long ride down the valley to deliver the bear to Ventura. Even with two ropes on the bear, it was no picnic to get that wild animal from Sespe to the coast, but they did it.

After the Civil War, Ramon bought the first six-shooter that came into the county, and he used it on bears when needed. He was also the owner of a Sharps rifle. When he took his two young sons along to visit a brother-in-law in Cuyama Valley, he carried all his artillery. One day, he and the kids were exploring a large thicket of willows not far from the Reyes's family dwelling. Ramon did not expect any problems so near the house and only carried four cartridges—one in the chamber and three extras. The brush was so dense Ramon had to part it with one hand and hold his rifle in the other. He cautioned the boys to stay close behind so they did not get lost in the tangle of willows.

Suddenly, a great grizzly came crashing through the trees. Ramon shot and missed. As he pushed the small boys to the top of a boulder and reloaded, Ramon made the shot of his life, with the muzzle of his rifle almost in the mouth of the bear. It ripped off the head. The noise awakened two more grizzlies from their rest, and they came charging. With his back against the huge boulder, Ramon waited for the first bear to get close enough he was sure he would not miss. That shot went through the heart of the bear. When the third grizzly was almost upon him, he fired again, and that one-ounce slug took the head off. This was too close for comfort for Ramon and his two small boys. Four shots and three bears was a pretty good record.

Other than Ramon, the grizzlies had few natural enemies. People were very careful and avoided all bears when possible. In the spring and summer, during the slaughter of cattle for hides and tallow, the bears and foxes did not even have to hunt. They had food just waiting for them in the killing places. The condors helped clean up the rest.

When Ramon Ortega's family built their adobe home near Ventura River, they needed lumber, and that was very scarce. He remembered an old adobe near the sycamore tree on the road at Sespe. (This was probably the Carrillo adobe built for the original land grant.) It was starting to fall down, but Ramon knew the building contained a large beam and several things the family could use in building their new house. There was no reason to let the lumber go to waste. He took a group of vaqueros to help load two ox carts, and they headed for the old house. It took them four days to make the round trip. They also took along several Indians to guard against bear attacks. Ramon's treasure from those trips was a heavy pine beam that had probably been cut and brought from San Cayetano Mountain. He salvaged all the wood he could from that old house and didn't leave anything of value for the bears.

When the Buenaventura mission was built, the Indians did the construction work. They put a stone ornament on top of the centerpiece of the fountain. It was carved in the shape of an *oso*. The Chumash made things they knew about, and the grizzly was one of them. Our state flag features a bear too. (Does that tell you something?) Yes, there were grizzlies aplenty in our valley.

Water

Before the Spanish explorers came down Santa Clara Valley, people lived along the streams. Water is essential to life, and life is better when it can easily be secured; thus, the Santa Clara River, Piru and Sespe Creeks, and Lords Creek all had villages nearby. The Tataviam and Chumash Indians welcomed the early Spanish explorers when they came down the valley and left diaries to record all the things they saw. The explorers camped near water also.

When the Mexicans petitioned the governor for land grants, every single one included good reliable sources for water. Once again, the Santa Clara River, Piru and Sespe Creeks, and Lords Creek were the centerpieces of the land grants.

As Americans followed their dreams of riches in the gold fields, they saw the possibilities of making new lives in the valley near available water—the Santa Clara River, Piru and Sespe Creeks, and Lords Creek. These streams were the most desirable places for new settlers. And those new settlers came.

Indian and Mexican families intermarried, made new homes for themselves in the adjacent area of the water source, and farmed the land, ran cattle, or started businesses. As Americans arrived, they just became a part of the community. Families were often far apart, but more clusters of homes were near the streams.

Some of the earliest American settlers were Ari Hopper and Ben Warring. Ari loved to hunt! When he found great hunting in the area just west of Piru Creek, he moved from San Jose. From 1868, he called this area his home. Hopper Creek and Hopper Mountain were part of the inheritance he left to us. Ari was not content to be alone in this new hunting paradise, so he wrote to his friend Ben Warring and invited him to come and join in the hunt.

Ben Warring and his twelve-year-old son, Hugh, soon arrived. Ben bought out a homesteader near Ari, and the Buckhorn Ranch evolved from that purchase. The Warrings are still well-known in the valley.

The last post office heading east out of the valley was Scenega (both spellings are acceptable in this area). It was about two miles east of the present site of Fillmore and was an early day stage stop. Of course, it served as the nucleus of a settlement, and eventually, you could pick up mail there. Kids attended Scenega School. Not too far from the stage stop was a real ciénega near the river. Water came to the top of the ground, similar to an artesian well. It was always wet and swampy, but the stage stop became known as the Scenega. The Americans could never spell very well, so good Spanish terms often got slight changes when they were put into print.

An 1875 directory for Ventura County showed everyone outside of Santa Paula as being in the Scenega post office delivery district. As settlements grew around Piru Creek and Sespe Creek, the people got their mail at Scenega. From Rancho Camulos to Scenega was a nice ride, but at least it was a post office for everyone.

To try and locate families in the right area, I checked census records. The 1870 census was enumerated as San Buenaventura. By finding a few names I know lived around Piru Creek, I can tell others living nearby; they were all listed by the same person, on the same day, so they were probably neighbors. Rancho Camulos's Ygnacio del Valle family had fifteen people listed; nearby was Indian Jose, a saddlemaker, and farmers Manuel Real and Santiago Dominquez. Indian Jose was the only one listed as being born here; the others were all born in Mexico. Others list occupations as sheep raiser, blacksmith, beekeeper, laborer, stockman, and station keeper.

Around Scenega and Sespe Creek, there were more Anglo names listed. Guiberson, Sprague, Lord, Edwards, and Stevens were added to Tico, Valdez, and Gomez. Many new settlers came by ship to Buenaventura and ventured inland until they found a place that suited them, so we found more Anglo families nearer the coast.

These sources of good water for home and ranch brought settlers together. Later, David C. Cook bought most of Rancho Temescal and formally laid out a town he called Piru, after the local Indians. The local settlers now had a formal name, but they were there long before Cook arrived. The town has never incorporated into a city, but their roots go back to Indian days.

When the railroad came down the valley about 1887, they needed places for train stations and wood and water for steam engines. When Mr. Ealy, the owner of the Scenega stage station, did not wish to sell to Southern Pacific, they went two miles west and found Sespe Land and Water Company eager to lay out a town, sell land for a depot, and start a new community. Actually, there were many people near Sespe, and they just fit them into this new enterprise. Two entrepreneurs were ahead of the game and took advantage of it and laid out towns around established communities, so they are credited with founding Piru and Fillmore. I guess it all depends on how you want to look at it!

Rancho Sespe

Fillmore has rubbed elbows with Rancho Sespe for many years; however, the kids and newer residents in town do not know the story of this historic Mexican land grant. As we head west toward Ventura on Highway 126, as soon as we cross Sespe Creek Bridge, we are in Rancho Sespe country. The old railroad sign for the flag stop at Keith is gone, but a large cluster of barns and outbuildings is still being used, and several dwellings can be sighted. One of the old bunkhouses has been relocated to the Fillmore museum complex in town and is a part of their museum square on Main Street. Highway 126 goes through the middle of the old ranch headquarters. However, the story starts much earlier.

The lands for Mission San Buenaventura extended from the ocean to Piru Creek, so at one time, John McNab's land, which became the Fillmore town site, was a part of the mission acreage. When Mexico decided they did not want to bother with the missions, the government started giving away the mission land in huge grants.

Carlos Antonio Carrillo lived in Santa Barbara and was appointed administrator for the Ventura mission. He had applied for a large chunk of the mission land in 1833 and was granted Rancho Sespe o San Cayetano. The land went from mountaintop to mountaintop on the north and south line. West to east. it started at the marsh of Santa Paula Creek near Mupu and extended to Piru Creek. The grant was about six and a half leagues long and three-quarters league wide, with the Santa Clara River running down the middle. A grant was similar to our American homesteads in that it required you stock it with cattle and build a dwelling. Carrillo did both.

If you read the history of Rancho Sespe written by Ynez Haase, you will learn lots of details about this old rancho. The house was adobe and built just south of the old sycamore tree on Highway 126. The pines from San Cayetano Mountain and Lords Creek provided large beams for roofing timbers. The tar seeps up Santa Paula Canyon were used for roofing material. By 1845, Carrillo had from three thousand to five thousand head of cattle, about the same number of sheep, and probably five hundred head of horses.

When Carlos Carrillo died in 1852, his estate listed about two thousand heads. His herds had diminished for some reason. A Santa Barbara attorney estimated the land should sell for at least $20,000. He said there were six sections of land with fresh water, open ranges, and fertile soil. In a few years, the unused adobe house provided building material when Ramon and Miguel Ortega removed the beams and rafters for their new house in Ventura. (The Ortega adobe is on Main Street near the Ventura River and is open for viewing.)

Josefa Carrillo, the widow of Carlos Carrillo, received most of Rancho Sespe as well as his heir. She lived about a year, and when she died, Thomas More and his brothers bought the rancho for $17,500. When the Americans took over California, many land titles had to go through the courts again. The More brothers did not get a clear title to six leagues of land that they thought they purchased. The government contended the Carrillo grant was for two leagues of land. There was a major problem over how much land Thomas More owned when his brothers dropped out of the deal.

After the gold rush of 1849, homesteaders were pouring into California and stopping on any land that caught their fancy. Later, when men built cabins on some of the land that More claimed as his, their cabins were burned, and the stock driven off. These outsiders formed the Sespe Settlers League and banded together to stay on "their" land. By 1877, the situation was getting dangerously wild. Seven of the settlers met, put on disguises, and went to More's ranch house. They set the barn on fire and waited for More to come out of the house. When More started for the barn to rescue the horses, he was gunned down and killed. The ringleader, W. A. Sprague, was sentenced to hang but only served a short sentence before he was pardoned and released. More's death brought the squatter controversy to an end, and Rancho Sespe began a new chapter.

More's wife and children inherited the rancho and the debts that went with it. There were additional family tragedies for them, but in 1888, the man holding the mortgage, Morton Hull, foreclosed and received clear title to the land. At his death seven years later, his son and daughter, Mrs. Keith Spalding, became sole owners of the 2,200-acre tract.

The days of raising cattle were long gone, and Rancho Sespe was now an agriculture ranch. Everything was done on a grand scale. Most of the land was planted with citrus, and they had their own packinghouse for processing the fruit. Worker housing was provided by the ranch with several clusters of small dwellings near the main barns. Rancho Sespe was the leading citrus operation in the state.

In the last forty years, the ranch has changed hands several times. As farming changed, the operation became very inefficient. The ranch was divided into smaller parcels and sold. The old worker houses were vacated after much protesting. Many of the workers were third generation and refused to leave although the small single-wall dwellings were unsafe. After several years, the current Rancho Sespe housing near Piru was built for agriculture workers, and the name is remembered through that housing complex

Several of the original ranch houses, a bunkhouse, and the barns can still be seen on Highway 126, but they are now rented and under new ownership. The old RANCHO SESPE is only a memory.

Sespe Township

So many little settlements from long ago are now just a memory or entirely forgotten. How many of you know that Sespe was a complete community in 1900? The *Fillmore Herald* issue on November 26, 1943, reported the last of the buildings had been dismantled and hauled away to make a chicken house for Robert Rollin on the Akers' ranch.

I guess Sespe was organized to get goods into and produce shipped from the old Rancho Sespe site when the railroad came through about 1888. There was a depot, a small Methodist Church, and a schoolhouse nearby. The last building to be torn down was the grocery store and post office. Lee Phillips was the postmaster from 1907 to 1932 and ran the grocery store for thirty years, until 1937. The redwood-frame building must have made a wonderful chicken house.

A marker for the Brownstone stop on Grand Avenue was only removed a few years ago. This stop was used for shipping Sespe brownstone from the canyon to the world market. Those stones were known everywhere. The Fillmore Historical Museum still has two brownstone columns holding up a sign at their location. Those columns were originally used to mark the door of Fillmore's first bank at the corner of Santa Clara and Central Avenue. I am so happy they have been preserved for us.

Just two miles west was the Sespe depot. Today, the two stops would seem to be very close together, but in the horse and buggy days, it was a long two miles. People living in that area found it very convenient to have a store and post office closer than Fillmore. Sespe was handy, and you didn't need to cross the creek to get to the store either.

With a train running in each direction night and morning, the Sespe depot was convenient for traveling to Santa Paula or Ventura on errands or to attend high school. If you needed to ship ag produce and oranges, the railroad was ready to take your money for doing that. A trip to Los Angeles was no simple matter from Ventura County, so it was nice to just get on the train and head to the city when it was necessary.

In 1906, Mr. Phillips delivered a load of groceries from town to the store at Sespe. The next year, he started working there. George Tighe, who sold it to the Ventura County Cooperative Association, originally owned the store. (The Association also had a store in Fillmore and one in Piru.) In 1917, Mr. Phillips enjoyed his job so much he purchased the store from the co-op and continued running it until 1937.

The Phillips family had living quarters in part of the building and did not move out until 1940. (I assume the new owners did not want to live there during those years.) After the Phillips family moved out, Mr. and Mrs. Walter Sommers lived there until the place was dismantled in 1943. No houses ever clustered around the store and post office, so once the building was torn down, there was nothing left of the town site of Sespe. It was a few years later that the school building near Seventh Street was moved or dismantled—probably about 1955, as I remember seeing it after I moved to Fillmore in 1947.

Another little community disappeared.

Sespe Overflow

The more you read, the more you learn. Recently I found my copy of the *Ventura County Historical Society Quarterly* for November 1962. (See, I told you I save GOOD stuff until I need it.) Harry Kenney wrote the whole story. His father worked land near Kenney Grove, and although he did not own the grove of oaks, it was named after him.

He wrote that the wet year of 1884 changed Sespe Creek into what we see now with a broad alluvial plain connecting to the Santa Clara River. According to him, it started raining during the night of January 28, and it rained almost steady for two weeks. The mountains were covered with snow down to the five-hundred-feet level. It was a cold rain! The last night of rain measured four inches with snow on San Cayetano Mountain.

When it turned warm, it was really warm. The snow quickly melted and added to the heavy runoff. I bet you could hear the rocks rolling down the creek then. Up to that time, the main channel of the Sespe was about 100 to 150 feet wide, from about Moe Fine's place down to where Sespe Bridge on Old Telegraph is now.

Usually, before the heavy winter rains started, they threw a rope across the Sespe to ferry over the mail when the water got too deep. The banks were about twenty-five to thirty feet high and formed a narrow channel. During the flood of 1884, it crumbled the banks down and filled up the channel to where it is now. That is the reason the Sespe overflows whenever there is high water. The overflow runs out toward the east. There was no overflow, and it never ran that way until 1884.

After the high water in 1987 and the Los Serenos flood, the ranchers above the bridge got some help from bulldozers and turned the water back into the overflow to protect their own property. Now that is usually the main channel. One of these days, we will have some heavy rains again, and Sespe River will go back to its original path to the Santa Clara. Man-made stuff only last so long!

We often look at the Santa Clara River and wonder what it looked like long ago. The center of the river is higher than the streets and new houses on the west side of Bardsdale Bridge. In the early days, before dams and houses were built along the river and creeks, the rush of water during the winter rains helped make a sort of channel down the middle of the river. It carried tons of dirt and sand to the coast. This sand kept the rocks along the coast covered, so there were more sandy beaches than we now see. In 2003, we had no way of making a channel in the river or have any control over where the water goes when it gets high. It often bounced back and forth from one side to other and took out many acres of orchards and farmland along the way.

This month, we are reading many items in the papers about the St. Francis Dam flood and all the damage it did in 1928. That flood brought huge amounts of mud and silt down the river and left the riverbed filled and very shallow. The Santa Clara has never been the same as the whole river was changed in less than five hours. Well, so much for Mother Nature, with a helping hand from Los Angeles Power and Light Company.

Telegraph

Often I think modern communication is way too much! Most people have a cell phone that seems to occupy their every waking minute. I have one but do not turn it on unless I need to make an emergency call if the car breaks down. When I am away from home, I want to be away from phone calls. I enjoy the silence when I am driving or walking. I am away from people (and the phone) because I want to be. Employers expect too much from their employees if they have to have constant, day-and-night phone calls. At the end of a regular workday, people need to be away from the job.

Last month, I found a report about Telegraph Road that goes from Santa Paula to Ventura. It runs near the railroad tracks for most of the way, from the east to the coast. The telegraph lines were used for rail communications and soon were utilized by the citizens too. It was much faster than the mail at that time. Our Fillmore Telegraph Road followed the telegraph lines down our valley for most of the way too.

Everyone used a wire for special things, from one family or business to another. For a maximum of ten words, you got a really good rate—I don't remember what it was, but seems to me it was about fifty cents. You soon learned to include basic information within the allowable ten words, for example, "Father very ill stop come quickly to see him stop love sis." It was all written without punctuation or capitals. After my mother's death, I found the old wire announcing the birth of my first baby, her first grandson, in 1949. (We could not afford a long-distance phone call.) She had carefully saved it in her book of memories.

Western Union was the company that was in charge. In the early days, when you went to their office, often located in the depot, they gave you a half sheet of yellow paper to write your name and address, the name and address of the person who should receive the message, and several lines to print out your message. They immediately sent it by Morse code over the telegraph lines to the office nearest the other address. As soon as it was received, that office printed it out, on another sheet of yellow paper, and had it personally delivered to the person and address as shown. Often the Western Union office hired a young man on a bicycle to ride "with the wind" to get that message delivered in a sealed envelope, so all correspondence was private except for the people working the lines.

The kid on the bicycle hoped for a tip to pay him for the trouble, but when the news was bad, I am sure he often did not make any extra money for his trouble. Frequently the news was about a death in the family, so a telegram was opened with dread. Often a delivery boy earned enough to pay his personal expenses and maybe help his widowed mother buy food and support younger siblings. (My mother had a cousin who dropped out of school to work as a delivery boy for Western Union.) During WWII, no one wanted the Western Union boy stopping at their house as it might be a death notice from the military.

The next step was being able to wire money from one spot to another. In an emergency, this was a big help too. Telephone calls were expensive, and often people did not have telephones. People lived far from town and banks, so one trip to the depot sufficed to send a fast message or money by Western Union.

When the telegraph wires were first strung, women were often the telegraph operators. By 1846, they were learning to operate and repair their equipment and do the job. Learning Morse code and using a telegraph key was no harder for them than it was for a man. Recently, I found a book about these women and their experiences in tiny isolated stations along the train tracks throughout the West. They kept trains on schedule, and freight sidetracked to permit a passenger train to run through—they were a very important part of the system. This was a better job than teaching or working as a domestic for most of them. (Do you know if Fillmore ever had a lady working the lines?)

Marconi invented wireless communications so messages could be sent without the telegraph lines. By the time WWII came along, messages could be automatically sent to a teletype machine that printed the messages out, and the man on the receiver did not have to learn Morse code. My husband spent several months in the South Pacific in charge of a machine on Iwo Jima and Saipan. At the end of the war, he knew before anyone else when his orders came through to head for home.

This month, Western Union shut down their offices. Now the trains are often automatically operated with electronic equipment. Everyone has a cell phone. The telegraph is no more! Well, it certainly provided a service for 170 years. Long live American inventors!

Communicating

Communicating is a basic human need and started with grunts by our ancestors almost before they were walking upright. Even today, toddlers often get frustrated when they cannot make them themselves understood by parents. It takes time and effort to get the sounds correct and easily understood in any language.

My grandmother was born in Texas long before modern communication technology. She told me about standing outside their small cabin after supper and yelling as loud as she could to a friend who lived a quarter of a mile away. Her friend would be waiting to hear her and then return the yell. Each would have preferred a modern cell phone for instant communicating, but those had not been invented. Those yells were the only way the two teens had to get in touch after chores were done as darkness descended. My grandmother had a voice that would carry a mile—well, at least a quarter of a mile—and I seem to have inherited that same volume and clarity. It serves me well in doing tours at Rancho Camulos.

By the time my mother was born in the Criner Mountains in Indian Territory, we were approaching the age of the telephone. My mother and her siblings walked about two miles around the hill to their two-room schoolhouse. A single telephone line was strung beside the road on the fence or slightly higher in the blackjack oak trees with a few low poles when necessary. The kids near the school were on the line with one phone company, and Mom's family was with another phone company. (Anyone with a little know-how ran a single phone line and got people in the area to subscribe to their service—that was a telephone company in the early part of the 1900s.) The kids figured out how to cross the lines so Mom could call her friend who lived near the schoolhouse. It didn't take the parents long to discover what had happened and fix the problem—at least they fussed at the kids and sent them out to fix the problem.

With one line for everyone to use, you listened for the old wall phone to ring with a short or a short and long or two longs or wherever combination has been assigned to your family. When anyone called, every wall phone on the line would ring, but only the family with the correct ring was supposed to answer. Mother eventually got into real trouble when she ran to answer their ring, jumped on top of her mother's wedding trunk to reach the receiver, and broke a hole in the round top trunk. Well, my mother was frequently in trouble, but it was fun while it lasted. (A few years ago, I gave that trunk to the Greater Southwest Historical Museum, and it still had the hole in the top. Three generations have laughed about that damage.)

August 15, 1899, the *Ventura Free Press* said that Fillmore was thriving and served by the Sunset Telephone and Telegraph Company. A county directory for 1914 proudly states names and numbers for 1,889 phones, and we know a few of those were in Fillmore and Piru.

Later, pioneers were able to follow the telegraph lines strung near the railroad tracks as they crossed the plains. The second group of Mormon wagon trains kept in touch with their Salt Lake headquarters about conditions along the way via telegraph at small stations in the middle of nowhere. It was a wonderful and quick way to communicate.

By the time we married in 1947 and set up housekeeping in Fillmore, the town was getting to be very modern. As soon as we could afford it, we put our name on the list to get a phone. The only thing available was a ten-party line, so it was in constant use, and you had to wait your turn. When we switched to a five-party line a year later, we felt very fortunate. A private line soon after was heaven on earth—we could use it anytime we wanted without having to wait for someone to hang up and free it for us.

The Southern Pacific depot had phone number 1 for many years. When you wanted to make a call and lifted the receiver, you waited until the operator said, "Number please." She would then connect your line to that number, and conversation could begin. I think Fillmore was the last town in Southern California to change over to the automatic phone system without an operator—eventually, even Catalina Island was changed. It made for faster service, more privacy, and was great. But it put a lot of women out of work too.

Women who did not become teachers often applied at the telephone company to become an operator. It was a good-paying job, easier than standing on your feet at the packinghouse, and eventually had benefits. And those ladies knew all the gossip in town! If you did it over phone, some operator had taken the call and knew who was calling whom and probably why, since it was easy to listen in. The job had a lot of perks.

Fillmore had a nice modern telephone office on Central Avenue that was in the brick building adjacent to the Nazarene Church. I think Charlene McGuire's mother started as an operator and worked her way up to be supervisor. Several other Fillmore ladies were operators and bosses through the years. It was a good job and assisted in communicating. People used phones for business and necessary messages.

At our house, kids were limited to phone calls about homework to a friend. Long distance was a costly item and used for emergencies only. A telephone was not for entertainment; it was for necessary use. Since our home phone was also used for our small business, our children were limited to three-minute calls. If they did not hang up when the egg timer sand had run through, I did a swift disconnect for them. With only one phone located in the kitchen, it was easy to stay in touch with what was going on and control it. (Yes, I occasionally did a quick disconnect if they talked to long. Rules were rules and needed to be followed at our house.)

I guess I don't need to tell you that phone use has changed drastically since 1950. It seems like everyone has a cell phone and can't walk down the street without using it to talk with people just two steps ahead. From watching other drivers, I doubt if any of them can drive without a phone at their ear, but it does not seem to improve their driving skills. And grocery shoppers certainly can't fill their basket without calling someone. I often wonder what people have so much to talk about.

How old-fashioned can you be! I guess I fit the bill as the oldest of the oldest. My cell phone is not turned on unless I need to make an emergency call from beside the road. When I am in the car or on a plane, it is quiet time for me. I do not want others intruding in my space for work or unnecessary conversation. I like being alone. I like talking person-to-person and reading body language and seeing the look in their eyes. I'm not sure that constant cell phone use is real communication! Well, I told you I am way behind the times.

A New County

One thing about trying to do any kind of research, you can easily get sidetracked to something else! I have a two-volume set of *The History of Ventura County* from 1917. So I thought I would bring you up-to-date about some of our early history before that time.

Most of you probably know that we were originally part of Santa Barbara County. Imagine how long it would take in a horse and buggy to get from Fillmore and Piru to the courthouse up there! When many of the local Mexican rancho owners were trying to prove title to their land after the United States took over, that is exactly what they had to do. Many thought they were lucky they did not have to go to San Francisco for ALL the meetings. With limited communication and transportation, life was very complicated.

W. D. Hobson went to Sacramento and lobbied to split the huge county into two parcels, and Ventura County was officially established January 1, 1873. It had over four hundred thousand acres, and the total valuation was estimated at almost $4 million. According to the *Signal* of February 17, 1872, the new county would contain two thousand square miles with a population of 3,500 and an assessment roll of $1.2 million—less than half of the original Santa Barbara County. There were three townships: Ventura, Saticoy, and Hueneme; three supervisors, and eight election precincts. Our end of the county was included in the Sespe election precinct. (It is my understanding that an early day polling place was the historic sycamore tree west of Fillmore.)

After the decision was made to form Ventura County, the local people asked for a few months' delay so they would have time to really get things organized. And they did! By January 1873, offices were organized, and things were ready to jump quickly and efficiently into county business. Immediately, the departments to record births, deaths, tax rolls, deeds, etc. were put into place. It worked out nicely.

The county rented offices in the rear of Spear's saloon on Palm Street for $720 a year. This location got things started. In May, bonds for $20,000 were sold to use $6,000 for a courthouse. The Catholic diocese offered three blocks of the old mission gardens as a site. Mr. Hobson did the brickwork, and T. B. Steepleton did the carpenter work. It was signed and sealed, and the building was delivered within the two-year time limit. (I have a gavel made from walnut wood that was reported to be part of the railing in the courtroom.)

These facilities were used until they bulged. By 1911, agitation began to build a larger building for the Ventura County courthouse.

Oxnard really wanted to become the county seat and offered their town square and $50,000 if they were awarded the honor. This built a fire under Ventura, and they quickly came up with $20,000 and land on the hill as a site. Two homes owned by the Blackstock family and one occupied by H. A. Giddings had to be removed to clear the land for building and get started.

The building and furnishings cost exactly $287,000. There was not a hint of any graft. Albert Martin of Los Angeles designed that courthouse, and it was the finest in California for the price. It stood on a hill at the head of the broadest street in the city leading from the sea to the downtown. It is now the city hall for Ventura, but it can still be seen from many parts of town and the train and the modern freeway. When it was built, it was a gleaming jewel set against the hill for passengers on passing steamers to see as far as fifty miles out to sea.

The structure is reinforced concrete with a facing of cream-white tile. Marble is used for floors and interior walls. That building is still impressive! It is worthwhile to wander inside just to feel the elegance and history. On my first trip to Ventura in 1947, I discovered the view from the beach, and I loved it. About ten years ago, the city of Ventura cleaned and repaired the outside so it is still a jewel. Every visitor should see the old courthouse on the hill.

The Fourth of July in 1913 also included the celebration and dedication of the new courthouse. It combined the opening of the new bridge across Ventura River and made for a very full day. No Independence Day was complete without oratory by some well-known person, and Francis Heney, a lawyer and politician of the state, did the honors in 1913. Our nation's birthday, a brand-new Ventura County courthouse, and a new bridge were all rolled into one day. Wow! You can't beat that!

Courthouse

Originally, Santa Barbara County also included all of Ventura County. When the del Valle family had legal things to sort out, it required a trip to Santa Barbara. Those sixty-five miles from Rancho Camulos were difficult and time-consuming by horseback or buggy. The road along the Rincon often ran in the surf, and during high tide, there was no road. Travelers had to wait for low tide to proceed. The stamina of your horse and the tide determined how long it took to make the trip. Regardless, all legal business had to be conducted in Santa Barbara, from recording documents to appearing in court.

In 1872, this huge area was divided, and Ventura County became a separate entity. At their first meeting, the board of supervisors voted to lease part of the Spear building at the corner of Main and Palm for office space. By May of 1873, $10,000 was available to put a building on land donated by the Roman Catholic Church. The courthouse would be located in the old mission gardens between Santa Clara and Meta Streets.

The first courthouse was built from brick, was two stories, and featured a clock tower. (The brick probably came from the brick factory in Ventura.) The jail was part of the main building. The construction contract went to W. D. Hobson. The citizens had every reason to be proud of it when it was completed. Later, a separate jail was added and the county hospital was built on the same property but faced out on Meta Street

By 1911, the bell tower was cracked and leaning over the entry. The supervisors decided it was unsafe and the building should be replaced. A bond election was called. The bonds for a bridge over the Santa Clara between Ventura and Oxnard passed, but the courthouse bonds failed. The citizens did not want to spend money on a new building. Soon it was determined that since the old building was unsafe, the supervisors had the power to build a new courthouse at its discretion. The grand jury did a thorough study and recommended the board to call for another bond election. This time it passed.

(When the old building was torn down, a piece of the railing in the court room was saved, and in 1980, Walt Taylor used a piece of it. That became the sounding block for the gavel presented to me when I finished my eight years on the unified school board. I will always treasure it as part of our past.)

The beautiful new Ventura County courthouse, at the north end of California Street, costs $287,000. It has long been the centerpiece of downtown. People going to the beach saw it, people traveling along Main Street saw it, and now tourists view it every day. For a public building, it is the most elegant piece of the past that we have in the county and well worth your time to stop and explore. The marble floors and walls and ornate hardwood banisters are beautiful. Fortunately, the city of Ventura saved it as their city hall, so it has not been demolished.

Ventura County had a terrible growth spurt a few decades back. At one time, we were the fastest growing county in the United States. The courthouse had records spilling out into every hall and closet and stacked as high as a clerk could reach. Once again, the supervisors called for a vote to build a new place for county business—not once, but twice, their bond election was turned down by the voters. But they figured out a way around the will of the people and built the large conglomerate of buildings on Victoria Avenue. Does this sound familiar?

The citizens still fuss about it, have to walk miles to get from the parking lots to a building, lose their way to any department or office, and mutter to themselves as they sort out where the jury selection will be held. But most will also admit, it sure works well, and we did need it and hope it will fulfill the county needs for a long time. (Sometimes elected officials have to do what is best, not what is popular.)

Fillmore Transportation

As the Southern Pacific surveyor traveled down the valley from Piru, he found the perfect place for another train station—one where water and wood could be taken on before the engine got the string of cars moving again. Mr. Ealy owned this hilltop (now called Adams Hill). He lived there and also ran the stage stop for a change of horses on the way to Ventura. He had a good spring of water behind the house, and he probably cut wood out of Pole Creek. Mr. Ealy had a small store for necessities and lived very comfortably. The hunting and fishing were excellent; what more could any man ask for? (In later years, Mr. Ealy would take the buggy to town to work and just head the horse toward home, give it a slap on the rump, and the horse would go back to the barn without a driver. The horse was hitched, the buggy ready, and Mrs. Ealy only needed to climb into her rig to go visit a friend later in the day.)

The railroad man noted there was a slope in each direction, so the train would have a downhill run from either direction after taking on wood and water. It was a perfect place for a train stop. The Southern Pacific representative promptly told Mr. Ealy that he had come to buy the whole property for the new railroad right-of-way.

It was soon obvious that the SP man did not know very much about Mr. Ealy. His approach was ALL WRONG! Mr. Ealy was in a position to name his own price if he wanted to sell out, but Mr. Ealy did not want to sell out. He enjoyed his setup, made a living, and enjoyed seeing the people who passed through on the stage or stopped by his little store, and he had no intention of selling. No amount of fast talking from the Southern Pacific man could persuade Mr. Ealy to sell. By the next day, the man had to admit defeat and go on down the stage road toward the west.

The SP man shortly passed a very marshy area Mr. Ealy had referred to as the ciénega. Perhaps there was an artesian well in wet years, but it was a wetland and worth nothing to the railroad. Within another mile, he slowed his horse and looked over a beautiful piece of land belonging to the Sespe Land and Water Company. They had about 3,300 acres. Most of it was in the flat before the next creek crossing, and he could see almost two miles toward the setting sun. The land the railroad needed must be near. He found this company was trying hard to start a town. They were making plat maps to subdivide a large area and sell lots. That Southern Pacific rep liked what he saw!

Well, the upshot of my tale, he bought land from Sespe Land and Water Company, the railroad company laid the track and put a depot at the corner of what is now Main Street and Central Avenue, and the town of Fillmore was born. All because of a train! (SPRR named the town after their superintendent in this area.)

Kenney Grove Park

The census for 1900 shows Cyrus and Elvira Kenney living in the Sespe area. He was sixty-six years old and came here in 1873. They lived on what is now known as the Hardison Ranch above Kenney Grove Park. His son, Harry, wrote a nice little book he called *Tales of Early Sespe Days*, and the Ventura County Historical Society published it in 1962. If I can get permission, I will get it into print again for the fun of sharing more tall tales about this end of Santa Clara Valley. In the meantime, I will repeat some of his stories for you.

Harry was twenty-three years old in 1900, so he heard many of these stories from his father while he was growing up. He remembered them and wrote them down for his little book:

> The Fourth of July was always a big event in the early days. Nearly every year they had a big picnic and barbecue in what was called "Kenney's Grove." My father never owned it, but a lot of people today think that he did. But my father always went to those who did own it and got permission to have the celebration there. My father and Mat Atmore always did all the preliminary work: hauled the water, fixed up the grounds, and put in seats for the picnic. Ari Hopper was always the man to tend to the big barbecue. He dug a big pit and roasted the meat on top. They did not cut it up into small chunks but into pieces about forty pounds. A big fire was built in the pit and kept going for about twelve hours. When the fire went down, they put the meat over the coals and roasted it. Old Ari tended to that. I tell you that was about the best meat that I ever ate.
>
> Old Ari was one of those loud talking old fellows, and when he got about two drinks of whiskey in him he sure could yell. He talked loud all the time, but at these picnics they used to get him to get up just to see how loud he could yell.

According to Harry, Ari could tell some real whoppers, too, about the bears and things that happened up Hopper Canyon. I will save those for a later time. Harry says,

> I believe it was about 1889 that they had a big Fourth of July celebration in Kenney's Grove. A special train came from Ventura and stopped right down south of the grove and let the people off. There was quite a parade and procession from Fillmore. They had a boat mounted on a wagon and had been celebrating before they left Fillmore that morning. A toy cannon was mounted on the boat and they were shooting it as they came. It was a breech-loader and had brass shells loaded with blanks. I guess the fellows shooting it were drinking a little too much because a shell got stuck, and they could not get it in the gun. Bradfield (killer of Joe Dye) took a little horseshoe hammer and tried to tap in the shell. He accidently hit the cap, and it exploded against his hand. They took him right over to Dr. Hinckley, who dressed him up. Bradfield lost three fingers, but anyway they had a big celebration and parade; and Ari Hopper barbecued five beef for the crowd.
>
> About 1908 Harry and Mr. Atmore were talking and decided it would be nice if the County would take over the grove of oaks and make a park out of it. The Sespe Land and Water Company owned the land and had priced it for $150 an acre for about twenty years, but no takers. It was worthless for oranges. When Mr. Atmore quietly approached Mr. McNab, head of Sespe Land and Water Company, about buying it, Mr. McNab needed a few days to think about it. When they went back the next day, the price of the land had suddenly inflated to $300 an acre and the local people could not raise the money. It was another 10 or 15 years before he finally sold the ten acres to the County for Kenney's Grove Park.

Many of you will remember when Kenney Grove was open to the public any time you wanted to go out. In the '50s and '60s, my husband and I often took the kids out to play or have a birthday party there. Several times in the early spring, our family took the tent and stayed overnight or just cooked our supper. It was so pretty that time of year. There was no lawn area or assigned spots to park. We'd find a pretty spot with tall spring grass and set up the camping stuff and have a great weekend near home. Usually, we could find miner's lettuce and make our own salad with a few tiny wild onions added. Pioneers had nothing on the Wrens! Being out-of-doors was the important thing for our family.

About 1963, the chamber of commerce planned a Fourth of July party out there, similar to the one Harry talked about in his little book. The barbecue was not as big, but I remember the Boy Scouts sold old-fashioned lemonade for five cents a cup (and they made several dollars from that for the troop camping fund), and Gene Wren planned kids games. Our youngest had just started school, but she found several neighborhood kids to enter the contests with her. We had tire rolling, and the little kids had lots of fun figuring out how to keep those big black tires going downhill from the starting line. (And they got as black and dirty as the tires.) Of course, we had three-leg and gunny-sack races, tug-of-war, wheelbarrow races, and all the old-time games we could think of. No one let a little dirt and heat ruin the day. Oh, what fun!

We hated it when they put in regular parking spots and planted the lawns—so much for the long-ago ways. We soon got used to having things cleaner and accepted the modernization of the park—at least we could still go out and use it. The last big improvement had been making reservations through the county, paying fees, and having to plan ahead. The park is no longer open for an impromptu cookout or late-afternoon play under the big oaks. Most of the time, it is reserved and used by people with camping trailers from out of town who love the beautiful old trees and isolation. But locals still remember the good old days at Kenney Grove.

Fishing

I guess when it was too cold for swimmin' in the Sespe, it was fishin' time.

The opening day of fishing season, May 1, was reason enough to quit any local job if the boss was obstinate enough to insist you had to work. Kennie Fine said the opening day of fishing and hunting season was an unofficial holiday for all the men around Fillmore, and it was understood before you hired on, in most cases.

Sespe Creek had a reputation all over Southern California. It was good fishing for trout and steelhead. And everyone came to check it out! Rooming houses were booked up, and you couldn't get a stool at the local cafés, so the city folks almost took over for a few days when the season opened. Kennie said it would get so crowded, "you had to take your own rock" to have a place to stand and fish.

The locals usually had a favorite fishing spot up the creek, and they packed in the day before and had a little privacy and elbow room when they wet their lines on opening day. They expected to get their limits and seldom were disappointed. If possible, these fishing holes were not divulged to outsiders.

After opening, fishing became a favorite pastime for local youths when their chores were done. The kids were close to both the Sespe and Santa Clara and were always ready to take an afternoon off to try their luck. Harold Balden grew up on the southwest corner of Central and Ventura Streets. From his house, it wasn't far by bike to the creek and his favorite fishing spot located near the present bridge on Highway 126. He told me it wasn't unusual to take one hundred trout out of that hole. Harold enjoyed fishing as long as he lived and was very good at it. The Sespe trained him well.

In 1969, the Santa Clara River was running full after some big rains and William Shiells Company lost over forty-five acres of prime orange orchard planted next to Ealy Wash and the river. The Santa Clara is noted for going where it wants to go, and this year, it wanted a new channel on the north side and started making it. As my husband, then manager for the ranch, watched whole trees covered with unpicked fruit floating down the river, Jim Shiells told him not to worry about it. He said, "I've sat on this bank when I was a boy and fished from this very spot and caught trout. We knew it used to be river, and now it is once again." It was too late in the century to make new fishing holes, and the water was soon gone, but the memory remains.

According to Kennie Fine, the favorite way of securing big steelhead was by spear. Now, spearing fish was illegal, immoral, and unconstitutional; but if you didn't get caught, it didn't make any difference. Every family had a good spear for taking steelhead, and it was used. When a family wanted fish for dinner, they usually had it. When the young men wanted some entertainment, they went to a shallow place and caught fish by hand—now, that is a challenge!

We all know that times change, but it is the wonderful memories that keep the old-timers sitting on the front porch with a smile on their face.

Peggy Hickman Hungate called this afternoon and told me the Fillmore schools used to have a FISH DAY during the '40s. It was a school holiday, and everyone went to the Sespe to fish—kids, teachers, administrators, everyone! The state built their first warm-water hatchery in Fillmore in 1942. It was located east of town and utilized both spring and well water with 60°F water that produced fast-growing trout. The original open ditches were divided into thirty ponds, and within a year, the fish were large enough to plant in lakes and streams, to the delight of fishermen. Trees were planted on both sides of the holding ponds and made a cool, shady place to visit during the summer. In 1968, the old open ditches were replaced with forty modern concrete ponds for both rainbow and brown trout. That local hatchery continues to produce over seven hundred thousand fish a year.

Tim Hagel gave me fishing information from 1908 when Richard Stevens Warehouse Company sponsored a fishing contest from opening day, May 1, to June 30. Of course, he was also selling all the fishing equipment you would need to catch the winner. Already, Fordie Pyle had brought in a twenty-five-inch trout with Julius Balden and Hess Elkins almost a tie for second place with fish just over eighteen inches. It seemed that fish were measured and not weighted during this time.

A fishing license cost locals a dollar. (If you want hunting stories, read Kennie Fine's book, *An Anecdotal History of Fillmore, California*.)

Gold

Recently, a friend asked me about the gold around here. I could only give her a vague answer, so this week, I decided to do a little research on that topic and pass it along to you. First of all, details and dates mismatch from source to source, but there is basic agreement. I will not be held responsible for any inaccuracy. As far as I can tell, this is the story:

A Peruvian named Echevarria, who had abandoned one of the privateer ships in Monterey Bay in November 1818, wandered south. He and a companion found gold near the headwaters of Piru Creek a few weeks later. In 1843, some Piru gold was shipped to the US mint in Philadelphia. Jonathan Warner, an early visitor to California, tells us that gold was found in San Feliciano Canyon on Piru Creek in 1841. Warner said he visited the placers soon afterward. The Piru gold mines never amounted to very much, but they still keep people interested in searching for it.

Antonio del Valle was granted Rancho San Francisco in 1839. It encompassed much of the San Fernando mission lands, and his family moved into an old mission adobe outbuilding at the junction of Castaic Creek and the Santa Clara River (near the junction of I-5 and 126). He died in 1841 shortly before gold was found a few miles south of his home in Placerita Canyon. His widow had her uncle, José Francisco de Gracia López as ranch manager. After his father's death, Ygnacio, the eldest son of Antonio, came from Santa Barbara to help his stepmother with the details on clearing title to the land, settling the estate, and running the ranch.

Uncle Francisco López was the one who dug up the wild onion at noon under the now fabled Oak of the Golden Dream. (Several others are also given the same credit.) The onion had small pieces of gold intertwined in the roots. Soon miners descended upon the land, seeking their fortune. When Francisco López and his friends petitioned to mine at this location, the letter was not answered for some reason. Within the next two months, Ygnacio del Valle requested relief from the Los Angeles town council from trespassers on their land.

Ygnacio was appointed magistrate of mines to keep records for tax purposes and settle claim disputes. He was the first person to make mining laws in the state. The court required he notify them immediately about claims. They also gave him permission to charge each miner on his land a one-time fee of eight dollars to cover water, pasture, firewood, and lumber for temporary shelters. Ygnacio never collected the fee, as the men were usually earning no more than a dollar a day, although the placers were extensive and a few small nuggets were found.

Ysabel del Valle soon married her current ranch foreman, Jose Salazar. The land was all in the family. He had several Sonoran miners working for him, and they took out two thousand ounces of gold in the first few months. Later, he placer mined $4,300 in one year, but he was the exception as few aristocratic Californios would soil their hands to mine.

When Francisco López got an answer to his letter about securing a permit to mine, it said they could not give him permission since it was on private land. He continued searching the adjoining area. He and Jose Rellane were granted Rancho Temescal in 1843. Rancho Temescal encompassed all of Piru Creek and Piru Canyon to the north. On these 13,320 acres, Francisco López found gold again. The two men held title until they sold Rancho Temescal to Ygnacio del Valle in 1855.

When López found gold in San Feliciano Canyon on Piru Creek, miners quickly arrived to stake claims to make their fortune. It was reported that one of them picked up a nine-pound nugget in the stream (not likely). A small amount of the gold found its way to the del Valle family, and it was put into small jewelry items and a medallion.

The Yankee invasion in 1847 made the Sonoran miners decide that home was the best place for them, and most went back to Mexico. The few who remained took off for Marshall's new gold strike near Coloma in 1849.

In 1887, David Cook bought the old Rancho Temescal to turn it into his personal Garden of Eden. His son George had a crew, and they continued to work the gold mines up San Feliciano Canyon. When the Cook family returned to Illinois at the turn of the century, the mines were retired again. They never made anyone rich although men put in countless hours of backbreaking work for many years.

During the Depression of the '30s, occasionally, out-of-work men would give it a try. Frank Erskine had a small flake of Piru gold that was given to him by two men who spent a week on the creek working the gravel for gold. I think he told me they had about five dollars at the end of the week to split between them, and they gave him the best specimen they found. He did not say, but I suspect he had grub staked them a couple of weeks, and that was their only way to repay him. He gave me that small flake around 1963, and I mounted it under glass on felt so the kids could easily see it. Many elementary kids were able to view some real Piru gold. When a teacher out there wanted to borrow it for his class, I was happy to lend it to him with a simple story for the kids. He left it on his desk, and it was stolen—so ends my story of Piru gold.

(I suspect we still have an occasional tourist who spends the day looking for gold up the canyon. If any of you have a good family story about looking for gold around here, please give me a call.)

Streets

Do you ever look at city streets and wonder who laid them out? Why the big difference? We've been in towns with streets wide enough you could park on each side and down the middle too. Then you find the ones who have old-fashioned angle parking with plenty of room for the new pickups that are so long. After that, you come to main streets the size of Fillmore's with angle parking and barely room to pass a long pickup if you meet a car from the opposite direction. From the pictures I've seen—but never experienced—in Europe, some streets are so narrow that a car can barely get through without hitting the walls on each side. Yes, streets come in all sizes.

I don't know why main streets were laid out in different widths. It is apparent the city fathers or the railroads or some passersby just made a road and added the businesses or houses as an afterthought. I know a few towns in Oklahoma, during one of the land rushes, had town sites laid out well in advance of the homesteaders, but few towns were that lucky.

I suppose in Fillmore, our Main Street and Central Avenue were laid out by McNab when he got ready to sell off lots when the railroad arrived. After Mr. Ealy refused to sell his hill and stage stop about two miles east of here, Southern Pacific was delighted to find John McNab in a selling mood and ready to start a town on his land. You just gotta find the right man at the right time, and Mr. McNab was IT for SP. When the railroad company completed the track, they had a place for a depot, and Mr. Nab had plenty of lots for homes and businesses. (He also had water rights from Sespe Creek for those homes.) The Fillmore Historical Museum has a copy of the original plat but no explanation about why the streets had a particular width. In the late 1880s, horses and wagons did not take up a lot of room, so wide streets were not necessary. The Fourth of July was about the only time that everyone came to town at the same time, so traffic was sparse most days. You didn't need wide streets. (Those men were not looking ahead for future growth and needs.) Now we are stuck with what we've got! Now we make do with what they gave us!

Residential streets are a different matter. A few of Fillmore's streets near the center of town are comfortable driving width, but none of them are extra wide. As transportation has changed and cars and pickups get bigger and bigger, it only makes sense to make the streets around new homes a little bigger too. Well, it makes sense to me, but evidently, not to the current city planners. In some of the new tracts, people park large boats and RVs on the street. You sure hope you don't meet a car in a section with all that stuff parked on both sides of the street. I guess the kids can manage to get through without a scratch, but for us little old ladies, it can be a harrowing experience—and we aren't talking on a cell phone either.

Developers want every inch of space to build houses, and I understand that. However, it seems like when our city fathers consider future development, the size of vehicles and safety of kids and pedestrians should all be taken into account. We should be making life easier in the future. It would sure be nice to have our residential streets a little wider for all concerned. We should not be proving that Fillmore is still a horse and buggy town!

The Tourist Guide

In 1898, P. Milliken complied the *Homeseekers' and Tourists' Guide and Ventura County Directory.* It is full of great information for any historian or genealogist. This was published at a time when new people in Southern California wanted to know about the area while they were looking for land and new homes. The railroad ran from Los Angeles to Ventura and Santa Barbara via our Santa Clara Valley, so it was easy to move and settle along the line. Once the railroad company completed a set of tracks and had regular service, people wanted to live near it. My own grandparents did the same thing along a railroad in Indian Territory. That is how the way life worked for early settlers anywhere.

This little book also included information about the post offices in the county. A few people in the northern section of the Piru precinct received their mail at Neenach. There is still a small store on that road across from Gorman to the Lancaster area. They had a long way to go to get mail but farther to vote. These men were listed as farmers and miners.

Juventino del Valle was postmaster at Camulos for about fifty inhabitants. Besides his family and their many employees, they had several laborers who came there for mail, along with rancher Ramon Castro and Patrick Galvin, the section foreman for the railroad.

Piru City was developing into a large community after David Cook started building and planting orchards. F. E. Woods had a store with general merchandise and the post office, so I assume he was the postmaster. The town had a depot with a telephone, the Western Union Telegraph Company, and the Wells-Fargo Express Company. There were two other stores, a blacksmith shop, and a carpenter shop; and Rev. C. W. Nelson was pastor of the Methodist Church. Leslie Gay was manager of the Piru Fruit Rancho, and his wife, Alice, ran the hotel. Piru was home to the Piru Trout Company with C. J. French as manager. (Do any of you know anything about this enterprise?) The people listed for Piru included many employees of the Fruit rancho, railroad laborers, ranchers, horticulturists, stockmen, and farmers, with a painter and harness maker thrown in for good measure. Piru City also got a new school building about this time.

Buckhorn had a beautiful school with a large bell tower, and W. F. Oglesby was the teacher there. Scénega School served the kids east of the current fish hatchery. On the other side of the river, the kids went to Willow Grove School. (Later a school was opened at Calumet Canyon for the kids who lived there during the oil-boom days around 1912.)

Fillmore was the next town just seven miles to the west. J. A. Guiberson Jr. was the postmaster for about eight hundred living around here. Citrus, apricots, honey, and beans had replaced most of the sheep and stock. The freight was measured by carloads with about 250 shipped in 1897. The fine sulfur springs just outside of town were never developed. (Does anyone have information about these springs?) John Grimes had a real estate office across from the depot and was also the Santa Fe ticket agent. Duncan and Stephens were the leading merchants and had the post office in their store with a telephone. The livery stable and blacksmith shop kept everything running smoothly. C. A. Harmonson had recently bought out the store of C. C. Elkins. Dr. J. P. Hinckley was the local physician, and he and T. F. Arundell and D. S. Linebarger were trustees of the grammar school. The town supported a constable and two churches, Methodist and Presbyterian.

Just two miles west of Fillmore, on the SPRR, was Sespe. This little town had Caroline Smith as postmistress with mail delivered to the store owned by her husband. Sespe had a Methodist Church, a school where Ethel Heanan taught, and the brownstone quarry. A little ways up Sespe Creek, early day oil wells were known as Kentuck field. The land was planted with citrus and deciduous fruit. Most of the people were listed as farmers, but George Henley, H. E. Peyton, and Owen Miller also got their mail at Sespe.

On the south side of the Santa Clara River, Bardsdale was doing its best to outshine everything. The post office delivered mail to over two hundred who lived in the surrounding orchards and hills. They had a Methodist Church and a fine grammar school. Most of the land was planted with citrus, and George Burson was manager of the packinghouse. A land agent and notary, J. R. McKee, provided reliable information about purchasing your own place in paradise. Adjoining the settlement were several oil wells. Most business was done in Fillmore unless the Santa Clara River was running high and the ford was impassable. Santa Paula had the nearest bank for the whole end of the valley, from Camulos to Sespe.

Yes, this end of the Santa Clara Valley was growing.

Piru

When Portolá and the early explorers traveled down the Santa Clara River Valley, they found several Tataviam Indian rancherias along Piru Creek. People always lived near a water source, and the Indians were no different. This was at the western edge of their normal territory. Farther to the west was occupied by the Chumash tribe. Piru was the name of the tule reeds that grew in the nearby river, and the Indians used them to make baskets. Soon the creek and whole area was called PIRU.

David Cook was the wealthy publisher of Sunday school and bible material in Illinois and was in poor health. His doctors suggested a warmer, drier climate might help him, so he started looking for a new home. When he found fourteen thousand acres of the old Rancho Temescal for sale along the creek and up the canyon, he bought it from the del Valle family and decided to build a second Garden of Eden for himself. He secured the water rights for irrigation of his new orchards and fields from Piru Creek and began planting. He planted only things that were found in the original Garden of Eden, required all his workers to refrain from smoking and drinking, and ran a tight ship.

As the railroad was being built down the valley in 1887, he requested they put a depot near the creek, and he would lay out a town around it. Since the railroad had just put a tiny depot two miles east at Rancho Camulos, they were not interested in another depot to pick up passengers and produce so near. Southern Pacific said no. They did not want the extra expense. However, David Cook was not one to take that answer, so he just built his own depot. He planned to ship fruit from his newly planted orchards and make it easy for the people in his new town to travel, so he WOULD HAVE A DEPOT. And he did

David Cook built a nice house on the main street in his new town so he had accommodations until his mansion was constructed. The first large house was near the new Methodist Church, and it was eventually used in many movie sets, as an assisted living facility, and a hotel. It is still an interesting place to visit or just view.

THE MANSION was the new home for David Cook for almost fifteen years until he recovered his health and returned to Illinois. He spared no expense in this large dwelling and imported workers and materials so his new home rivaled anything in the East.

Piru was a thriving community for several years but eventually settled into a small town as times changed. The old PIRU FRUIT RANCHO was abandoned, the gold mines yielded smaller nuggets, and oil drilling was less active. I still love to drive five or six miles up the canyon and see the remains of olive orchards that still cling to the hillside as a reminder of the good old days.

Piru Co-op

Ramona Tourists

After a weekend in Hemet at the Ramona Bowl, all the old stories about Helen Hunt Jackson's *RAMONA* came to the surface again. Our own Rancho Camulos and the Hemet/San Diego area have both claimed that book as THEIRS since it was published in 1884. (And of course, I KNOW it belongs to Camulos.) A new book, *Ramona Memories*, has a very logical explanation that I figured out for myself over a year ago—the old adobe in the story is the house and grounds at Rancho Camulos, but Mrs. Jackson took the liberty of any fiction author and put it in a location much farther south. I was delighted when I found an author that agreed with me. Well, maybe I am agreeing with her.

After the book was published in 1884, those eastern tourists flocked to California and Rancho Camulos to see where Ramona lived and loved her Alessandro. The stage made regular stops at the ranch, but by the time the book was really the thing to read, Southern Pacific had finished the railroad tracks down the valley to Ventura; and those tourists could ride in comfort from Los Angeles to Camulos. The train made scheduled stops at the Camulos depot, and locals used it to go to Ventura to shop or for business. After Ventura County separated from Santa Barbara in 1873, the courthouse was located there and was handy for legal things. The train got them there in the morning and brought them home late in the afternoon.

When tourists got off the train at Camulos, it was only a few hundred yards across the road to Senora del Valle's adobe home, with Mexican servants, beautiful rose garden, chapel, and fountain. They had already read the book and knew how things would appear at the ranch. These tourists were usually there at mealtime as they waited for the next train and expected to be fed. Doña Ysabel expected to feed them—that was the custom in 1884. A hostess never waited for company to leave before calling the family to the dining table. Whoever was there at mealtime was served. Camulos was known far and wide for the hospitality they extended to everyone, but they had never expected the huge flood of tourists that descended upon the ranch in the late 1880s.

One story said when tourists insisted on seeing the REAL Ramona, one of the ranch girls gave them their money's worth by posing as Ramona. I bet she charged them a quarter if they wanted to take her picture. As soon as Senora del Valle learned of it, she put a stop to that!

(Two years ago a lady, who stopped at the museum for a tour, insisted that she was a direct descendant of Ramona. We explained that Ramona was a fictional character from a book, but the lady kept insisting. Since she paid us five dollars for the tour, we decided she could think anything she liked. Later, the docents agreed that perhaps she was a direct descendant of the original, fictional Mexican Ramona girl on the ranch. Hey, you never know, so don't argue with an expert.)

After a few years, the del Valles were forced to close the ranch to tourists or go bankrupt showing their hospitality. Cash was always in short supply, and food was expensive. Besides, Ysabel was weary of the questions and prying about their private lives—all things that well-bred Californios would never speak about. So tourists were no longer allowed on the property. Local family and friends were welcomed as always, but outsiders were turned away, and tourists had to be content to view the "home of Ramona" from their train windows.

After the ranch was sold by the del Valles to August Rubel in 1924, the hospitality returned until the death of both Mary and August. Once again, Camulos became off-limits to tourists, friends, and family. After the earthquake of 1994, the Rubels returned to the ranch and put up a welcome sign when the old buildings were opened as museum and a national historic site.

The little depot is gone, but there are plans to reconstruct it in the future. The original sign on the end of the tiny building and platform is in storage. The railroad company hopes to restore the train tracks from Piru to Camulos, so it will be similar to the old days. The old Mexican land grant has gone from a time of having too many tourists to having none to hoping to get them back again to support the Rancho Camulos Museum. Yep! We've gone full circle again! Life is like that.

Chapter 2

FARMING

Olives

Crops in our part of the Santa Clara Valley change and change and change. In the late 1800s, David Cook came to Piru and planted many different kinds of fruit trees on the old Rancho Temescal property—the Piru Fruit Rancho was about 1,000 acres out of the 14,000 of the land grant. The *Homeseekers' and Tourists' Guide of 1898* lists Mr. Cook as having 200 acres of oranges and lemons, 200 acres of apricots, 135 acres of peaches, 100 acres of prunes, 70 acres of vineyard, and 150 acres of olives. (I assume the grapes were table grapes since Mr. Cook was against any alcohol for consumption, so surely it was not used for wine.) They also had figs, walnuts, chestnuts, almonds, pomegranates, and persimmons. At that time, Leslie Gay was the general manager for the fruit company. It was a big operation.

When Mr. Cook envisioned his personal holy land, olives were an important part of it. You can still see the remains of those olive orchards along the road to Lake Piru. There were several olive groves closer to Fillmore along Highway 126. A friend told me there was an olive press located at the end of Fillmore Street on the north side of the railroad. I think it was built by C. C. Elkins in 1903. Later, the old building became Dewey Garden and Feed Store.

Rancho Camulos grew olives as well as everything else needed on the ranch to feed the del Valle family and their workers. Olive oil was an important item in their kitchen. The old millstones are still visible at the corner of the winery, so look for them when you take a tour of the museum. Rancho Camulos bottled and sold the first olive oil in the United States. They were always in need of cash, and a good-quality cooking oil brought a premium price.

Cured olives are the best things in the world for nibbling. Local families still have their own recipes for pickling both green and ripe fruit. Now, olives are sort of like Oklahoma persimmons before they are cured—they will pucker your mouth beyond belief! I am sure that many local kids had great fun with introducing the fruit to visiting city cousins in the summer. They only got one chance with that joke, but it was fun while it lasted.

One summer, a friend and I decided to cure our own olives. She found a place where we could get permission to pick the fruit. I secured a five-gallon crock for the curing, and we were in business. We quickly discovered that picking olives was a time-consuming job—an olive isn't very big, and two inexperienced pickers made slow headway. It took us the whole afternoon, but when we had about three gallons of fruit, we decided that was enough for both families for the year. We brought them home to wash in our garage.

Peggy Guiterrez Hickman Hungate traced her ancestry back seven generations in Piru, so I assumed she must know a lot more about curing olives than this Okie girl! At least she had the Elkins recipe for doing IT. On the first day, you soaked the fruit in strong lye water. The next day, you soaked the fruit for two days in weaker lye solution. Then you started washing in plain water and washing some more before you drained them.

It was all downhill from there. Now, every twenty-four hours, you washed and covered them in fresh saltwater, with each day using more salt. After a week, you could begin testing to see if the lye was gone. If not, you made more saltwater and soaked for another twenty-four hours.

Changing the water and the washing was my job since it was being done at my house. Occasionally, I forgot. My children were small, and I often had other things that required my attention. So I was not very faithful, but I sort of kept to the recipe. The five-gallon crock got heavier every time I tried to drain those olives. That fruit was not looking very good by the end of a week. It was moldy and scummy beyond belief. Neither Peg nor I really wanted to taste the stuff to see if we'd removed the lye or not. By the end of the second week, we thought it was time to throw out the whole soggy mess and chalk it up to experience. Neither of us knew what we were doing!

Gene and I were often at Lucky and Maggie Balden's house. She had the most fantastic home-cured olives you've ever tasted. Her brother, Dick Elkins, made them and shared. Oh, how we loved those olives. Peg says that Keith Warring and Simon Carrillo know how to cure olives too—well, best of luck to them because us gals sure didn't have the knack.

If you ever have the privilege to eat super good home-cured olives, please remember how time-consuming they are and compliment the cook. (I still have our original recipe for the memories it affords, but I shall not use it again. It is better to quit while you are alive and ahead.)

Horses and Tractors

Henry Ford wrote about his business life and published the book *My Life and Work* in 1922. He was an interesting man with new ideas and was destined to make it BIG in the United States. We all know how successful he was with the assembly line that made the Model T car, and then he produced tractors in the same way. He wanted to help the many farmers in America. His first tractors went to England and, in 1918, sold for $750. The next few years, the price went up and down as he made changes in them. When fuel cost and problems arose, he just solved them and would not take NO for an answer. By the time he opened a new modern plant at River Rouge, he was able to produce tractors for $395. He wanted farm equipment to be cheap so power would go to all the farms.

Hauling lemons, 1911

Henry Ford felt the farmers did not need new tools; they just need power to work the ones they had. He felt that doing everything slowly by hand meant most farmers only made a bare living, and their products were never as plentiful and cheap as they should be. It was a waste for a man to spend hours walking behind a team when a tractor could do six times as much work.

In order to sell this mechanizing idea to skeptical men in their fields, Henry did some detailed math about how much a tractor would save in a year. He really worked on the financial end of things so farmers would understand that buying a tractor would be to their advantage. The following info comes from his book:

In the very early days a Fordson cost $880 and Henry figured the "wearing life" was 4800 hours. He worked with 4/5 acres per hour. He thought, the depreciation

per acre would be .221 cents; repairs .026 per acre; fuel
cost (kerosene at 19 cents, 2 gal per acre) .38; 3/4 gal oil
per acre .075; driver at $2 a day, 8 acre .25. That gave
him a total cost of .95 cents per acre to plough with a
Fordson tractor.

To prove his point, he gave the cost of plowing with horses.

Eight horses cost $1,200 with a working life of five thousand hours.
The depreciation of horses per acre was 0.30; feed per horse, 0.40 per
acre; feed per horse for idle days not used, 0.265 per acre; and two
drivers and two gang ploughs at $2 per day figured 0.50 an acre. The
cost of plowing with horses per acre was $1.46.

Using a tractor, you could plow the same acres in about one-fourth
the time and use only the physical energy necessary to steer the tractor.
He sold the idea of letting steel take the physical burden off every man,
and I guess he did a good job of selling. Henry Ford was convinced
that a farmer must either take up power or go out of business. He felt
farming should be a kind of business and not just a rural occupation
that needed more hours in most days. He wanted farmers to have time
to spend in other business or some leisure.

Henry Ford said, "We shall have as great a development in farming
during the next twenty years as we have had in manufacturing during
the last twenty."

In 1926, John Peres was the local Ford dealer with a building on
Santa Clara Street. (In case you want to call him, his phone number was
246.) His ranch trucks with a starter would cost you $510. Touring cars
were $520. Fillmore always kept up with the latest and most popular
models.

Gene was only twenty-one years old when he went to work for
Balden Ranch Company in 1948. Julius Balden was probably close to
eighty at that time. One morning, when Gene stopped his tractor work
to take a cigarette break, Julius mentioned it to him. Gene's reply was,
"Didn't you have to stop to rest your team when you plowed in the early
days?" After that, Julius did not say any more about the midmorning
work break. Gene climbed back on the Ford tractor and finished disking

the cover crop. Julius Balden was a fine old gentleman and lived a few more years, but he was also frugal and did not like time to be wasted. Changing times are harder on the elderly—and don't we know that!

Stage Stops

I often look at the roads, fields, and mountains and try to imagine what they looked like two hundred years ago. There were no fields or orchards, and our grandkids may have to just remember OUR stories about the time when the whole end of our valley was orange groves. (Aren't we lucky to have lived during this time!) Ag crops have rotated several times through the years, and unfortunately, we are seeing another of these changes. In the very early days, mustard was about the only thing seen beyond sagebrush and grass.

Often, an early day story will mention about the height of the mustard in a wet year. It was said a man needed to be on horseback to see over the top, and a small child could be lost in it. Sooooo that is a likely story! Well, it may also be true! Last week in Ventura, I stopped near a vacant lot about half a mile from the river. The mustard growing there was at least four feet high, so guess those old stories really are fact!

Roads are another story! The original footpath down the valley was used by the Portolá expedition and was probably an Indian trail. That group visited several Indian villages at Castaic, Camulos, Piru, Sespe, and Lords Creeks. They called the road the King's Highway to honor the king of Spain. We still claim the camino real all the way down the valley to the ocean.

Most freight came by ship to be offloaded in Ventura and brought into the valley. Sometimes it came from the San Fernando mission, but the roads barely accommodated a Mexican cart or wagons. It was slow and tedious to get anything delivered or hides and tallow shipped out. It was a big deal when the stagecoach was able to maintain a regular schedule. Out by Blue Cut, the road was steep and ran at an angle across the face of the cut. It was a difficult pull, and it was not unusual for the stage to turn over and dump passengers in the dirt and mud.

There were several stage stops in different places at different times. San Martinez Canyon had one. Camulos had one. Scenega had one. Now we look for a gas station to keep our horsepower going, but a stagecoach needed fresh horses every few miles. If it was a rough road, they changed horses more often. Passengers rested at the house while four or six fresh horses were put into the traces.

Trying to get to Santa Barbara along the coast route was even worse. There you were controlled by the tide since much of the way was in the surf. If the tide was high, you were forced to wait for it to go out enough that the horses and coach could proceed along the sand. Recently, I found a picture of a couple and a buggy along that route. The man was driving the horses and buggy through the many rocks at the edge of the surf in the Rincon section, and the woman was walking behind. (Now why am I not surprised at that picture?) Perhaps it was so rough she would rather walk than ride! I don't know why, but he was driving in the buggy, and she was walking!

One of my pioneer women's stories is about a young wife who lived on an army base near Yuma, Arizona. When her husband was transferred, the army provided an ambulance (enclosed wagon) for the women to use for transportation to the next post. The couple had a very young baby, and the jolting over stones was awful on both mother and baby. They had befriended an Indian couple, and when her baby was born, the Indian woman presented it with a traditional cradleboard. The young army wife put her tiny babe into the cradleboard and suspended it from a crossbow inside the wagon. The baby was in a swing and very comfortable for the rest of the trip. Oh, the things we learn from others!

Last weekend, we drove to see the wildflowers for the second time this year. They are spectacular! The rains have been good, and everything that can bloom is blooming or getting ready to burst into flower. The yucca and Joshua trees are showing color, so it won't be long for them. The poppies make our eyes hurt; they are so brilliant. Lupine and other things are a mass of color in many places.

Imagine what the pioneers thought the first time they came to Tejon Pass in the spring and saw those hills—it would be much the same as this year. From a distance, it looks like someone has thrown buckets of paint on a canvas. Even after we see it, it is hard to believe. If you have time this week, take a drive up to Gorman, go out the back way on the Old Post Road to 138 toward Lancaster, and go at least ten miles along that route. Although it is outside the Poppy Reserve, the fields of grain are framed with blooming poppies in every fencerow. It is worth the trip. Next year may be dry, so you better see the flowers within the next week while they are in full bloom.

Cold Winters and Smudging

Smudging in an orange orchard

The past two years, Fillmore and Piru have experienced fire and the recent flood, with all the "wonderful" experiences that go with both. I guess we should get ready for a COLD year in the near future. That is about all that is left for the farmers to endure this year. Southern California has cycles of drought, flood, cold, and heat—and the fires are just thrown in to keep us all honest when building a campfire in the Sespe.

That thought made me start thinking about the cycle of cold that started about 1947 or 1948, when we had cold winters for five or six years. We had just married. After a few months, Gene quit the oil fields and went to work for Balden Ranch Company. We've been farmers ever since and love it. During over fifty years in ag, Gene has had several opportunities to work at other jobs, but he loved farming; it provided a living for our family, and he stayed in the business. He often said, "I never worked a day in my life. When you love your job, it is not work!" He worked for Balden Ranch Company for eighteen years and William Shiells Company for thirty-one years and loved every day of it.

Gene's first farm job was with Harold Balden, and he quickly learned about ORCHARD COLD! Harold was a good teacher when it came to farm operations. He had lots of progressive ideas about raising citrus.

At that time, farmers protected their valuable citrus crops by smudging. During the winter, everyone in Fillmore listened to Terry Shaffer give the nightly frost report for different sections of the valley. Things just came to a standstill when it was time for the evening radio predictions. If you happened to be at a dinner meeting, someone would listen and come back with the report to share. I think Terry Shaffer did the report from his home in Santa Paula. It was part of the National Weather Service, as I recall, and he was ACCURATE! (Remember, this was all before satellites and TV weather as we know it now.) I assume Terry got high- and low-pressure readings from the National Weather Service and then was able to make his own local predictions. A few years ago, funding was lost, and that program was retired as we had known it.

Our area was divided into several sections; Terry gave the temperature predictions for Santa Paula, Fillmore, Rancho Sespe, Bardsdale, Lower Bardsdale, and Piru. He did the whole county, but I do not recall the other nearby districts. It is amazing how much difference there might have been among these local minidistricts, but each announcement was important to the farmer living there. The orchards within the city of Fillmore seldom got cold. The Balden homeplace (now Balden Plaza Shopping Center) did not even have thermometers to check the cold;

it just never got cold in that location. Julius Baldeschwieler chose well when he bought that land and planted his twenty-acre navel orange orchard. It never froze. Those huge orange trees were about one hundred years old when they were pulled out to make way for progress.

When Frank Erskine was manager of the citrus packinghouses about 1915, there was a freeze so bad the smudge pots did not help at all. It was so cold for such a long time, the sap in the trees froze, and many of the trees split and died. He said it sounded like gunshots when they exploded. About ten years ago, we had another of those very cold nights, but the trees did not freeze. The next week, along Guiberson Road, you could see trees near the road that looked like a fire had gone through them. As the super cold air came down those little canyons on the south side of the road, it froze the leaves on those trees, and it looked like they had been burned. Once the air got into the orchards and started to warm up, it did less damage. The trees next to the road were in bad shape. The next tree was in a little better shape, and two or three trees farther down the row looked even better until the "burn" faded out. It was a very interesting phenomenon.

After you cross the river and head to Bardsdale, the temp gets lower as you head west toward Santa Paula. By the time you are out of Bardsdale proper, you hit Lower Bardsdale, and it is often five degrees colder than near the church. Often, individual orchards vary several degrees depending on the lay of the land and how close it is to the river or little canyons coming out of the foothills. That is why Terry Shaffer's reports were so important.

In the long ago, by midnight, orchard owners usually knew if it was going to be a cold night and time to watch the thermometers closely. Recording thermometers were tested for accuracy and then placed in the orchards before winter. The man responsible for checking them would start his route. Driving his pickup down the designed row, with flashlight in hand, he stopped and walked through the citrus trees to find and read each thermometer. If he was checking a small block of fruit, the time between checks might be spent visiting with other farmers in the Bardsdale smudge shack and having coffee. If you had several locations to keep track of, you did not have much visiting time.

The men drifted in and out all night, exchanged information, and did their job. By the time they warmed up from the outside cold, it was time to make another run back to their orchard.

If they got some east wind, the temperature rose, and everyone went home. If it was a clear night and very still, they had to be alert to how quickly the temperature fell. It was a guessing game, and all played by the same rules, which were no rules at all when it came to the weather! The men who had wind machines started those earlier than the men who lit smudge pots. A wind machine worked well if there was a layer of warm air above the orchard to pull down, and there usually was. However, one year, when it was exceptionally cold, they brought in helicopters to move the air and save the fruit. The ceiling was over five thousand feet that night with no warm air above the orchards. Some owners spent a lot of money in a very short time for nothing.

Lighting smudge pots was the dirtiest job in local farming. The pots were set between the trees in one of the rows, or alternate rows, depending upon how cold that location usually got. The men had a special torch for lighting the pots. After the oil caught fire, they adjusted the air vent to control the amount of heat the pot provided. A full pot would burn about ten or twelve hours. Once the pots were burning, it was time to watch the thermometers again and see if you could keep it above freezing. Lemons were more susceptible to cold than oranges, so you needed to start earlier in a lemon orchard.

The coldest time of the night was just before the sun came up. Often the temperature in an orchard dropped a couple of degrees an hour or two before sunrise. When the sun came up and it started warming, it was time to go through the orchards again and close the vents to put out the flame in each pot. By the time that was done, the pots cooled, and it was time to refill the pots and get ready for the next evening. (They never filled a pot that was still hot or had a flame—men were badly burned when they forgot this safety precaution.) It was not unusual to have three or four nights in a row when you had to smudge. When we had a prolonged cold spell, the boys in each family helped, and often high school boys were called upon to light and fill pots and maybe skip school the next day to sleep.

Smudge oil was one cent a gallon and available from the local Texaco refinery on the east side of town. It was a by-product of their operation. It could also be bought from the Seaside Refinery in Ventura. Old smudge oil tanks can still be seen in several locations around Fillmore. Bulk oil was brought to the tanks and then transferred to the farmer's rig to haul to the orchards as needed.

Women hated smudge season. That oily black smoke seeped through windows and doors in spite of all. White lace curtains quickly became a dingy gray and needed frequently washing. Everything was soon covered with light soot and was dirty to handle. It was just something they all put up with to save the crop if your husband owned an orchard. If they lived in town, it was just something they had to put up with!

In the early 1900s, if you owned ten acres, you made a living. If you owned twenty acres, you made a GOOD living. If you owned more, you could have a big house, a new car every two years, and send the kids to college. It was the heyday for citrus farmers, and it established old-line family dynasties around here.

We were fortunate to live in a little house next door to Harold and Mary Balden on First Street when Gene went to work for them. There was just a driveway between the two houses. Harold had figured out the temp differences between his home and the family's outlaying orchards. He had a preset frost alarm in his backyard that rang a bell in their bedroom at night when it got cold. Then he knew it was time to get up and start his orchard routine. It was not long until he rigged up a bell from his bedroom to our bedroom. When his frost alarm went off, he could roll over, press a button, and then it was Gene who got up to go check on the thermometers and call Harold only when if they needed to light the smudge pots.

We had several years when the coldest weather was between Christmas and New Year's. Several holiday dinners had no men at the table. They had to check thermometers, light pots, fill pots, and come home for a short nap. During the workweek, they went back to work when there was something pressing to get done. Those were long winters.

Often after several hours of checking thermometers, a gentle breeze would start, and the men knew there would be no need to light the pots. These guys really learned all the nuances of the weather and their orchard. It was time to go home and back to bed for the rest of the night.

Before the days of down coats and special winter gear, smudge clothes consisted of long underwear and your oldest pants and throwaway jacket. It was a COLD, dirty job. If Gene got home early and came to bed, he was an absolute Popsicle! It took an hour to warm him up enough that he could go to sleep. (We still laugh about how cold he would be when he got home.) If they had to fill pots before he came home and was covered with oily grim, a hot soak in the tub helped to warm him, but what an awful ring that left with the Fillmore hard water!

By the time our first child was born a couple of winters later, it became routine to move the baby bed into the kitchen each morning during smudge season. Our baby bed had double drop sides, so I removed the mattress and bedding, folded the sides together and rolled it into the large kitchen for the day. When all was reassembled, our baby was perfectly happy with the new surrounding while his father slept to get ready for the next night. In a one-bedroom home, you just do what you gotta do! It was quite an experience for an Oklahoma girl!

Once again, times changed! The Air Control Quality Board outlawed the old-fashioned smudge pots. If farmers wanted to continue using smudge pots, they had to purchase a different style with less air pollution. One of the chemical companies came out with heat blocks to be used instead of pots. They were expensive, hard to light, and did not put out enough heat. Smudge oil was no longer available, so diesel was used. That fuel costs over a dollar a gallon. Most citrus farmers decided they could accept a small amount of frozen fruit and lose less money than it would cost them to light up the pots. Now in a real emergency, ranchers turn on their irrigation water to help warm the air. If it is not cold for a long time, most of the fruit will survive. Several years ago, the sprinklers put a coating of ice on every orange. When the sun came out, the ice magnified the heat from the sun and often burned the rind. Sometimes you just can't win! (It was a beautiful sight.)

A few years ago, the bottom fell out of the fresh fruit market. Orchards provided a very poor living, and many trees were pulled out. After the fruit was picked and packed, it did not bring enough to even cover that cost, and many farmers received a bill from the packinghouse instead of a check for selling their fruit. Farming has always gone in cycles. Winters go in cycles; rainy weather goes in cycles. Why would anyone want to be a farmer anywhere in the United States? Well, just ask my husband!

Crops

In 1840, Ventura County was cattle country. The hills were covered with sheep and cattle, and the horses needed to herd and work them. Grass was abundant, and wild mustard was as high as a man's head. The whole area was divided into large Mexican land grants called ranchos. We still carry many of those old rancho names with us: Conejo, Camulos, Temescal, Saticoy, Santa Paula, Calleguas, Canada, Los Posas, Ojai, Santa Clara, Tapo, and Simi. The drought years of 1861 and 1862 just about did away with the livestock. After two years of very little rain, there was neither grass nor water for cattle and sheep, and they perished by the hundreds. Three-quarters of the animals died during that time. The huge ranchos were sold off in smaller pieces to settle debts and pay taxes. Eager buyers and homesteaders could not wait to get their slice of the pie. This ended the rancho era for Ventura County.

With the demand for wool during the Civil War, sheep ranchers recovered a bit, but never again were the great herds of cattle seen on the hills. The smaller landholders turned more to agriculture. Even Rancho Camulos found their best cash crops to be wine grapes, dried peppers, and apricots; and they had the first oranges planted in Ventura County. They had a market for all four. Farmers grew the things needed by each family for food and added large fields of various crops for their cash.

By 1878, the alluvial plain of the Santa Clara River supported great fields of grain with smaller plantings all along the valley. One reporter said, "As we drove through that region, it seemed as though we were gazing upon a vast sea of grain, with here and there, dark spots looming up like a distant island and contrasting strongly with the billowy waves of green barley on every hand." The dark spots were fields of corn. That year it was reported 29,262 acres of barley and 5,310 acres of corn with 2,000 acres of wheat in the Colonia area alone.

Barley grew to three feet in height with heavy heads of grain. Artesian wells provided water, and farming was good. Many farmers had a large herd of hogs. The corn they raised was used to fatten pork that could be shipped from Hueneme. The Patterson Ranch had 1,500 hogs, though most farmers seemed to have from 50 to 300.

Farther inland, beekeepers were starting to produce some of the finest honey around. Tom Arundell up Pole Creek and the King family up Piru Canyon became well-known for their superior product. Ventura County had over 4,500 stands of bees and shipped 420 tons of honey around the world. In 1876, Rancho Camulos planted several acres of seedling oranges to see how they would grow in Ventura County.

By 1890, farmers were trying out new things. They discovered lima beans grew exceptionally well in the cool air along the coast, and the fields of barley turned into fields of beans. Oxnard shipped more lima beans than any other place in the United States. It was estimated we had fifty to sixty thousand pounds of beans hauled to Port Hueneme and loaded on ships there.

Drying apricots

Small orchards of apricots grew well. When it was found the sun dried the fruit perfectly, more orchards were planted. A few commercial apricot driers were built, but they were soon retired. Sun-drying was the fastest and cheapest way to preserve the fruit, and we had plenty of sunshine. Dry-land farming of apricots suited the foothills and places with less water. During the summer, families came from adjoining towns, camped out, and work side by side with local people to pit and dry apricots. During this time, English walnuts found a good market, and soon large groves were producing nuts.

Nathan Blanchard had fifty acres near Santa Paula, and he wanted to plant budded oranges there. With the success Camulos had with growing and shipping seedling fruit, Blanchard felt sure a good market would evolve for seedless navels—and he was correct! By the early 1900s, the valley had many acres of citrus fruit with packinghouses and trains moving the fruit to market. Barley, corn, hogs, and apricots were dropped to make way for a new crop—acres and acres of oranges and lemons.

By the 1940s, there were few of the old apricot orchards left. Upper Ojai still had a few and some near the top of Grimes Grade, but the Bardsdale apricots were all gone, and the land was planted with citrus. Lima beans and walnuts were phased out in the 1950s when row crops and oranges brought a better price. Around here, most of us only remember oranges, oranges, and oranges in our end of the valley.

Our kids grew up with a father who farmed citrus, and they all loved going with him to irrigate so they could walk in the furrows of water. They walked through orange groves on the way to school and threw fruit that had dropped from the trees. They looked forward to April when the trees bloomed and the night air carried the unbelievable fragrance into their bedrooms. They enjoyed fresh orange juice for breakfast in the morning. Oranges were an integral part of their world. Wasn't it the same everywhere? (I often said if my husband had a cut on his arm, it would bleed orange juice!)

With the turn of the century (2000), we are starting another big shift in plantings and other rotation with farmers looking for a better cash crop. Every farmer needs to make a living. They expect market prices and weather to affect them, and they can absorb a bad year, but they can't last long when the market crashes and oranges are not worth what it costs to pick them several years in a row.

So we come to another major change in our valley. Our beloved orange groves are being pulled out as fast as bulldozers can push over the trees. Row crops, mostly peppers, are planted and soon harvested. Companies with large holdings of nursery stock are using the bare land as a storage place while plants are grown and sold. When I stand and look over our valley, it puts tears in my eyes to see the oranges quickly being destroyed. But I am glad that the land is staying in farming, so we are lucky in that respect.

The farming industry will always change. That is the way with farming. I wish it had waited another 20 years. Now where will we be able to drive in the evening with the car windows down just to smell the orange blossoms? Some things are never forgotten. This is the end of an unforgettable era. (Now in 2017, the avocado farmers are facing the same thing as a terrible hot spell of over 116° for several days is making their trees drop all the fruit. Let's hope next year will be better.)

Mustard and Honey

Many stories tell about wild mustard growing as high as a man's head. When the vaqueros were looking for cattle, they had to be on horseback to find them. A person walking could easily get lost when the plant was so heavy and tall.

Harry Kenney wrote the following:

> After a year of heavy rains in 1885, the hills and our valley were covered with wild mustard. When it ripened, Mr. Chormicle got it in his head that he could harvest it. He found a company in the east that sold mustard for making mustard plasters and arranged a contract for the seed.
>
> Mr. Chormicle took an old header and removed the sickle blade and used the reel to beat out the seed. He harvested several thousand pounds around the country and shipped it. His only expense was for the horses and one man to run the header and another to sack up the seed. It was a good year for him. As far as I can find, this was the only time the mustard made money for anyone.

I found that about the same time, honey was also a major product of the county. The Arundell and King families both had large apiaries soon after they arrived in the valley. W. H. Hunt and A. A. Jepson were raising bees in 1874. By 1880, the county directory showed John Corey, Brice Grimes, and Robert Strathearn as bee raisers.

Harry Kenney tells a story about his father who had a big honey crop and a neighbor who also had a lot of honey to be shipped. When they found they could ship it to Seattle and get a cent a pound more than selling it in San Francisco, they started making plans. They found a steamer that had brought down a load of lumber to Ventura from Seattle. The boat was going back empty and needed ballast. The captain agreed to take the honey for no charge and use it in place of rocks for ballast.

When they got to Seattle, they missed their return boat because the buyer was late finding them to pay for the honey. They had to wait a week before they could secure passage back to Ventura. However, it was a fortunate mishap as their original boat sank in Puget Sound and was never heard of again.

By 1916, the census showed several people who sold honey. Minnie and Sarah Holley, John Hassheider, Cyrus Young, Charles Brown, Frank Batty, and Nathan Stone joined the old-timers. Honey was a good cash crop for many years.

During the last fifty years that our family had camped up Sespe and Piru, we saw many hives. Often local bears that were hungry for dessert had overturned some. Often many hives are brought into the orchards and along the river by beemen out of state. They winter their bees here in anticipation of the orange bloom, and they can sell orange honey when they get ready to return to their home states where the cold would kill many of their little friends.

It won't be long until the sage blooms, and we will have local honey from that too. A few years ago, the Bennetts upgraded their honey operation and opened a new plant near Piru to process their honey, so that industry is alive and well. They recently retired but left their bees in new hands. Anytime you want local honey, drive out to their place, near the old Buckhorn School building, to purchase it. Our best wishes to the new folks for keeping an old-fashioned industry from the mid-1800s going into another century. No other crop has survived from that era

Oranges

Oranges and citrus farming have been so much a part of my life that I can hardly realize that others are not aware of the details the way I am. When I came to Fillmore and married in 1947, I still remember coming around the curve on Highway 126 and seeing the first Newhall Land and Farming orange orchard. What a surprise to see a big tree with beautiful orange fruit hanging on the limbs, just waiting to be picked—and there were lots of trees! That day was a new awakening for me as my new husband was soon worked as a ranch hand for the Balden Brothers' ranch and later managed the William Shiells Company for thirty-one years. Yes, ORANGES were going to be a big part of the rest of my life!

As a docent at the Rancho Camulos Museum, I found that old rancho had planted the first oranges in Ventura County so long ago, and they still have several seeding trees that nursery growers use to start their new trees. Yes, an orange tree does start with a single seed planted, and it grows to be budded into the kind of orange they want to harvest.

The navel orange was the most popular orange for eating and was often the most important Christmas gift found by children in their stocking on the twenty-fifth. They were big and sweet and a treasure. Valencia oranges are the most wonderful for juice, and a ton have been squeezed in my kitchen in the past sixty years. Gene always kept a five-gallon bucket of fresh oranges ready for the morning meal.

A picture from 1893 shows tall orange trees with pickers on ladders and a long canvas sleeve hanging from the top of the ladder. The picker pulled the orange and dropped it into the sleeve to softly roll into the box on the ground. Soon they were using a large picking sack that pickers slung over their shoulder to hold the oranges until they released the bottom of the bag and let the fruit fall into the field boxes. Mechanical harvesting is still a thing in the future. Good fruit needs good pickers to get it to the packinghouse.

California sold the idea of growing oranges and making a fortune to folks back East before the turn of the century, and I suppose that was the first real boom for our state. It didn't take long for the ideal weather to encourage people to move to Southern California, buy ten acres, and get rich. Many learned it was not quite as easy as they thought, but many more loved it and did make a good living, built nice houses, and sent the kids to college on orange profits.

Originally, marketing was a big problem as each grower sold his own fruit, but they solved that challenge when they formed a co-op and called it Sunkist. Iced cars of Sunkist oranges traveled from California to New York and stayed fresh and made money.

Securing water to keep the trees growing was easier as small irrigation companies were organized and water assigned as needed. Horses for plowing were replaced by tractors, and open-furrow irrigation was changed to sprinkler systems to utilize every drop of the precious water. Every industry changes with the times to stay competitive and make a profit, and growing oranges is no different. Many different farming practices were tried—some worked and some did not. Trial and error still works.

When you have out-of-state company visiting, just give them fresh orange juice with breakfast and watch their expression when they discover that bottled stuff should be poured down the drain and be almost illegal to even sell if you live in real orange country! LONG LIVE FRESH ORANGE JUICE! There is nothing like it.

Chapter 3

SCHOOLS

Now and Then

I can never get far from the schools around here. The new Mountain Vista site is shaping up, and we still hope it will be ready for kids early in 2006. (So much for the August 2005 completion date!)

Do names like Sespe, Ciénega, Willow Grove, Buckhorn, Montebello, Bardsdale, and Mountain View bring kids and school buildings back to your memory?

I think the first school in this area was Sespe School. It was located on the east side of the creek up the canyon about half a mile. When the district got more kids, probably after the railroad and depot arrived in Fillmore, the district was divided and a school was built in town near the present Bardsdale Bridge. Sespe School was moved to the west side of the creek for the kids there. The Fillmore Museum has a picture of a schoolhouse built with long boards that had been donated by a local rancher, but he didn't want the lumber cut, so several of those board stuck out several inches or a foot near a corner. He wanted to be sure he got his lumber back in long lengths when the school was torn down and moved.

By the time I arrived in Fillmore in 1947, Sespe School had been relocated on Seventh Street near Sycamore Road. The rancho Sespe kids attended there with the other neighborhood children.

Mr. Ealy had a stage stop and store at the top of Adams Hill about two miles east of Fillmore. The school at the bottom of the hill near the railroad was called Ciénega! Yes, that area is still called Ciénega because of the rising groundwater. During the past year of heavy rain, those forty acres were the last to dry out. There may have been an artesian well there in the early days before water was being pumped for irrigation.

The district just across the river from Fillmore, on Guiberson Road, was Willow Grove. Yes, there were lots of big willows near the school. The old school building was moved a few feet east and incorporated into a nice dwelling about twenty years ago, but it still remains near the original location.

Further east on Guiberson Road, Montebello School provided education for the kids during the early oil boom. The school building was placed on a bluff overlooking the road and is now used as the William Shiells Ranch Company office. They restored the building several years ago to its original look. It is a real treasure to have in our community. Kids from Shiells Canyon and Calumet Canyon walked about a mile to get to school.

Before Piru had a school or a town, Temescal School welcomed kids from Rancho Temescal and Piru Canyon. Mrs. Lechler had the Fustero kids among her students. This site is now under Lake Piru. Buckhorn School still stands on State Highway 126 as a residence. I guess when the town of Piru was platted, they soon got a school in town for their kids.

I don't have space this week to talk about Fillmore's brick Sespe School or Bardsdale School, but they are both an important part of our school heritage. Neither of them were up to earthquake standards, and so they are no longer used for schools; however, neither had much damage in the earthquake of 1994, so who knows what building codes are necessary? Still, we can't be too careful with the lives of children either.

As Fillmore grew, a new building provided additional space at Mountain View School. This old building was big, with the first floor sort of a half basement. The windows looked out at ground level so the kids had plenty of light. The second story was accessible by steps on the front. Many schools were built in a similar style at that time. They had a big fenced play yard and equipment. After San Cayetano School was completed, the old Mountain View building was closed and was vacant for a short time before the large lot was sold to developers for houses. It was about 1958 when the big move was made to the new site. The kids started school in the Mountain View building but were eager to get into new, modern classrooms at San Cayetano. Miss Hiberly was principal and marshaled everyone on moving day. Each student collected their personal items, and with their teacher ahead of them, everyone walked up the street and into their new room. Oh, what a day that was for all of them!

The developer tore down the old building and sold some of the lumber. We have several of those full-cut two-by-six pine or redwood beams in our patio. They are almost knot-free and old-growth timber. You can't buy lumber like that anymore. I think of that old school every time I rest on the patio.

Soon we will have a new Mountain Vista School opening in Fillmore, but I bet the kids don't walk to it with their books on opening day. Times change!

The First Sespe School

Early day schools are interesting to me. According to Clara H. Smith, who taught in the Sespe school district, the first Fillmore school was built about 1874. The school district included children in Sespe Canyon down to the Santa Clara River and the settlers who were living in the Fillmore section of the valley outside the Mexican land grant. The schoolhouse was located near the future site of the Bardsdale Bridge.

Hartley and Ida Sprague hauled the lumber from Ventura with a team and wagon, and their father, F. A. Sprague, did the construction work. It was twenty by thirty feet with three windows on each side. The windows allowed light and heat from the sun for warmth. It had the usual water bucket with a tin dipper. One of the older boys filled the bucket from the creek each morning. A bookcase on the left side of the door was filled with 150 volumes, many of which were far beyond the reading ability of the students.

The children sat in rows facing the teacher, whose chair and desk were on a raised platform in front. An extra desk was on the right of the teacher to be used for any unruly student who needed closer supervision. The district was fortunate to have a manikin, which showed the relative positions of the different organs of the human body. Here the children of the early settler learned according to their inclination and the skill of the teacher. Reports for the period show students named Goodenough, Jepson, Kellogg, Kenney, Akers, Fine, and MacIntyre. The school records and census do not show any foreign-born children attending Sespe School.

The first teacher was Clara Skinner, followed by Clara Larson, Augusta Stevens, Maude Fisher, Ryal Sparks, and Mr. Jordon. While the ladies dismissed the kids with a formal count; Mr. Jordon always said, "Get out of here!" Teachers were employed for eight months at a salary of sixty dollars per month. Records show they taught for one year and moved to another district. Ms. Anna Parsons was a superior teacher, and she stayed two years before moving to the Santa Paula school system.

About 1879, the building was moved to be more centrally located for the students. The lonely site was on the east side of the creek about one mile north of the present railroad bridge. There were no trees or shrubs but plenty of sage brush in the playground.

At that time, the chief agricultural products were grain and cattle for the market and grapes, olives, and garden produce for home consumption. Students were frequently kept home to herd cattle or help with the farmwork. After the railroad was built in 1887, a water company was developed, and Sespe Creek water was used to irrigate new citrus plantings.

Students walking to school needed to be close to their school. As more people moved into this area, the large district was divided into three schools. One school was built farther up the canyon on the west side on Grand Avenue. Another was named San Cayetano and located on Seventh Avenue on Rancho Sespe for the Mexican workers' children. The original school building was moved again and put in Fillmore for the students in town.

As Fillmore grew and the district needed larger accommodations for education, the little schoolhouse was bought by Dr. J. P. Hinckley, who moved it to town and made it into a drugstore with a home in the back. It continued in service for sixty years before it burned.

Many things have changed since the first school was started in 1874. The most important have been getting rid of segregation, improving teachers' salaries, and making education available for everyone. Many citizens berate our schools today, but the kids with caring and interested parents still do well. If education is important to the family, it is important to the student. Maybe things haven't changed so much after all!

The original San Cayetano School

Teachers and Schools

In order to do more writing about the history of this area, I need some help! My next project will be finding the facts on some of the old-time teachers and schools in Fillmore, Bardsdale, and Piru.

Recently, I received an e-mail from a lady in Missouri who is doing family genealogy, and one of her ancestors was a Fillmore teacher. That reminded me it was time to start collecting facts and information about a whole bunch of the early teachers.

I will be calling and talking with retired teachers here in town, but I know many of you former students will have charming stories and memories about your teachers. What do you remember about Petey Weaver, Dulcie Arnold, Mr. Ross, and Vera Fremlin for starters? Did your father tell you things about his school days and the teachers at Buckhorn and Willow Grove? Where did Grandpa attend school?

Please give me a call with little things you will share with us, and I will have a start on TEACHERS for the history book. (I did not go to school here, so I can't do this alone—I need YOUR help immediately.)

The old school buildings at Buckhorn and Bardsdale are now used as dwellings. Montebello School is now the Shiells Ranch office. The Willow Grove school building has been moved a few feet and additions put on so it no longer looks like the original structure, but the old schoolhouse is an integral part of this attractive home on Guiberson Road.

Many of the original schools sites have completely disappeared. San Cayetano School on Seventh Street at Rancho Sespe was torn down many years ago and citrus planted in the old play yard. The Mountain View site in Fillmore became an early day subdivision, but the Wrens have some beautiful clear redwood timber from the old building on the patio roof. Sespe School at the end of Grand Avenue has disappeared too. Ciénega, east of town near the Santa Clara River, no longer exists. The school site in Piru has changed locations, and their Temescal School up the canyon is under Piru Lake. The tiny school at Torrey is long gone, but it served a purpose during the oil boom.

The school population changes as times change, and communities grow or disappear completely. Transportation makes the necessity of a school within one or two walking miles of students unnecessary. Now we just put kids on a bus and take them to a more centralized school location. Both Piru and Fillmore advance students originally rode the train to Santa Paula to attend high school before, about 1910. Now you really had to WANT an education to make that daily trip. It was much easier when the Fillmore high school district built a building and hired teachers.

Anyone with early day stories about schools and teachers is requested to give me a call so I can add to my "Facts, Fun, and Fiction" in Fillmore and Piru. If I can get some good stuff, I will use it in a column in the near future.

Chapter 4

WEATHER

Cool Houses

We got a good laugh this week (April 2005) when we received a letter from Edison about saving us $200 during the summer if we signed up for something about summer brownouts! I don't know if the joke is on us or them. We still live á la natural—without air-conditioning! It did make me think about ways the pioneers did things to accommodate the lack of artificial cooling.

We rented the little Hinckley house on First Street when we married in 1947. It was built for Kate Hinckley's mother so was a bit old-fashioned in design. It had a big kitchen, very small living room, and one small bedroom. The back porch was screened, so one end could be used for sleeping during the summer. The other end had plenty of room for a washing machine and rinse tubs. As newlyweds, we didn't have much, so small rooms were okay. It worked well for us. One corner of the kitchen had a tall door about twenty-four-inch wide that opened to slatted shelves. This cupboard was vented to the outside and also the roof. It was used as a cooler for food as the air circulated, with the hot air going up and outside. And it worked pretty well if it was not really hot. I am sure that Grandma Cruson used it as long as she lived or got an icebox that would hold ten pounds of ice.

Trees were planted around every house with the idea that shade in the summer would help keep certain portions of the house cooler. People knew where they wanted shade in the summer and where they wanted it in the winter. The changing seasons often determined where the trees were planted.

Windows were always the double-hung type so the tops could be lowered to remove the warm air in summer. The old kitchen building at Rancho Camulos has a large square hole in the ceiling that vents hot air from the abode's cucina straight up and outside. A window on the west brings in ocean air and circulates the hot air out the top. Even in 1850 they knew how to make nature work!

When possible, rooms were provided with cross ventilation for additional cooling at night—you were bound to get a breeze from one direction or the other. Every kid knew it was cooler on a linoleum floor than anywhere else during the day if you wanted to be inside. A nice patch of lawn under a big shade tree was even better.

When electricity gave every house a few wall plugs, fans made their entry. The old cardboard or palmetto fans were discarded for a fast breeze from an oscillating twelve-inch fan. The hum was enough to put the baby to sleep, and a wet dishtowel could be hung on the side of the crib for further cooling. If the baby was ill, a block of ice might be bought and set in a dishpan on a chair to help cool things.

The iceman brought a block of ice on a regular route to put into the icebox.

(An icebox was a wooden box with shelves and a place at the top for ice.) It would keep the milk and potato salad and the leftovers from lunch from spoiling. It was better than just the air cooler. Soon refrigerators were the best invention since sliced bread! With a few trays of ice, kids had cool lemonade. The milk stayed cold. Water was so much better than drinking it warm from the faucet. Mothers found it hard to keep the door closed on the fridge so things were often not as cold as she desired. If kids were really hot, they could stand with the door open a long time to select a snack and cool off at the same time. (Some things have not changed.)

In the Midwest, once it got hot in the summer, windows and doors were never closed. The old single-wall houses needed all the ventilation they could get in the summer. You learned to live with the heat.

In Fillmore, it was a different story. That wonderful, great, blessed coastal breeze usually arrived by midafternoon and saved the day. Better-built houses here did not heat up so much during the day. The first morning activity for mothers was to close up all the windows to save the cool night air. Then they had to keep the kids from running in and out every two minutes and opening the doors to let in hot air. When the west wind came up, they had to open all the windows and doors and start cooling the house so everyone could be comfortable to sleep for the night. Then in the morning, they closed up every window and—well, you see how that goes!

We live in a house that is fifty years old. We have added all the insulation possible in the attic and walls. We have installed double-pane windows. We have a bedroom with windows on three sides that open wide. We have mostly tile floors. The hall has a huge fan that sucks out the hot air at night. It goes into the attic and out the vents and allows the cool evening air to flow through the open windows. We have ceiling fans and moveable ones to place where needed.

Yep, every morning I close up the windows and shut the doors. Then later in the day, I open everything—hey, I guess you've heard this story before. But we do live very comfortable (most of the time) without air-conditioning, so guess Edison won't be sending us $200 this summer. Well, you win some and lose some, but we love it. Now if I could only get Gene to agree to sleep out on the patio------.

(My brother lives in Oklahoma, and a few years ago, he was working on the plumbing for a bathroom in a huge old home dating from the early 1900s. He discovered the walls were insulated with cotton seeds.)

Tornado Party

This spring, we are all aware that EVERY section of our country (and world) may be exposed to a natural disaster. Iceland has some very active volcanoes throwing ash into the air and making air traffic a mess this week. The "controlled" Mississippi River is flooding thousands of acres of farmland in addition to small towns and cities. The earthquakes in Japan, with the tsunami, have dealt those people more misery than they deserve. The tornados have wreaked havoc through the Midwest the past week. Living in California, we are always aware of brush fires that can quickly burn miles of forests and hundreds of homes.

I feel pretty experienced in local things. My first big earthquake occurred in 1952. We were living in an old frame house that moved around a lot but did not come apart, so we had minimal damage. Our second child was only two months old, and I had a hard time getting to her crib while Gene was trying to get through the moving door to comfort and protect our three-year-old. The Wrens have been very fortunate to only be on the edges of earthquakes, and we've never suffered major damage. When the last big one woke us in 1994, we discovered we were in good shape, put on our clothes, and went to San Cayetano School to report for work and do what we could for those who needed help. The town was a mess, but we all worked together to get back to normal in a few years.

Big brush fires along Guiberson Road put many acres of ranch property and family homes in danger, so we learned to fight fire. Foolishly, Gene stayed with his fire hose on Jim Shiells's house after the firemen abandoned their lines and pulled back to the road, but the house escaped damage. Many times our family helped load and unload precious items into our car as flames came down Pole Creek or burned along the south side of the river. That is just what friends do to help when there is a need.

In 1978, we were on the receiving end of help when the creek made a new path through Los Serenos. (When we bought the house in 1955, several old men told Gene it was too close to the creek and not a good location. However, we had a paper from the VA/federal government that said it was a safe spot, so we did not worry about Sespe Creek ever flooding our home.) Fortunately, the water was not in our houses very long, so we did not get the total damage that occurs when rivers flood and house are underwater for weeks at a time. We were so appreciative of the many friends who came to help us shovel mud, tear out walls, and get us back into our home. It was hard to believe so many people came to assist. For the first time in our lives, we had to ACCEPT HELP instead of being able to provide it. That was a totally new feeling for us.

A few days ago, a friend called me to turn on the TV and watch the storms around Ardmore, Oklahoma, where I grew up. It was different to be able to see the situation as it was happening. In a couple of hours, I started calling to check on my brother who lives in rural Ardmore. Yes, they had ten friends and family members in his concrete storm cellar. The tornadoes that day were small and only touched down in outlying areas, so there was no major damage. The golf-ball-sized hail damaged every car not under a roof, and it also ruined many, many home roofs. I guess that will provide work for many contractors for the rest of the summer.

When I called a cousin in Ardmore, it was hard to believe her story: they had over twenty people in their small storm cellar for ninety minutes. The last to arrive was a family of three, parents with a ten-year-old son who was almost hysterical. My cousin's house was the third one where these three strangers had asked for shelter; the first two had told them they did not have room enough to let them in. My family was ready to double-deck them if necessary, but no one would be turned away. I asked Cousin Phyllis if she felt like the Christmas story when Mary and Joseph were looking for shelter. (Since none of their friends were pregnant, they did not get a baby during the tornado, but you never know what to expect.) She had board games and room enough on the floor for the kids to play games until things passed over and it was safe for everyone to go home. She could not believe that anyone would turn away a family under these circumstances—me either!

Everywhere there is a natural disaster; you hear stories about people who come to the aid of strangers and those who don't. I like to think that in Fillmore, no one would be turned away. I also hope the city will get an emergency siren working so we know when we need to run for safety if the dam breaks. Oklahoma has the best system of tornado sirens, and often the people have a twenty-minute head start on finding cover and protecting themselves. I wish California could match that!

But I am glad we seldom need to have an impromptu TORNADO PARTY, but it is the newest thing throughout the Midwest.

Snow

When you get a group of women (or men, for that matter) together doing something that is almost automatic, you get rambling conversations. Eventually, those bring forth a single topic that will start each one remembering, and then you get a flood of stories. If you are peeling peaches to can, quilting or exercising, or maybe just drinking coffee, it gives plenty of time for the mouth to bring forth and illuminate!

Our topic today was snow in Fillmore. And we all had our stories. A couple of us were old-timers, a couple were younger native daughters, and we had one gal who had only lived here for a few years. She almost didn't believe us when we started telling about the big snows in past years.

I remember a snow in January of 1949, I think. We had only been married for a couple of years, and I was recently removed from Oklahoma and Midwest snows. According to what I had been told, this part of California did not have snow! Baloney! I saw it! It was heavy and wet, and it was cold. It had to be California snow. I was expecting our first child in about four months, but Gene had a coat that was large enough for me to button around my expanding middle, so he took me exploring in our recently acquired used car. It was great fun.

Then the next snow that I remember arrived in about 1956 or 1957. We had moved into a new house in 1955 with two small children, and it was exciting to see big flakes of the cold stuff falling. We were afraid it would melt before morning, so we awakened the kids so they could see it. As I recall, the kids were not as excited about it as the parents. It was another time of fun.

In 1970, our son was coming home on army leave before heading for Vietnam. Several wanted to go along with us to LAX to meet him, but his sisters stayed home to wait for him. Everything went according to plan until we left Los Angeles. Then the rain turned to snow, and we had another one to remember. It was slow driving, and we stopped at a restaurant on Lyons Avenue for coffee and a call home so the kids would know we were all right (before cell phones). Most of the freeway traffic was stranded there. We overheard a highway patrolman say they were closing the road, so we quickly returned to the car and headed out before the barricades were put up. We wanted to get home!

Of all the weird experiences we've had through the years, driving on the freeway in heavy snow (without chains) and not a single car in sight tops the list. Imagine eight traffic lanes with an occasional center divider and not another car or truck or even tire marks to show the way. Now that was weird!

It was slow going to the old 126, but we made the turn without slipping into a ditch and now faced two lanes toward home. Without a single track to follow, it didn't make much difference if we had two lanes or eight lanes. It was totally uncharted territory. We were real explorers for about a mile. As soon as we got to that first big curve, the headlights spotted truck after truck in the ditch beside the road. Some were jackknifed, and some just slipped into the drainage ditch. But those trucks were all dead in their tracks. At this point, it became man against the elements, as the snow continued to come down so heavy we didn't try to look at each flake. The windshield wipers kept most of it cleared so Gene could see. Fortunately, he is a good driver. He slowly maneuvered us past the trucks and up that first long hill and stayed somewhere on the road. In due time, we gingerly approached Piru, and the snow became lighter toward Fillmore. We'd made it in spite of everything the weather threw at us! I still know that somebody bigger than you and I took care of us that night.

It was a beautiful sight next morning. An orange tree covered with snow is pretty spectacular, and Fillmore had lots of orange trees then. After a couple of days, it was all gone, but it stayed in my memory. We don't get snow very often. It doesn't last very long, but we talk about it forever.

A few years later, Gene and several local men went to Los Angeles to a basketball game. They were extremely LATE getting home, and wives were worried or mad and still waiting up for them. The men all told the most unlikely of stories: they had gotten into snow over Weldon Grade! Yeah! You bet! However, the *LA Times* confirmed it the next morning, but one of the men never went along with them again.

I think our new history of the valley should include some good snow stories. Everyone has a story about these big snow events, so please write them down or call me so we can include a whole chapter with pictures. I am sure every family has some special memories, so help me save another group of stories. (And don't forget to keep working on your family history for me.) This BOOK will only happen if everyone helps.

East Wind

Everyone in Fillmore takes the East wind for granted! We have it every year. Sometimes it seems to blow for ten months out of the year, and other times it is a three-month occurrence. If you haven't lived with it, you can't believe it! It is sort of like the tale about grunion hunting when we get hot east winds in winter, but both of these things happen in Southern California. Most of us Oklahoma immigrants have learned to accept both of them as truth. (The only doubters are the ones who have not experience both of them.)

One year, our daughter Kathryn decided to do her science fair project on the East wind. (Do you remember when we had Bill Brisby as the science teacher who built up an outstanding program for our kids doing science projects?) She had to do lots of research without the help of a computer. She took daily reading from the weather station at the county fire station, made charts and grafts, and the whole family learned a lot about the East wind.

I was amazed to find out that it is also a naturally occurring phenomenon in Israel and Switzerland, so there are three places in the world where devil winds blow. Our early California history usually lists them as Santa Ana wind. Regardless of what we call them, they blow hard and hot. Coming from the desert, we expect them to be hot; however, it is not the desert that make them hot.

As the air high above the earth drops down from thirty-five thousand feet to the top of mountains and then flows over them to the valley floor, it is the atmospheric compression that produces the heat. (When a gas is compressed, it becomes hot—an old law of physics.) The streams of air pours through mountain passes and canyons like water and is further compressed and heated before it flows into the valleys. Since the circulation in a high-pressure zone is clockwise, we get winds from the north and northeast—thus, EAST WIND.

Of course, this is all mute this past week since the front was a cold one from Alaska and came from a low-pressure zone, and that east wind was not very warm. Weather can be very interesting. In my next life, I will take the place of Dr. Fichbach or Dallas Raines. I'd love to be a weatherman—lady!

While the East wind keeps the air superdry and encourages brush fires, when we get a low along the coast, we get moisture. Do any of you remember grandparents who told you "Tomorrow we will get some rain" after they noticed a large ring around the moon? That may just be fog or ice crystals in Southern California, but in the Midwest, it will often bring showers the next day. A ring around the moon certainly shows ice crystals in the atmosphere with moisture in some form.

Fillmore should soon be getting some beautiful sunsets. Now that the time has changed and winter sun sets about five or five thirty each afternoon, we will also see those gorgeous red and orange sunsets. I am not sure exactly why winter brings them, but a few clouds will reflect and make a picture to remind us of God's beautiful handwork. I love them.

One year, when we were living with my grandparents on the farm, we made an unscheduled trip to the cellar because the "clouds had a lot of wind in them." When the heavy rain hit, we found safety in our earthen cellar. I am sure that my grandparents would not have gotten out of their beds if they had been alone, but with a young family in the house, they were cautious. When the storm had passed and we started back into the house and our warm beds, I saw a lunar rainbow. The clear air and full moon made it light as day outside at 2:00 a.m., and there was an honest-to-goodness rainbow! They are very rare, but I got to view one in Oklahoma.

Every house in our part of Carter County, Oklahoma, also had a lightning rod. It was a strong iron pipe, or strap, that ran from above the highest roof section, down the side of the house, and into the ground. In case lightning struck the house, it would run into the ground and not hurt us. Although we had lots of lightning, I never heard of it striking a house or barn. Maybe we were just lucky.

One year, when we were camping with the Boy Scouts at Horseshoe Lake, we had a terrific thunderstorm on Mammoth Mountain, and lightning did strike a tree at the head of the lake and near our tents. What an explosion! It sure did get our attention, and the next day, we found the tree split by the electrical current. With metal tent poles, I never felt safe during a storm after that. We did hear of two campers who were killed when lightning struck while they were leaning against the tree with their backpacks' metal frames touching the bark. We did not repeat that story to the boys but filed it away in our list of things not to do when camping.

I've often thought about the excitement when the weather people saw the first satellite pictures from space showing clouds for hundreds of miles and being able to actually SEE weather in the making—what an experience. Yes, I would love to be a weatherman.

Floods Long Ago

Nature has a way of making us take notice of the drastic changes in the weather. Severe droughts gets our attention, but natural flooding is just as bad.

L. M. Hardison wrote a good description of the flooding in 1883 and '84, and here are some of the highlights. In mid-December of 1883, he moved his family to the Herculean Oil claim on the south slope of San Cayetano Mountain at the 2,600-foot level. Early showers in October and November had the grass greening up. By the first of January, it was six inches high in some places.

December brought high East winds, so the family had a difficult time erecting a tent on the floor that would become part of their new cabin. They eventually lowered the tent six inches to reduce the surface facing the wind and to give them enough canvas on the ground to weigh it down with stones to help hold it in place. They started erecting the cabin around and over the tent. Toward the end of January, as soon as the roof was finished and anchored with two cables, it began to rain.

The drought of 1877 was still in the minds of everyone. After the howling winds, many old settlers thought they were in for another dry year. Then the rains started. By February 8, they had gotten twenty inches, and it cleared for a few days. Mr. Hardison started for Los Angeles on February 13 with his span of mules. He needed to buy a wagon and was heading back home with his new rig on the fifteenth. He stopped in Newhall for the night, and it started to rain. During the next four days, they got ten inches of rain and four inches of snow. All the roads were washed out, and there was no traffic in any direction.

Mr. Hardison and a friend, Frank Whittier, left the wagon and rode the mules toward home on the nineteenth. They caved off the banks of many washouts to get the mules across. The road along the bluff east of Piru Creek was gone, so the men and mules took to the riverbed. The mules soon broke through the hardened mud and were mired in quicksand several times. The men pulled on the ropes around the neck of the mules and got them to roll over on brush several times until they found firmer ground. It was dangerous for both men and animals until they were able to get back on the road.

At Sespe Creek, they stayed all night with Mr. Kellogg. The next morning, all the community gathered to watch the crossing of the raging stream. No one expected the small mules to withstand the current and be able to swim across. If anyone took bets, they lost! Mr. Hardison and Frank Whittier, straddling the two mules, made the wet crossing without mishap. The stage did not cross until twenty-four hours later. By now, Santa Paula had been without any mail for a week. The floodwaters swept huge trees downstream. One-hundred-year-old oak, sycamore, and cottonwood trees were uprooted and floated down to the ocean. Many cattle, sheep, horses, and hogs were drowned or mired by the mud until they died.

On the seventeenth of February, the waiting family experienced a cloudburst during the night. Water and debris rushed down the gulch behind the cabin and nearly reached the house. The fireplace would not draw, so they could not light a fire against the cold and dampness. They were glad to survive this cold, wet storm and see the sunrise.

Mr. Hardison had been gone from home for ten days. The trail to his house was filled with debris. He had to take to the ridges and work around dangerous slides to get home. He found his family well but uncomfortable as everything was wet. The wind had driven the rain under the shake roof to soak clothing and bedding and damage the dwelling.

On March 7, and for several nights in succession, it rained and cleared up in the morning. These showers continued until they had seventeen rainy days in March.

The river and creeks washed away acres and acres of good farmland and left it filled with rocks and stones. Nearly all the bridges in Southern California were swept away. Horses were mired to the saddle blanket if they stepped out of the beaten path. Cows and hogs almost dropped out of sight in their muddy pens. Things were a mess. It was July before the fields were dry enough to plant corn, and it only made a fair crop. Other things were never planted that year.

From the cabin window, the Hardison family had a fine view of the Santa Clara Valley below. It looked like one great lake as far as the eye could reach. The rainfall at their cabin reached seventy inches in sixty days. No wonder it flooded! Through the years, it has not been unusual for either the railroad bridge or the highway bridge to wash out during a wet season—occasionally both! According to one source, the Sespe cut a new channel west of the creek in 1884. That continued to be the main channel most of the time until 1978. At that time, the Sespe tried to reroute itself above the North Fillmore section of town. It straightened out a curve in the creek bed and cut a new easterly path to the Santa Clara. This time, the full force of the water came in front of my house in the Los Serenos tract in the rush to pour into the Santa Clara. Many houses experienced flooding at that time. Afterward, the occupants had all the work and worry that comes with drying out, salvaging, and rebuilding. The citizens of Fillmore rallied around and helped their friends and neighbors for many weeks. The property owners along the upper Sespe wanted the water to stay in the channel on the east side, away from their land, and with their bulldozers, they helped it. With government assistance, a dike was constructed to protect the houses on the east bank from future flooding. The dike needed repairs during the rainy season two years ago, so it is false security, but we continue to close our eyes to what the river and creek can do to everything near their banks.

When we bought our Los Serenos house in 1955, local old-timers told us it was located in a flood plain for the creek. Our GI loan required a statement from some government agency that there was no danger of flooding, so we laughingly signed the loan papers and felt okay about the deal. After 1978, I looked many times for that piece of paper to frame and hang on our wall to remind us that thirty inches of water and mud in the house "was not considered flooding." Well, we live and learn. I expect the people buying new homes along the Santa Clara and Sespe will be reminded one of these days. Government assurance means nothing to floodwater. When the river and creek are in flood stage and decide to change course, you better grab your stuff and move to higher ground! I know.

If we get an El Niño next year and lots of rain, old-timers will listen, and when we hear the roar of the Sespe with boulders tumbling downstream and hitting one another loud enough to be heard a quarter of a mile away, we know there is water a-comin'. Newcomers will have to go down and watch the muddy water and debris rise higher and higher until only the tops of the shaking bridges are showing and the current is taking everything in its path. The Santa Clara will make waves jump three feet high and spread out a mile in width. When newcomers see that and stay up all night watching from the safety of their homes, then we can call them OLD-TIMERS. History has a way of repeating itself. Welcome to my world!

Santa Clara River flooding

Sespe and the River

The more you read, the more you learn. Recently, I found my copy of the Ventura County Historical Society Quarterly for Nov. 1962. (See, I told you I save GOOD stuff until I need it.) Harry Kenney wrote the whole story. His father worked land near Kenney Grove, and although he did not own the grove of oaks, it was named for him.

He wrote that the wet year of 1884 changed the Sespe Creek into what we see now with a broad alluvial plain connecting to the Santa Clara River. According to him, it started raining during the night of January 28^t and it rained almost steady for two weeks. The mountains were covered with snow down to the 500 ft. level. It was a cold rain! The last night of rain measured 4 inches with snow on San Cayetano Mountain.

When it turned warm, it was really warm. The snow quickly melted and added to the heavy runoff. I bet you could hear the rocks rolling down the creek then. Up to that time, the main channel of the Sespe was about a hundred to a hundred and fifty feet wide from about Moe Fine's place down to where the Sespe Bridge on Old Telegraph is now.

Usually before the heavy winter rains started, they threw a rope across the Sespe to ferry over the mail when the water got too deep. The banks were about 25 to 30 feet high and formed a narrow channel. During the flood of 1884, it crumbled the banks down and filled up the channel to where it is now. That is the reason the Sespe overflows whenever there is high water. The overflow runs out toward the east. There was no overflow and it never ran that way until 1884.

After the high water in 1987 and the Los Serenos flood, the ranchers above the bridge got some help from bulldozers and turned the water back into the overflow to protect their own property. Now that is now the main channel. One of these days we will have some heavy rains again and Sespe River will go back to its original path to the Santa Clara. Man made stuff only last so long!

We often look at the Santa Clara River and wonder what it looked like long ago. The center of the river is higher than the streets and new houses on the west side of the Bardsdale Bridge. In the early days before dams and houses along the river and creeks, the rush of water during the winter rains helped made a channel sort of down the middle of the river. It carried tons of dirt and sand to the coast. This sand kept the rocks along the coast covered so there was more sandy beach than we now see. In 2003 we have no way to make a channel in the river or have any control over where the water goes when it gets high. Flood Control wants it to be natural, so you better not do any work in the river bed. The water often bounces back and forth from one side to other and takes out many acres of orchards and farmland along the way.

This month we are reading many items in the papers about the St. Frances Dam flood and all the damage it did in 1928. That flood brought huge amounts of mud and silt down the river and left the riverbed filled and very shallow. The Santa Clara has never been the same as the whole river was changed in less than 5 hours. Well, so much for Mother Nature with a helping hand from Los Angeles Power and Light Company.

Droughts

IF you are a farmer, you probably look outside first thing every morning to see what the weather looks like. This often determines what work you will be doing. You probably have your own set of weather signs you go by to supplement what you learned on the TV news. A friend once read my grandmother's little 1895 diary and asked me, "Why does she always start off telling about the weather?" Obviously, this lady was not a farmer, and I had to explain to her how important weather is in the life of any farmer.

I don't know which has affected us the most, drought or flooding. Today, I will talk about the droughts that changed many lives.

From 1862 to '64, a drought killed three-fourths of the cattle and livestock in Ventura County. There was no grass or water for many months. That caused a major change in lifestyle. The huge land-grant ranchos were broken up and pieces sold off to pay debts and taxes. Cattle-breeding stock was never replaced, and things began to change with more agriculture.

The Civil War in 1861 brought a great demand for wool, so sheep were brought back into this area. At that time, wool was the best way to make money, so the industry prospered for fifteen years. In 1877, another drought fell upon the county. Many sheep died. One owner at Saticoy started his flock of eighteen thousand animals toward Soledad Canyon, looking for food and water. Many, many of the sheep died along the way as they slowly walked up our valley. They stopped for water at Castaic, but there was still no food. The last few sheep died that night. Imagine the odor in Santa Clara Valley with so many decaying carcasses. This was only one flock of many that perished. That drought took care of the sheep/wool industry in Ventura County.

In our own lifetime, we recalled years of drought too. We were inconvenienced with the pumping from wells and the water from

Northern California, but cattle and sheep did not die from lack of water. Often they were trucked to better pasture for food. They did not starve to death.

Southeastern Colorado had a two-year drought in 1891 after several unusually wet years. That part of the state is like our area for normal rainfall. It so happened my paternal great-grandparents went to Two Buttes in Colorado to homestead during the wet years. They were getting ahead with good crops and gardens and the increase in their stock. My great-grandfather and four sons each filed homesteads on 160 acres of land. When the drought started, they soon lost it all. By the second or third year, they had one team of horses surviving to get the family of twelve to Indian Territory. That year, Prowers County, Colorado, population went from six thousand to seven hundred. The homesteaders all starved out. Only sections of land that could be irrigated near the river remained in farming. The balance went back to smaller cattle operations as the land was now fenced and divided into smaller units.

Last month (July 2002), we drove through this same section of Colorado. It is again in the middle of a terrible drought. The ground is bare. The little creeks or streams are dry. There is neither food nor water for livestock or crops. The cattle were spread out and finding very little grass, and often they were being fed where they collected around a portable water tank. Times are repeating themselves. I can only imagine what it was like for my family in 1893 as they struggled to survive. They left behind three family graves, their dead stock, and the dream of owning land.

Many Oklahoma immigrants in Fillmore remember the Dust Bowl days in the Texas and Oklahoma Panhandle. The soil became so dry after several years of little rain that the wind picked it up and blew it to stack up against anything outside. Fences and farm tools were often completely covered by fine dirt. It mounded like snow against the side of houses and barns. Neither people, crops, nor animals could survive; so people had to move. The federal government started a program to help the remaining farmers learn how to save every drop of water that fell and use it on their fields. They made low contour terraces that held rain and watered the crops. Not a drop was wasted. Soil conservation districts were formed to help teach farmers methods for improving the land and securing better yields. It took several years, but a few farmers refused to give up and survived as they learned to cope with the change in the weather. That drought changed the way the land was farmed from the 1930s until today.

Every drought affects farmers, ranchers, and the urban residents who use the limited water. It's okay to look out the window each morning to see what the day will bring. Maybe it will be rain.

Rain and Drought

One of the stories from Rancho Camulos is about the year they started to enlarge the main adobe home. Since they had ninety acres of grapes, Ygnacio del Valle wanted a place to make wine for both home and retail market. They always needed a cash crop, and wine was one of their early one.

About 1860, they started on the project. They dug a basement/cellar as the first step in their split-level addition. Well, as most constructions projects turn out, about the time they got a good start, it started to rain in Ventura County. That year, it rained and rained and rained. It was recorded we had thirty days straight of rain. When I started work at Camulos several years ago, we would laugh at the thought of this area ever having that many consecutive days of rain. After last year (2005), we now know it is certainly possible, so that sort of ruins my story. Eventually, the unauthorized pond/cellar beside the house dried out, more adobe bricks were made, and the four-room addition was completed.

The next year was dry. It was so dry that it was thought to be a real drought. The second year was just as dry. Pastures were eaten down to bare ground and livestock started to die from lack of any water. By the end of the second year, three-fourths of all the livestock in Ventura County was dead. It was so bad around Rancho Camulos that Ysabel asked Ygnacio if they could drag off some of the decaying cattle so it did not smell so bad at the house.

One man with seventeen thousand head of sheep near Saticoy Springs heard about some water and grass near Lake Elizabeth. He was desperate to provide food and water for his animals and decided to slowly herd them up the valley and into that area. By the time he got to I-5, he had two head of sheep left. All of them had died along the way.

This drought ended the rancho era for Ventura County. Many of the big Mexican land grants sold off large holdings to Americans who were flooding into the valley. The old land-grant families needed cash to pay their two years of accumulated debts. American authorities insisted they prove their title to the land again so they needed lawyers. There was no money to buy cattle to restock the old pastures. The United States government wanted taxes paid in a timely manner. Our county soon turned to agriculture.

Now the point of my story this week! Does any of this weather sound familiar to you? Last year, we set a record for rainfall in Ventura County. This year, we can barely beg an inch of moisture from the skies. I hope the dry spell does not continue for several more years, but it may. Fortunately, we have enough water to maintain homes, farming, and the limited animal population; but we really need to be careful and not waste a drop. (Hurrah for the city who is working on plans to recycle waste water from the new sewer plant and use it on school lawns and parks—that will cut down on the amount we need to pump from underground. The more we can save, the better off the water table will be for future pumping.)

YEP! HISTORY DOES REPEAT ITSELF!

Weather

I am a weather nut! I've always enjoyed looking at clouds and watching the sky and doing my own prediction about what we could expect. I suppose this comes from living with grandparents on the farm and having the weather not only control what we did but also what sales from the crops and garden would be in a few months. I come from generations of farmers, and weather was an important factor in their lives.

Grandpa knew what the wind looked like in dark, gray clouds on a stormy night. Grandma was sure that a red sunset meant we'd have wind the next morning. They were usually right too. One year, I encouraged one of our girls to do her science fair project on the EAST WIND IN FILLMORE. I don't know if she had fun, but her mother sure did. We researched the wind phenomena in other parts of the world and recorded it in town for several months. (Yes, two other places on the globe have their own East wind—Switzerland and Israel.) The heat is not generated from blowing across the desert. It is generated when the wind drops down the side of the mountains and is compressed as it gets to sea level, and it is this compression that heats the wind up!

One spring, I was visiting in Oklahoma, and my brother called me to take our mother to his house and be near his storm cellar as there was a tornado in the area. We went next door, and I got Mom settled into a comfortable chair while I observed the clouds outside. What a fascinating afternoon for me. The tornado went around us, so we did not go to the cellar, but I saw the most beautiful clouds scudding along for two hours. They were in layers of all shades of gray, from almost black to a light smoky color. Some were very low, and each layer was moving in a different direction. It was beautiful to watch, but eventually they gathered and all blew away and ended the show for me.

I've wondered many times what Dr. George Fishbeck thought the first time he saw the global picture after the first weather satellite was launched (ABC TV). Years ago, he was a favorite of mine, and he loved to give a lesson on weather at least once a week or when he thought it fit into his prediction for the next day. What an improvement when these meteorologists could see what was happening over the globe and figure out how it would affect us in California.

This column got started last night when I was reading a girl's diary about her growing years following a father who was in the army from 1878 to about 1900. They lived in New York, Michigan, Kansas, Oklahoma, and Texas. It was a short book, so it didn't take long to go cover to cover with it. The back section had almost fifty pages of detailed notes. In these notes, I found the following about a bad Norther they lived through when they were stationed near the Mexican border in Texas in 1883. They had just arrived, and it was ninety-nine degrees. The next day, they had snow. Now, that is a real NORTHER! The signal officer telegraphed her father who was in charge at Fort Ringgold. He reported it would be getting very cold overnight. Her mother got out the blankets and flannel underwear for her family, and they still almost froze for a couple of days.

The notes said, "This warning from the signal officer about the approaching Norther is an interesting confirmation of the efficiency of the fledging weather early-warning system established by the Signal Corps of the U. S. Army. After the American Civil War the army began an extensive project to install a military telegraph system linking the frontier posts. In concert with this system Congress authorized in 1870 for certain telegraph stations to have army operators trained in weather observation and equipment in order to furnish data to centralized collection points. The meteorological observations systems provided public warning of approaching storms and dangerous weather changes to farmers and sailors, resulting in an enormous benefit to the public good and nearly universal praise from citizens. By 1879 the system was very sophisticated, with 133 stations making observations and reports. This system is generally the progenitor of the National Weather Service of today."

Gee, I wonder if Dallas Raines and Fritz Coleman on TV know about this! Maybe I should send them an e-mail.

One year, when we were living on the farm with our grandparents, we made a run to the cellar. When the thunderstorm passed and we started back inside to our beds, a full moon produced a lunar rainbow. That has been the best weather experience of my life!

Blizzard

In this modern day, we take so much for granted! We expect to have electricity at the flip of a switch. We know clean water will run from any faucet we open. We know sewage will be drained away and processed and trash is hauled on schedule. We know telephones are in every pocket (hand or ear) to instantly contact anyone, anywhere, anytime! What a world we live in.

It hasn't always been that way! I was fortunate to grow up at the end of the olden times—the pioneer times were being phased out for the country people, while the people in town enjoyed the new, modern way of living. This gave me a great perception on both worlds. The odd thing about it all is that I enjoyed both worlds and never felt cheated that I went from fancy town living to country living all in the same day. That was just the way IT WAS.

Living on a farm with grandparents made me very aware of the weather. It controlled the work for the day, our income for the year, and what happened to us. It was an integral part of living. It was noted every morning as work was planned. It determined how we dressed for school and what we ate for supper. It was a part of our lives!

My grandparents were great weather predictors. After living in Indian Territory for all their married lives, they KNEW the weather. They looked at clouds, felt the winds, and had an idea about what to expect for the day and the coming week. It was all just experience. After we got a battery radio, they never missed the evening weather report—it was important to them. Cash was scarce, so the battery was saved for the news, weather, *Amos 'n' Andy*, and maybe the *Grand Ole Opry* on Saturday night. It was not used to entertain two grandkids who had books to read and games to play by lamplight.

Recently, I read *The Children's Blizzard* by David Laskin. It is the true story about a blizzard in 1888 that killed about three hundred people in the Dakotas, Minnesota, and Nebraska. It came suddenly after a day of spring weather. No one expected it. No one was prepared. After a long and cold winter, a day in January was a warm spring day. Everyone wanted spring to arrive. The men took care of livestock and outside chores, and most of the kids went back to school in light clothing. It was an enjoyable day.

Kids usually lived less than three miles from school. Most of them enjoyed attending class and missing home chores during the day. It was a time to learn and socialize with friends. As the day progressed, very young teachers in the one-room rural schools became alarmed as the weather changed so quickly and drastically. Some turned out school early to let the kids start home before the new front hit. Others were too late and kept the children at school, hoping to ride it out, but when the roof of the schoolhouse was blown off, they tried to get the kids to the nearest house, which often was only a quarter of a mile from the building. One town got together a caravan of wagons and came to rescue the kids and get them all home. Every school, teacher, and student had a different set of circumstances and just did the best they could. Many did not live through that event.

The wind picked up the snow and turned it into fine particles, which made for whiteout conditions. In the extreme cold, snow particles froze eyelids and plugged up noses on humans and cattle. Once you left shelter, you were totally lost. It is like flying in dense fog with no way of knowing any direction. While parents worried, teachers and kids tried to survive. The next day, groups were found in haystacks, in small groves of trees, under overturned sleighs, or out in the open where the bodies were clutching each other for comfort. It was a terrible sight. A few who survived the night dropped dead the next morning as they rose and started toward home. Others lived a few weeks before dying. Some survived with the loss of limbs. There were many heroes. There were many fatalities.

This story contains detailed information about the weather and the conditions that brought about the awful cold. Record temperatures as low as –70°F were shown in some areas. Now that is COLD! The blizzard blew through to South Texas with freezing temps all the way. Predicting the weather was a new science and primitive.

Our National Weather Service had not been organized. After the Civil War, the military knew they needed to know more about predicting weather and set up a series of recording stations along the new telegraph lines in the North and West. These army men took regular reading of temperature, wind speed, and barometer pressure and sent their information to a main station in Saint Paul, Minnesota. The first graphs and barometric plottings were made and forwarded to Washington, DC. The experts there sent back predictions for the nation, and our weather reporting began. The biggest problem was the time lapse from the original readings and getting out the weather news to the stations, who then flew a flag of white with a large black circle to indicate severe storms or weather. That was their only way to notify people.

While the military was getting stations organized and making recordings, the civilians in Washington started their own set of rules in new offices. Now as we all know, you can't have two bosses and get good results. The terrible aftermath of the blizzard in 1888—amid much squabbling, finger-pointing, and dissensions—brought the two groups together in 1890 under the Department of Agriculture, and the National Weather Service was officially born. The Army Signal Corps was out when President Ben Harrison asked Congress to put it all under civilian control. And Congress agreed. This was the start of our current weather predictions and information that people still need. It did not solve all the problems, as we well know from the hurricanes in 2005, but it helped.

I am still the local weather prophet for the Wrens! My family knows that when I start sneezing badly, in two or three days, we will have allergy-laden East winds. Old habits die hard.

Western Fires

In reading about the recent fires in western Texas and Oklahoma, the devastation in Cross Plains, Texas, clearly brought up old memories to me. I was born near there in 1928. My father worked for the Amerada oil company, and we lived on a company lease with six or seven houses. It was sort of like the old Torrey lease here. Families often lived near the job. These houses were located in Coleman County and a few miles from Cross Plains. I was only eighteen months old when my father was transferred to Hobbs, New Mexico, so I do not remember anything about the land and our home except from family pictures.

Two years ago, when Gene and I drove back to my family reunion in Oklahoma, we made a zig down into Texas so I could see the area where I was born and where my grandmother lived before her family removed to Indian Territory. We drove through the little town of Cross Plains and looked at the short grass prairie and scrub brush. I imagined the day of my birth when my mother was driving to visit a friend and her labor started. My grandmother had come to be with her daughter for the home delivery, and Grandma immediately got them turned around and headed back to home. I was a second child, and Grandma did not want to make the delivery beside the road. Mother was doing the driving. Woe is me! I am glad I was not driving a car when my labors started. But Mother got them back home and prepared for my arrival.

I enjoyed seeing the little town near where I was born. The old oil company housing leases have all vanished in the ensuing seventy-five years, so we did not see the actual site. I hope the people still living in Cross Plains can recover and rebuild after the current fires. Life has been hard for lots of people in 2005, so let's hope 2006 is better.

Our first thought last week was anyone should be able to control a grass fire, but with the winds in that area, fire is not controlled as we expect it to be. Fire is not a common thing around Cross Plains either. They are not used to fires and are not trained to control them. Oklahoma has no county fire department, as we know them. Some areas have small volunteer departments with a fire truck in a central location and ready when volunteers need to use it. Bake sales and fundraisers help the men secure needed equipment, but they receive almost no county money to keep them in business.

I am not sure how the state of Texas handles rural fire departments— and maybe they don't have them either. There is little need to fight grass fires as they soon burn out, unless it is a time of drought and high winds. Then the fires are uncontrollable. Citizens are not careful with open fire, fireworks, open burning of trash, etc. They continue life in the usual way. In Southern California, we are all aware of being careful with any fire and avoiding brush fires, but it is not the same everywhere.

The people in Ventura County and Fillmore should appreciate our good fire departments in both town and the surrounding areas. I hope we never see Piru in the situation of Cross Plains—destroyed!

While we all complain about our taxes, let's also remember what we are getting for our tax dollar—lots of protection! (And remember to buy insurance to cover your home from fire and flood.) It is always better to BE PREPARED.

Late Rains

Sespe Runnin' Full

Wow! Isn't it good to see SUNSHINE again? A week or more of the early June gloom may not be over, but at least there is a sunny break. It is reported that Thomas the Train is sold out, so town will be full of those city folks for another weekend. Locals don't mind all the visitors when they can see our town is getting something in return for our inconvenience. It is essential Fillmore & Western Railway work with local business and citizens to make it all run smoothly. It is thinking about our spring rains and the Rancho Camulos Museum art show that got me into this column.

April in 1926 brought Fillmore a lot of rain. It seemed very late, but weather does seem to repeat itself. We certainly had lots of late rain again in 2006. The 1926 *Herald* reported almost four inches in February to bring the total up to 11.96 inches. The government rain gauge was located at the home of Richard Stephens on Central Avenue across from the high school. The last heavy downpour had both the Sespe and Santa Clara running strong. I don't know if there was any rain in March, but April reported over six inches early in the month and another good drenching in May. The April rain was the greatest storm since 1919, so records were made to be broken.

In 1919, those 6.6 inches washed out all the bridges in the upper section of Piru Creek and marooned oil workers for several days. The Hopper Creek washout stopped all traffic on the impassable road. The Sespe could be heard from some distance as it rolled boulders toward the Santa Clara. George Henley's Sespe camp rain gauge filled with 9.5 inches during the week. There were heavy slides on the road to his resort and camp, and he opened the road up to Pine Creek so oil-field traffic could get into their well sites. Joe Russell lived three miles farther up the canyon from Henley, and he recorded 13.5 inches. No wonder the Sespe was running full. For a brief time, the Santa Clara River was almost to the top of the old Bardsdale Bridge.

Castaic Bridge was damaged, so traffic was detoured via Grimes Canyon from Fillmore. This was before the grade had been cut from 18 percent to the present 6 percent—can you image driving that steep, unpaved road just to leave town? I suspect many families just got by with what they had in the pantry until other roads were open. By the end of the rainy season, Fillmore had recorded 20.14 inches of rain. Well, many things have not changed in eighty years.

Regardless of the light rain early Sunday morning, about seventy people gathered on Tietsort Hill for Easter sunrise service. Paul Goodenough was in charge of the singing on that celebration day.

The late Easter was soon forgotten, and opening day for trout fishing was on the mind of most of the men. State Game Warden Emerick estimated between two and three thousand persons along the Sespe for the traditional May 1 opening. Los Angeles had discovered fishing on the Sespe, and those guys flocked to the creek. Approximately 1,500 people entered Henley's camp by noon on Sunday. On top of everything else, Fillmore had an earthquake early Monday morning that was felt by all the campers. The recent rains had loosed many boulders, and the sharp shake sent rocks onto the steep roads up canyon. A cloudburst on Sunday caved in a wall on the bank of Coldwater Creek and made the Sespe muddy. It was not a good opening day for fishing on the Sespe, so people from out of town soon left for home. Locals knew the creek would soon clear up, and then they could really wet a line and catch their limits. And they didn't worry about those city guys. The weather in 1919 controlled everything.

Locals still experience many of the same natural phenomenon of heavy rain and earthquakes. Still, hope springs eternal that someday we will have good fishing in the Sespe again, the trail up the creek will be open to the public, and traces of the old brownstone quarry and Henley's camp could be explored. Dreams, dreams, dreams!

Chapter 5

ST. FRANCIS DAM FLOOD

The ninetieth anniversary of the St. Francis Dam disaster in our valley was celebrated in 2018. Let me give newcomers in Fillmore a brief report: Los Angeles built a dam on a small creek and canyon called San Francisquito in 1927. It was north of Canyon Country. Even then, Los Angeles needed more water. Their far-sighted and self-educated engineer, William Mulholland, found a likely spot for a dam to hold Sierra runoff until the city needed it during the summer.

A great arch-shaped concrete dam was stretched across the little canyon. The reservoir was filled with diverted snow runoff, and the resulting storage was enough to then provide Los Angeles with water for a year. It contained thirty-four thousand acre-feet of water with a surface covering six hundred acres. Before the dam was built, the water from this little creek flowed into the upper reaches of the Santa Clara River and eventually to the ocean between Ventura and Oxnard.

Mulholland seemed to have a great talent for knowing about rocks, earth, and water. It was a natural thing for him. He was very successful with the Los Angeles projects. Engineering tools and testing equipment were almost nil in the 1920s, so engineers learned by hands-on work.

The dam was completed, and a drought two years later confirmed the wisdom of the planning. Early in March of 1928, a small seep on the face of the dam was reported. After an inspection, it was agreed there was no problem. Edison had several substations in the area connected to the dam providing electricity for Los Angeles County and the Santa Clara Valley

On March 12, 1928, at 11:57 p.m., the lights in Los Angeles flickered momentarily. Saugus Substation had the Lancaster transmission line short out, and this brought the resident personnel to emergency duty. People living near the dam felt the earth move and thought they had experienced an earthquake. There was major trouble.

The dam broke. A wall of water 185 feet high started down the canyon. It took the liquid avalanche five minutes to travel the mile and a half to Powerhouse No. 2. The first few miles, the depth varied from 100 to 140 feet, and nothing could withstand the violence of the flood wave.

Remains of the dam

The water followed its natural course down the canyon, across Newhall and the Santa Clara River, across Highway 5 to Castaic Junction, and down our valley. It took an hour to go ten miles. At the head of our valley, it was about one hundred feet high and moving at eighteen miles an hour. It swept away everything in its course—homes, people, orchards, and bridges.

Edison had a camp of men at Blue Cut—the narrow place in the valley east of Camulos. They were working on new lines, and the camp was located back away from the river on a slight slope. Most of the 185 men drowned in their tents before the night watchman could alert them to a problem.

When the police and firemen at the lower end of the valley were notified of the approaching water, they began trying to wake rural families and those in towns to move to higher ground. Telephone operators made as many calls as possible to alert people. Several individuals provided outstanding service and helped save many lives. The Piru area was hard hit. For some reason, the local Fillmore police chief, Earl Hume, did not receive the phone call that would put him on duty. By the time a man in a car arrived to alert Fillmore, the water was starting to rise, and it was too late to help Piru. He started ringing the old fire bell to wake residents and let them know something was very wrong. Bardsdale Bridge was immediately washed out by the spreading wall of water, and those living near the river were swept away.

Basolo home

In Santa Paula, many people were able to move to higher ground before the twenty-five-feet wave came through. It floated houses to the school grounds on Harvard Street. The flood reached the coast at 5:30 a.m. It carried tons of debris into the ocean, and the wide gray band of water stretched out to the Channel Islands. Now it was time for the cleanup to begin.

In less than six hours, hundreds of lives were changed forever when the St. Francis Dam broke. Until the recent 9/11 incident in New York, it was one of the worst disasters ever recorded in the United States. The Santa Clara Valley and the riverbed were changed forever. The stories will be handed down for generations about families that were lost and families who survived by some miracle.

The best estimates and records show 420 people lost their lives and over ten thousand agricultural acres were destroyed. The bridge at Saticoy was the only one left standing—everything else between Newhall and Ventura was washed away! The road along Blue Cut was gone. Where the road was not washed away, it was covered by mud and debris. Everyone was involved in the rescue operations.

Within an hour after the flood passed through, the American Red Cross was setting up canteens and organizing kitchens so people could be fed. The Newhall Red Cross opened a canteen at 3:45 a.m. and notified Los Angeles about the need for help in the valley. Soon, the National Chapter was alerted and help was arriving. Southern Pacific ran trainloads of rescue workers as far as possible on the washed-out tracks. The Southern California fuel and truck companies donated gasoline and equipment without charge. The Auto Club rushed transportation to the valley, and sixty Los Angeles policemen patrolled the area to keep out sightseers. Help arrived immediately, and there was plenty to do.

Local people were checking on their relatives and finding survivors in the process. Even before daylight, survivors were straggling into nearby houses. Often they were completely nude, as the force of the water had torn every shred of clothing from their bodies.

The August Rubel family had only owned Rancho Camulos for four years, so they were newcomers to this part of the valley, but they were one of the first groups to start rescue operations. The few nude survivors from the Edison camp got their immediate attention and help. Although over seven hundred acres of their land and orchards were washed away, the Rubels were giving food and clothing to the Edison men. Their ranch equipment and workers searched the wreckage for victims and removed tons of debris for weeks.

As soon as workers could see, they started finding survivors clinging to trees, utility poles, on rooftops, and half buried in the mud. Several families disappeared completely. No trace was ever found of any of them. Sometimes a single member survived to tell their story. Bodies were taken for identification by the county coroner, Oliver Reardon. Rescuers heading for the river to start work remembered the damp smell that wafted in the early morning air long before they could even see the devastation. The cleanup effort continued until August, when the last bodies were discovered by a farm crew. Most of the bodies were identified and buried.

While Boy Scouts are renowned for being prepared, after the flood in 1928, the local troop was called in to a duty they were not prepared to do. As usual with Scouts and kids, they rose to the occasion and met the challenge!

Early in the morning, the scoutmaster contacted his boys to meet him down by the foot of Bardsdale Bridge. It had been washed away, but the area needed to be searched. Toolie Palmer, Curt Fisher, Oscar Defever, and Jack Ipswitch, with the rest of the troop, were soon there for duty. The boys were formed into a long line to canvas the north side of the Santa Clara River. After walking almost to Piru, they found one dead horse and headed for home.

Toolie Palmer recalls they were sent to the school gardens for the rest of the day to work. These gardens were planted in the area now covered by bleachers at the high school football field. There were tables and benches, and soon bodies were being brought there before being taken to the morgue in Santa Paula. Although the kids did not find bodies in their work, others were finding the remains of many local people who did not survive the wall of water that swept down the valley.

The Boy Scouts were asked to use a hose to wash off the deceased so they could be identified and appropriate action could be taken by the adults. This was something that none of them had ever expected to be called upon to do. Everyone in Fillmore was involved in the aftermath of the flood, and everyone did what was necessary.

Americans seem to always rise to the occasion. (There are many books and stories about this tragic incident available with many, many details if you are interested.)

Rebuilding Bardsdale Bridge across Santa Clara River

Chapter 6

OTHER STUFF

Blue Laws

I'd bet most of you do not remember the blue laws. I don't know why they were named that, but they were local ordinances that said no business could be open on Sunday. They were enforced in Fillmore until about the mid-1950s, as I recall. Sunday was a day to go to church or go somewhere with your family or visit the neighbors. It was NOT a day to go shopping, buy gas, or go to the grocery store. Adults had all week to do those things, and on Sunday, the shops were closed so the owners had a day of rest too. When you think about it, that wasn't such a bad idea!

Like most things, if you don't know any difference, that was just the way it was. Stores had always been closed on Sunday, so we all thought it was supposed to be that way. We were all newlyweds at that time—at least, we hadn't been married more than a couple of years. We lived from payday to payday, did some serious budgeting, and planned meals without leftovers. My pantry contained what I expected to cook for the two of us the following week. Our little kitchens did not have much storage room, our purses did not have much money, and we fed our husbands frugally.

If we had unexpected company, it was a real scramble to feed them. When we lived on the farm, my mother just went out and killed another chicken to fry, but living in town was different. If company came soon after we'd grocery shopped, we could manage, but if it was near the end of the month, food might be more than a little sparse. One friend told me about finding her cupboard bare soon after she married. She had very little of anything to put together a meal except for potatoes. She dug into her sack of spuds and baked enough for everyone and served them with sour cream to go with the other little items for the table. Her guest got their first introduction to baked potatoes with butter and sour cream, and that meal was a big hit. They loved it.

It always worried me that I might not have food to cook if friends stopped by unannounced. In those days, people visited when they had time, and it was never necessary to make prior arrangements. Many of us did not have phones to call ahead, so it was very acceptable to just drop in. We soon learned to always have a little extra stuck back in case we needed it to feed company over the weekend and all the stores were closed.

I don't know if the blue laws were rescinded or eventually just ignored. After a few years, the gas stations and grocery stores were open seven days a week—that was a relief! It was a comfort to know we would not be caught in a lurch when we needed extra food. Many of us still try to plan ahead just in case we need to feed visiting friends. (But come to think of it, I don't remember the last time anyone dropped by the house to see us without letting us know in advance they would be there for a meal.)

CCC

CCC camp up the Sespe

Recently, we were watching JEOPARDY after dinner, and one of the questions asked was, "What did CCC stand for?" It seemed a rather simple question for people with IQs so high on the charts, but none of them got the correct answer. When I occasionally know a right response, I get pretty excited. I kept prompting them with CIVILIAN CONSERVATION CORPS, but nothing happened. They all lost, and I didn't get any points either! Once again I was reminded that I am getting old and often remember things that are so out-of-date with younger people.

Soon after Franklin D. Roosevelt and the Democratic Congress took office, the CCC was set up. It was part of the emergency program of 1933 and helped many young men and communities benefited from their productive work. About 2 million men served before it was abolished by Congress in 1942.

When the bottom fell out of the stock market in 1930, suddenly there was very little work for men. You can still see movies about men begging on the street corners or selling apples and pencils—well, that really happened. There was no welfare to take care of you. It was a do-it-yourself project. You were fortunate to have a job paying a dollar a day for ten hours work, seven days a week, and no vacation or sick time. If you didn't like it, you always had the option of quitting. There was a long line waiting to take your place.

The CCC gave young men the opportunity to work for room and board. Everything they needed was provided, and they could collect thirty dollars a month, rain or shine. Medical care was included. The men needed very little of their money, so twenty-five dollars was sent to their families back home each month. Their work kept many people from starving. The duties for the CCC boys were to plant trees, build dams, improve roads, fight forest fires, construct buildings and lakes, and prevent soil erosion of the lands in our national forests. This work provided the tools to teach the men trades they could use in industry when their enlistments were completed. It was a good solution to a national problem.

After a young man enlisted, he was given a departure date when he was to show up at the railroad station with no luggage—just his comb, a toothbrush, and the clothes on his back. An army officer met them there with a roster to check off names and assign them a seat in the Pullman car. The train was set up with a military kitchen and four enlisted men to do the cooking. Some of these kids had full stomachs for the first time in many months. A porter made up their beds at night, and they travelled first class all the way. What an experience for most of them.

When they arrived at a military complex, they were physically checked from head to foot and given new GI clothing with the brass buttons replaced with regular ones. The old WWI uniforms were in use again. After smaller units were formed, assignments were made and the boys were put back on the trains headed for (?) again. At the end of the line, they were loaded into open trucks and taken to their final destination to start work.

The larger work camps had barracks to accommodate about eighty men, an administration building that included an orderly room, a mess hall, a dispensary, a supply room, and a motor pool. The recreation building had a pool, a Ping-Pong table, a library, a canteen, and a post office. Although this was a civilian camp, it was run with military style.

Fillmore had a CCC camp a short distance up the Sespe. One of their major projects was to build a road so the area was accessible by car for several miles. Everywhere in the USA you will find small bridges with the distinctive CCC mark and a date on the approach. Lakes and recreation buildings and picnic grounds show their touch. Many community buildings have a cornerstone with the same mark. These young men helped improve civic parks, roads, and structures. Over a period of time, Sespe Creek took its toll on that road, and it is now gone; but for many years, locals enjoyed the easy access for family outings.

Kenneth Fine said the local boys did not like the CCC because they got all the girls. I guess their Sespe Canyon camp was within walking distance of Fillmore, and they came to town occasionally.

These young men learned a trade that helped them get a job when their enlistment was up and they went home. When times became better, this training was invaluable and was put to good use. They were the older, experienced men in the military when WWII started. They were proud of their work and had something to show for it. A few surviving elderly men can still tell stories about that period in their lives.

While researching at the Ventura museum library last week, I found the rest of the story on the Fillmore CCC camp. As happens with so much historical research, while you are looking for one thing, something else jumps out of the paper for you. As long as I have been telling you about the CIVILIAN CONSERVATION CORPS, I'd like to finish up.

The first camp in Ventura County was located at the entrance of Sespe Canyon and was known as Camp 560. It was composed of 224 officers, state forest service employees, and enlisted men.

The camp consisted of sixteen squad tents to sleep ten men each, two headquarters tents, and two officers' tents. The mess hall was one hundred feet long and thirty-two feet wide. The enlisted men all came from Indiana and were between the ages of eighteen and twenty-five. They received thirty dollars a month and enlisted for six months.

Clothes, medical, and food were furnished. The mess sergeant was allowed thirty-three cents per day per man for food. (I wish I could find a menu and see how the cook managed for that cost. I bet the boys were fed well too.)

According to the *Fillmore Herald*, "the camp was welcomed by the local people who did everything possible to make the sojourn of the young men as enjoyable and pleasant as possible." There was another camp at Newhall Ranch and one of the largest near Santa Paula.

Some of the projects listed for the Fillmore area were as follows:

- Repair and completion of the old wagon road running from Torrey to the Simi Valley and Santa Susana district
- Brushing out Lords Creek
- Fire trail west of the lookout station on Santa Paula peak and a new fire trail from Sespe to San Cayetano
- Reestablishment of the road to Grassy Flat by way of the Big Sespe
- New road to Squaw Flat and Sespe Hot Springs to connect with the present road at Tar Creek
- New lookout station on South Mountain

If this was not enough to keep them busy, the camps listed the welfare programs and athletics; library service including newspapers, magazines, periodicals and writing materials; education; religious service; camp exchanges; radio receiving sets; and miscellaneous games. (Perhaps the trip to town where they got all the girls—according to Kenneth Fine—was considered one of the miscellaneous games.)

Currently, we have the CALIFORNIA CONSERVATION CORPS that often help with disaster cleanups and fires in the state. This group still maintains the concept of military rules as originally established but has expanded to include young women and is mixed racially. It, too, deserves our support when they work around Fillmore.

It may be an old-fashioned idea, but giving people the chance to work, learn new skills, and receive monetary help is still THE WAY TO GO!

CCC camp up the Sespe

Kelp

In the '50s, when we went to the beach, we often found it littered with seaweed. The kids loved it. There were long ropes of stem, huge leaves, and the large hollow balls that made the whole plant float underwater. Often we could see the kelp cutter working offshore. It was sort of a wheat combine working on water. There had to be a big scythe deep under the water in the front to cut this massive plant, then a paddlewheel pulled the cut kelp into the barge. All the stuff that did not get loaded soon floated to the beach on the next high tide. It made a mess, but kids loved it, and with a little imagination, they played their own games with it in the sand and water.

Kelp was used in a host of food products—Jell-O, medicines, paper, beer, and cosmetics. I don't know where they harvest kelp in this century, but it sure isn't along the Rincon. I'd bet they killed a good thing by cutting too much of it.

Biologists from Santa Barbara to San Diego are now working to recarpet the ocean floor with giant kelp that has largely disappeared from the region. Less than 25 percent of the kelp beds remain along the Southern California coast. Millions of dollars have been spent trying to solve the problem the last thirty years. Now we know what does not work but know very little about how to fix the problem.

Like coral reefs and tropical rain forests, kelp is a critical habitat. Its floating canopies provide shelter and feeding grounds for marine life. Without it, the fish population will continue to shrink. Private agencies and the government have tried to restore the kelp beds to no avail.

Divers have tried hand-planting thousands of seedlings. When that did not work, they scattered spores. Giant nets were draped over the baby kelp beds to try to protect them from being eaten by marauding sea urchins and fish.

Giant kelp in the Northern Hemisphere only grows along the California and Alaskan coasts. It requires very cold water to thrive. Several episodes of warm-water La Niñas have not helped. Overfishing has not helped. Harvesting it for our use did not help. These things combined have killed out the kelp beds. It comes down to a balance of nature in the ocean. We need lobsters, sheepshead fish, and sea otters that feed on the sea urchins. Those sea urchins are the thing that feed on the tiny kelp plants.

After many experiments, Tom Ford of Santa Monica seems to have come the closest to being successful. He cleans the ocean floor of sea urchins. Then kelp is planted, and he also adds mesh bags filled with kelp leaves, which release millions of spores into the water. His original eight-kelp plants have multiplied into an acre. If he can keep the sea urchins out long enough for the kelp to take hold, he will eventually get the balance of nature restored in his little spot of ocean.

Although El Niño and La Niña are probably a natural occurrence, when that was combined with overfishing and kelp cutting, everything went haywire. We need the cold water. We need a kelp forest that brings in the fish that, in turn, keeps the sea urchin population under control—now that is balance! Good luck, Tom Ford! We wish you well and hope we've learned a lesson from overcutting kelp along the Rincon.

We want kids to always have a few strands of kelp along the sand when they go to play at the beach.

255 Monorail

Sign for the monorail

Fillmore got the jump on Disneyland and their Land of the Future before that entertainment project was even a figment of Walt's active mind. This town has bought snake oil and wonderful ideas since its inception. Now let me tell you the real skinny about a major, supersized, before-its-time idea. According to Edith Jarrett and county newspapers, here is the story!

In 1927, Fillmore was trying to sell itself as the perfect small town for business and growth. The motto was Fortune Favored Fillmore. We still proudly use that on occasion. We are still a wonderful small town. In 1927, we were even smaller, but the chamber of commerce wanted to bring in more people and more business, and grow.

In May, a fast-talking fellow in a suit and tie arrived in a big Packard. His briefcase contained a full set of plans for a monorail from Fillmore to Sespe Hot Springs. This gentleman was J. S. Coombs, vice president of the Sespe Development Corporation based in Delaware. He was the model for the main character in a musical to be written later titled *The Music Man*! When Mr. Coombs opened his briefcase and removed the drawing for the Monorail System Rapid Transit Rural Line, the people in Fillmore knew their time had come. At last, they would be on the map for the place to go as tourists rushed in to ride the monorail to Sespe Hot Springs to a spa, a hotel, and a chance to soak off their ailments. The boron and sulfur in the water was sure to cure anything. Hadn't the Indians and hunters used the springs for years? As the hot water mixed into the Sespe, you could select the temperature you wanted—from boil-an-egg, where the water came out of the ground, to barely warm downstream. Yep! Let the good times roll!

Everyone in Fillmore knew someone who had soaked at the hot springs and came back talking about how much better they felt. Dr. Ernest Basher came out with Coombs and said he represented a Los Angeles medical group interested in being a part of this spa project. It wasn't long until most of the city fathers wanted to participate and sponsor the project.

The twelve directors of the chamber of commerce were listed on the new letterhead stationery with a picture of the monorail. A billboard appeared in a pasture just west of town—the full color was quite an eye-catcher! The fine print mentioned summer home sites available through W. E. McCampbell, a local real estate agent. It would be only thirty minutes from Fillmore to a modern sanitarium and spa.

Mac was appointed by the company to sell shares at one hundred dollars apiece, so you could invest in a summer home site and help build the monorail at the same time. Owen Miller would no longer need to rent riding horses and pack trains for folks to get to the hot springs.

Soon there was a rumor of a Sespe Light and Power Company that would put a dam on the creek to provide electricity. Then maybe they would extend the monorail over into Bakersfield. Then maybe they would extend to Hueneme and develop a deepwater port. And maybe people would live in fortune-favored Fillmore and commute to work in Los Angeles. Everyone was sure the moviemakers would swarm in to film our clear sunshine—what a deal!

This is the first recorded incident of Fillmore's search for tourist and the easy money that might come with people from out of town; however, it is not the last!

All of Fillmore was excited about the idea of building a monorail from town to Sespe Hot Springs in 1927. J. S. Coombs, vice-president of the Sespe Development Corporation, had great ideas, plans drawn, and was ready to start work. All he needed was a little capital to get started. He had stock for sale in one-hundred-dollar shares, and Fillmore provided the eager buyers. It was a done deal.

The June 17 edition of the *Fillmore Herald* reported that work had begun.

Stakes with strips of red cloth marked the route west of Sespe Creek. Frank Buren, president of the Sespe Development Corporation, and his engineer, J. O. Groves, who had recently arrived in town, would supervise the job. A meeting was held at George Roberts' cigar store to organize the Monorail baseball team to help advertise the new monorail system. The chamber of commerce printed up several small items to advertise the project, and the money would go to support the work. During this time, a crew extended the trail across West Fork and set up the main camp at Grassy Flat. The rocky trail required dynamite to blast a place to set the posts for the monorail. A horse pulled the sled with a gasoline air compressor on it to power the drills. Work had started.

With the project underway, more and more believers brought their checkbooks to W. E. McCampbell's real estate office to buy stock and consider purchasing a home site. Now was the time for the required traditional dedication, and plans were made for it. The ceremony would be near the sign at the terminus of the monorail just west of town.

On July 16, 1927, a little platform appeared. It was properly decorated in red, white, and blue with a big flag, basket of flowers, and a silver-plated shovel. The chamber of commerce chairman, John McNab, and the eleven other directors assembled on the platform in their summer straw hats. After an invocation, the Fillmore Quartet sang, and then the speeches began. Coombs was in fine voice that day. The *Fillmore Herald* quoted part of this discourse. He mentioned that San Francisco might eventually be the northern terminal of the system. He reminded the large assemblage how much they would have made if they had invested a hundred dollars in Henry Ford's auto project at the start of the Model T age. He stated the monorail would be built and completed within twenty-four months to make the hot springs water available to those who desperately needed it for better health.

Dignitaries of local organizations, the state of California, and Southern Pacific Railway were near the platform while Pathé News took movies. Mayor W. H. Price had the honor of turning the first shovel of dirt. His comment was "We've had enough talk about this. Let's get to work." The quartet sang again, and the momentous event was concluded.

Within a week, the president, vice president, engineer, and everyone associated with the new company disappeared; and they even took the silver-plated shovel with them! Items sold to boost the monorail continued to sell through September 2. When the chamber of commerce held their meeting on September 30 and made an inquiry as to what had become of the monorail project, there was complete silence. The project had dropped into the black hole of space and lost forever.

Even in 2004, we don't know where those scoundrels took the money, but they sure lit out for parts unknown. People were so embarrassed at being taken, there was never a howl from anyone. No one was ever prosecuted.

An antique trunk may still disclose gold certificates from a salted mine, but not a single share of stock for the Sespe Hot Springs monorail company can be found. (The Fillmore Historical Museum would love to have a share for their collection. Please contact them if you know of one.) Time marches on, but some things do not change in Fillmore.

Newspapers

Newspapers have long been the life blood of every community. You knew you HAD A TOWN when someone started printing a weekly paper with an occasional EXTRA when a bank was robbed or the sheriff was gunned down.

In Ventura County, the first weekly was the *Signal*. The date of establishment has been lost, but it was run by Shepherd and Sheridan until it was taken over by new owners in 1879, and publication was stopped early in 1900. In 1875, the *Free Press* started printing, so now the county seat had opposing views for the citizens.

Through the years, every town has seen papers come and go, with names like *Hueneme Herald*, *Republican*, *Vidette*, *Ventura Democrat*, *The Observer*, *Ventura Independent*, *The Expositor*, *Golden State*, *Chronicle*, *The Ojai*, *Courier*, *Sun*, and of course, our own *Fillmore Herald*. A few have survived, but most have merged or just plain gone out of business.

The *Fillmore Herald* was started by H. G. Comfort in 1907. Fillmore was booming and rapidly moving forward, so Comfort did his best to promote local interests and opinions and sell some ads. He sold out to Hoffman and Wagener in 1911. I am not sure when Ham Riggs bought the *Herald*, but he is the one I always think about when the *Herald* is mentioned. When I arrived here in 1947, Ham ran his favorite weekly from a tiny building on Fillmore Street near Main Street. It was an old-fashioned shop with a noisy printing press and the distinct smell of ink—and ink everywhere. When I had occasion to enter the shop, I was never sure if I would get out without ink on my dress, but I loved the smell. Ham printed a newsy weekly with a couple of regular reporters who covered city, political, and social events. If it happened in Fillmore and Piru, you could read about it in the *Fillmore Herald*.

I still love to read old papers that tell about kids birthday parties, baby showers, weddings, vacation trips, and everyday things that happened in a community. Most papers are now much too modern for me, but we take two dailies and read a lot to know what is happening around the world, in the USA, and in California.

Gene and I both come from families who valued a daily paper and read them thoroughly. During the late '30s, I rode a bus to a country school. Every day a family of kids got on the bus with one of them holding a neatly rolled newspaper. About a mile down the road, when the bus made another stop to pick up their cousins, that newspaper was thrown near an old mailbox for the other family to read. Two families were sharing the same paper on a regular basis. When times are hard, you manage the best you can to keep up on the news. Most of us had no electricity or radios, so a newspaper was the best way to stay up with current events.

I think Fillmore can be proud that we have one of the oldest newspapers in the county—the centennial of the *Herald* is only five years away, and I hope I can write a column for that special edition. Regardless of the hard times or competition, it will continue printing even if computers have replaced real ink. (The *Herald* closed down just one year short of their centennial.)

Living in 1900

Do you ever stop to think about how much the US has changed in the last hundred years? Well, actually 101 years. Let me give you a few statistics from 1905.

There were only eight thousand cars in the nation. (Our neighborhood has that many today, with most parked in front of my house.) The United States had 144 miles of paved roads. (The WPA made major road improvements in Oklahoma roads during the Depression. By the time WWII started, the majority of the rural roads were passable, but my grandfather occasionally got a midnight call to bring his team of mules out to pull one of those cars out of the bar ditch.)

In 1905, more than 95 percent of births took place at home. Most places had a local midwife to attend a birth, and a doctor was called when needed. (Mrs. Davis did many deliveries for Fillmore women.) Ninety percent of the physicians had no college education. Instead, they attended medical schools that often were substandard. It was a do-it-yourself project or learn by doing for many of these men, who usually had another job on the side. Heroin, morphine, and marijuana were sold over the counter at the corner drugstores.

The leading cause of death was pneumonia, tuberculosis, diarrhea, heart disease, and stroke. The last two are still the cause of many deaths in the US. Babies often died from summer complaint—diarrhea. Only the rich had screens on the windows, so every house had flies and mosquitoes to carry disease and germs, and people did not know any better. The average life expectancy was forty-seven years.

One in ten adults could not read and write. Only 6 percent had graduated from high school. Anyone who had the opportunity to attend college or normal school (teacher training) was held in high esteem. It was a privilege to attend school.

I know you ladies cannot imagine it, but in those days, women washed their hair once a month and used borax or egg yolk for shampoo. Rainwater was saved for this special event. My grandmother's family used lye soap and always had the nicest hair after a vinegar rinse.

Only 14 percent of homes had a bathtub. The rest used a good old number 3 washtub. Long, long ago (1400s), the monthly bath started with the father and a tub of warm water, and each male had a bath according to age. (Yes, the same water.) Then mother took a bath, and the girls were scrubbed according to age with the baby being last in line. That water must have been THICK after ten or fifteen baths. No wonder the old saying was often repeated: "Don't throw the baby out with the bathwater." The poor little thing must have been about as clean as a mudhole after that kind of bath. And no wonder less than half the children lived past the age of two or three.

A three-minute call from Denver to New York costs $11. Only 8 percent of the homes had a telephone, so you used the neighbors' in an emergency. The average worker made between $200 and $400 per year at twenty-two cents an hour. A professional accountant brought home about $2,000; dentists, $2,500; and mechanical engineers, about $5,000.

Sugar costs four cents a pound; eggs were fourteen cents a dozen, and coffee was fifteen cents a pound. When possible, each family had a garden for fresh vegetables. Eighteen percent of homes had at least one full-time servant to help with the laundry, housecleaning, kitchen, and babies. With no electricity to run our modern-day appliances, it is no wonder Mama needed some help.

Now think twice before you wish for the good old days! I would enjoy having some domestic help at our house, but that is about the only thing from the above facts I would even think about—yes, we have made progress in lots of ways. Would any of you ever want to go back? I doubt it! Be careful what you wish for.

Suffrage

Last Friday was Women's Equality Day, and it slipped by unnoticed in Fillmore except for a few of us ladies. It was the eighty-fifth anniversary of women's right to vote. Since I have been very interested in the lives of women and collect books about how they lived since the 1700s, watching the way times have changed for the ladies is remarkable.

It isn't really remarkable! Women have fought, yelled, and pulled on the coattails of men since this country was founded. In every generation, we find a few girls who wanted more than marriage and kids. They also wanted to work at jobs that were only open to men; they wanted equal pay for doing the same work, and they wanted the chance to prove themselves. And they are still doing that in 2005 (and 2020).

When the Nineteenth Amendment to the Constitution was ratified, it opened the door for women to vote. Once that door was opened, other things gradually started to change. Change does not come easy within a society, but it does come. Eventually, the Equal Rights Amendment would be accepted and approved!

My own great-grandmother went to court to protect a small inheritance from being taken in payment of my great-grandfather's bad debts. (He kept trying to farm when he was not a farmer, and he was never successful at that.) Great-Grandmother Margaret eventually used that money to help the family move to Colorado to homestead, but she had control of it. Other women of that time had brothers, fathers, or relatives who took over and took care of the money for them. Most women had no say over their own money even when it was inherited from her father.

In researching, I discovered another lady at about the same time who went to court and put on file that she owned cows given to her by her father when she married. She had saved until she had enough money to buy a horse and buggy, and these things belonged to HER. Then she milked the cows, delivered the milk on a regular route, and spent that money as she chose. What a hussy!

If you talk to a high school girl now, she probably does not know that women could not vote, control their own money, or work at any job other than teaching school or being a maid. And when they married, they were out of a job. Married women were not permitted to teach. Women were paid less than a man teaching a classroom at the same school. Women were never hired as school administrators, policemen, or firemen. Very few owned a business of any kind or became a professional, such as a doctor or a lawyer. There were always a few, but not many. The ones who made it did so against really big odds. Who remembers when girls played half-court basketball? And how about playing tennis, riding a bike, or hiking in long skirts! Thank goodness for Amanda Bloomer. Oh, yes! We've changed!

It was in the late 1960s that Title IX was born and girls were given the right to the same kind of athletic opportunities as boys. What a boon that has been for the United States in the Olympics and world competitions. What a boon that has been for girls who just enjoyed the exercise and competition.

We've seen our own daughters struggle to advance into fields that were reserved for men only—and they made it! We've seen a year when Fillmore was governed by women! Around 1976, Deloras Day was our city major, Marie Wren was president of the school board, Mary Tipps was president of the chamber of commerce, and the Reynold's daughter was postmaster. And you know what? We did a pretty good job—at least we weren't any worse than the men who had held the jobs before us. We didn't solve the problems of the world, but neither did the men, so I guess we were at least treated equal.

Women should be able to do anything they can qualify for. I don't expect requirements to be watered down for them in any way, but if they can swing the deal, then they ought to get the job. For the women who do not want to enter construction or be a fireman, it is fine to stay in an office or teach or work where they want, but if they want to be a fireman or a contractor, they should have the opportunity. If they fail, they are in good company because a lot of men have failed too.

Yes, the right to vote has been good to us. The eighty-fifth anniversary of suffrage slipped by, but a few remembered. Now it is up to each of us to do our best and reach for what we want to do and be good at it. Voting is very special, and every woman should exercise her right.

Post Office

Of all the things I really miss about the good old days, the postal delivery service is near the head of the list. It was really a big deal when the government started RFD—rural free delivery. Before that time, everyone had to go to a post office and ask for their mail. In the West, the post office was often the corner of a small store or perhaps a home near the crossroads. Rancho Camulos had a post office at one time. Merchants were usually happy to have the postal window in a corner of their store. When people came to pick up their mail, they usually bought small items they needed, so merchants picked up some extra sales. The post office was a good place to exchange news about their neighbors and community activities. It was expensive to send letters. It took a long time to get mail from one place to another, and there were not many separate post office buildings outside of larger towns.

The original FAST MAIL was delivered by Pony Express in1860, and that lasted less than two years. The two thousand miles from St. Joseph, Missouri, to California was covered in about eight days. Riders changed horses about every ten to fifteen miles. When the railroads tracks were connected across our nation, people, mail, and freight traveled from coast to coast. The Pony Express quickly went obsolete, but it served a real purpose during its time. Mail service soon improved. The neighborhood store continued to be the gathering site for mail and news.

Home delivery of mail started in the larger towns in 1863. However, Congress did not authorize rural free delivery, or RFD, until 1896. It had taken the Grange several years to get this passed, and every rural family appreciated it. Farmers could buy a mailbox from Sears for forty-nine cents and mount it beside the road near their house. After RFD was installed, rural people did not need to go to the store, so often this was a downer for the merchants. RFD encouraged improved roads and raised land values and changed the way people communicated with both letters and printed material.

Many large items for a family were ordered from Sears or Montgomery Ward twice a year and delivered to their front door. After the fall harvest, money was counted and winter clothing was ordered with a Christmas surprise if finances permitted. In the spring, live day-old baby chicks were brought by the mailman to be quickly tucked under waiting brooders. (I can still hear the cheeps of those yellow balls of down as they were taken out of the box to be fed and watered.) The farmer saved time by ordering his chicks direct from a hatchery. They would provide lots of eggs and Sunday dinners for the next year. The whole family enjoyed looking at the seed catalogs and helping place the order for bare-root fruit trees and the latest variety of seed corn and beans. The girls always asked for one packet of flower seeds, so the seed catalog was well worn by the time the order was mailed. Orders were usually delivered in a timely manner, and everyone was happy. (Perhaps not the speed that we expect now, but still, in a timely manner.)

When we lived on the farm in the late 1930s, the mailman brought letters and the *Capper's Farmer* magazine to our mailbox mounted on a post at the corner of the road near the house. If we needed stamps, money and a note were left in the box for the mailman, and he left change as required. It was a very convenient way to do business when we had only mules and a wagon for transportation to the post office in town seven miles southeast.

A few years later, we moved into town, and by 1945, I left for college. My laundry was sent home each week for my mother to do with her Maytag wringer washer. Laundromats were still in the future, and there was nothing near the college that was economical, so my laundry went by mail. I had a heavy-duty box made especially for that purpose. It was made of heavy, stiff cardboard that was almost like thin wood. I washed my personal items in the dorm bathroom and dried them on a line strung over my bed, but larger things were sent home. After putting in the sheets, towels, and dresses, and the deep lid slipped over the box, I fastened two heavy straps that held the whole affair together—one went around, and one went end to end. On the top, there was a special frame where I slid in the label. One side of the label had Mom's address, and the other side had my college address. That label was turned back and forth and used for two years. The post office never failed to get my clean laundry back to me. It costs about thirty-five cents to mail each time.

When I married and moved to Fillmore, our little house on First Street got mail TWICE a day during the week and once on Saturdays. Mr. Grady was usually our mailman. He walked many miles in Fillmore and must have held the marathon record for town. His leather bag carried the mail for half the town. His bag was seldom full except when Christmas cards were in season. We had very little junk mail and no catalogs except for Sears Roebuck and Montgomery Ward. Everything was important first-class mail. If something special did not come in the morning mail, it would probably be there in the afternoon delivery. We knew that Mr. Grady would bring it as soon as it was received at the post office. A small truck brought packages. If something was really big, we picked it up ourselves at the post office.

As I remember, it was in the 1960s or '70s when a mailman discovered his golf cart was good for hauling around his mailbag. The idea caught on quickly, and they soon advanced to a bag/cart system that is now used by many delivery people. The mail got heavier with all the junk stuff; delivery was cut down to once a day, and in forty years, we have evolved to the present system.

Imagine! Mailing a letter for three cents and receiving mail at home twice a day. Yep! Times do change.

Stamps

Last week, I did not finish telling you about the post office. I found that post offices were located at Camulos with a del Valle in charge; Sespe, near the ranch headquarters; Scenega, at the stage stop and store owned by Mr. Ealy about two miles east of Fillmore; and Buckhorn. None of these has survived to modern time.

The Piru post office had three names through the years. At one time, it was called Piru Rancho, then Piru City, and finally, just Piru as we know it now.

The county also had postal delivery stations at Matilija, Wheeler Springs, Lyons Springs, Griffin, Nedo, Nordhoff, Timberville, Penrose, Ozena, Stauffer, Roblar, and Triumfo, with none of them still in service. If anyone knows exactly where they were located, please give me a call. In Ventura County, our little post offices were sort of like schools—not many miles from the people they serviced, unless you lived far back in the mountains.

The first postage stamps featured George Washington and Ben Franklin. Since 1847, we've had just about everyone and everything printed on our stamps. Originally, it costs five cents to mail half an ounce less than three hundred miles and ten cents over three hundred miles. By 1855, they changed the charge to three cents for up to three thousand miles. The Pony Express hauled mail for a couple of years starting in 1860, and it was expensive, but got mail to the Pacific Coast in about eight days. By 1863, mileage was not considered in mailing letters.

It doesn't take very much paper to weigh half an ounce, so everyone was happy when Congress changed the rate to two cents for one ounce in 1885. When RFD started in 1896, the rate was still two cents per ounce anywhere in the US. That rate remained unchanged until 1917, but it went up to three cents as a war emergency for two years in WWI and then was dropped to two cents again. The three-cent rate began in 1932 as a depression charge. We did not get another rate increase until 1958. Wow! Twenty-six years for three-cent mail! No wonder I remember three-cent stamps! By then, the airmail rate was ten cents, I think.

From 1958 until 2004, every two or three years, the postage rate rose. Usually, it was just one or two cents, but now we are paying thirty-seven cents for an ounce of mail with restrictions on size and thickness of the letter. (We are up to forty-nine cents in 2018.) Anything beyond the standard size adds additional cost. As new equipment has been developed to automate the service, the requirements have changed. As transportation has improved, service has been curtailed. As working conditions have changed, employees have received better salaries. The way stamps are sold has changed from buying one or two a week to buying a whole sheet or a roll of one hundred. We don't even have to lick them anymore. We can buy special LOVE stamps for Valentine's Day or wedding announcements and have a selection of designs for Christmas.

The pioneers on the trail WEST sent letters home as they met a wagon train going toward the East. They always wanted to keep in touch with families. When they finally arrived out here and settled, a letter from their folks back home often took six months. They did not know if those mentioned with an illness were still alive or not. It really was old news that had traveled by ship and across Panama or by wagon cross-country. But it was still news from home, and every letter was treasured and shared. News from Washington, DC, about elections or war was just as long in arriving. It was a long ways from coast to coast.

The Pony Express cut delivery time down to a few days; then the telegraph was strung beside the railroad, and there was instant news from place to place. National news was sent by telegraph with both women and men working around the clock to send and receive messages. A wire was used for important news between families—births, deaths, arrivals, or special events. It was expensive to send ten words, so you learned to write carefully with the basic information. (For example, FATHER DIED THIS MORNING FROM ACCIDENT STOP FUNERAL MONDAY STOP LOVE SIS.) It costs less than a phone call, and often people did not have access to a telephone. Western Union always got a wire delivered as addressed. When you sent a wire, you were sure it was received. Young men worked for Western Union and delivered wires via bicycle all over the country.

Now people enjoy collecting stamps and learning more about them. Some people still enjoy writing letters; everyone enjoys receiving them! E-mail is fast and easy for those working on computers, but there is still nothing like going to the mailbox and finding a pretty envelope with a carefully folded sheet inside covered with a handwritten message. Letter writing is a lost art, but I have enjoyed the best of times. My grandmother taught me that letters keep a family together, so I keep writing. Try it! You might like it! An old-fashioned thank-you note is always appreciated. (That reminds me, I have one to do today for our Thanksgiving dinner invitation.)

PS: How many of you remember V-mail? No, not *e-mail*, *V-mail*! During WWII, many of us wrote letters to our guy overseas every day. (My garage still has a bundle tied with ribbon.) A V-mail letter was a very lightweight onionskin paper that you purchased at the post office with an airmail stamp. You wrote your letter on one side, and then it was folded along printed lines and sealed with the long military address written on the other side. If we were lucky, it would be delivered in a few days, but if the guys were in the middle of something, it would take several weeks. Thankfully, the government tried very hard to get mail delivered. Oh, how those letters were treasured.

County Fire Department

Once again, a friend has come to my rescue! He brought me information about the Ventura County Fire Department, and I will share with you.

In 1928, the population of the entire county was sixty-two thousand. The Ventura Avenue area had fifty-eight new oil wells, and the St. Francis Dam had broken. The new fire district was formed in May by a vote of 230 to 47. The board of supervisors appointed Walter Emerick as the fire chief for the district. He had been the fish and game warden for several years and had tried to enforce fire laws and use property owners with volunteers to fight fire in the unincorporated areas, so he was the perfect man for the new job.

Emerick was considered the best brush firefighter in Southern California. He wanted to set up protection measures and equipment prior to fires occurring in the county. He planned to spend county general fund money before fires started to prevent them. The state attorney general ruled it could not be done. Our supervisors then took the issue to the public, where it was approved, and the Ventura County fire protection district was formed.

During the 1928 fire season, they had thirty-seven fires, lost six houses, and had 2,820 acres of vegetation burn. Their first budget was $20,000—a far cry from the current budget of $106 million. (Currently, we pay approximately 1 percent of assessed valuation for property taxes. From that amount, 10 percent goes to the county fire department.) The DEPRESSION hit the next year, but they still managed to locate ten stations around the county.

The original station was in Santa Paula in the county agricultural building at 845 Santa Barbara Street. Ojai joined in when the district was formed, and they also put a station in Piru. That pretty much covered the unincorporated county. Soon they added stations in Ventura Avenue, Port Hueneme, Moorpark, Thousand Oaks, Camarillo, Simi Valley, and Oak View.

Piru was Fire Station 3. In the 1920s and 1930s, Piru had a bank, a grocery store, a meat market, a furniture store, and a newspaper. It was a thriving commercial center. In November 1928, Fire Chief Emerick attended a meeting of the Piru chamber of commerce and proposed his new district take charge of the current fire equipment in Piru and add more as funds were available. The locals thought it would be fine to relinquish their two small pumpless Ford trucks to the county department. Hugh Warring, owner of the Piru Water System, agreed to install fire hydrants when the county assigned Piru a pumper.

In November 1930, the Piru station received a Dodge fire truck with a pump and a 450-gallon water tank. Fire district personnel at Santa Paula built the pumper. The next year, the district people built a firehouse on Market Street. It was eighteen by thirty and made from concrete block with a red tile roof. It costs $179.15. In 1950, Harry Lechler's father sold the department a lot on Church Street for $500. The current station was the first building on the block and has served the area well.

Volunteer Frank Bowdle was Piru's first fire chief. Later, he was hired and was the first paid personnel at Station 3. He operated a gasoline station, where he also lived, at 4072 Center Street, which was then Highway 126.

Piru is now Station 28. It has three shifts of three men per shift working a twenty-four-hour rotation. We are fortunate to have them. The fires last year just reminded us of how fortunate we are to have a county fire department—many midwestern states and counties WISH they had the protection we have here. (More next week.)

When the Ventura County Fire Department was organized in 1928, communications were very primitive compared to what we now have. Lookout towers around the county were used to look for smoke and catch a fire as soon as it started. The tower on Triumfo Peak helped the Los Angeles county department. In 1931, one on Santa Paula Peak was staffed during the fire season. This tower later became a mountaintop radio transmitter. The operator evacuated during bad east winds for fear the large glass windows would blow out. In 1967, the Sence Ranch brush fire burned off the roof and wrecked the radio transmission.

The South Mountain tower operated until 1974 and houses several emergency agencies' radios. In 1934, federal work–program funding provided the fire district with its own phone lines to connect the six stations. The phones were used until the new radio system became available in the late 1940s. When the radios were first installed, they used the same frequency as the sheriff's department. In 1951, the fire department received their own frequency.

The second mountaintop communication tower was on Red Mountain. It went into service in 1970, and those old phone lines were replaced by a microwave system in 1980. As technology advanced, so did the communication of the fire department.

In the early days, when there was an emergency, people called their nearest fire station to report it. Wives often manned the phones when the fellows were out on a call. Soon, several stations went into one place, and by 1974, everything was under one dispatch system at Camarillo. By 1983, calls to 911 took over for reporting any fire.

Hand crews have always been the first line of defense in firefighting. In 1929, four hundred men and one truck fought a major fire on Sulphur Mountain. During the Depression, several labor camps constructed fire roads and firebreaks. The CCC camp in Sespe Canyon did a lot of work in our backcountry. In 1942, the fire district hired its first hand crew. These young men fought fire, repaired telephone poles connecting the stations to headquarters, and did valuable work in the county. Even the bracero program provided workers for hand crews when the need arose. From the stories I've heard, when there was a really big fire, local boys stayed at home to avoid being drafted into a hand crew. Some looked forward to going out to fight fire, but others were happier to be at home.

Only three years after the department was formed, the first bulldozer was purchased. It was a Cletrac Model 40. It opened up many fire roads and trails. The firemen were experts at improvising and figuring out how to make do. Slowly more equipment was added with blades, graders, and trailers to haul things where they were needed. On occasion, the agricultural department provided a truck to move tractors or dozers. Everyone worked together to get the job done.

When Chief Emerick reported the need for a fire truck in 1928, he discovered the budget had not provided for one. He solicited one hundred dollars from the Ventura County Mutual Fire Insurance Company and pledges from others to get a fire engine. Emerick reported a new Ford truck, capable of going sixty miles an hour, would cost $755. Fire Commissioner Orton, on behalf of his Ojai Gasoline Company, furnished all the gasoline and oil for the new truck at no cost. These men took their job seriously, and they were willing to put their money where their mouth was.

Commercially built chassis were made into fire trucks at the Santa Paula fire shop by firefighters. Many of the trucks were on Mack chassis and painted red. They were open cabs with no windshields until 1931, when a state law was passed requiring windshields on all trucks. The pumpers used 300 to 600 gpm centrifugal pumps or rotary gears. The water tanks were 350 to 500 gallons. Ladders were built in the shop and cost five dollars each.

Our Ventura County Fire Department district has come a long way. We are proud of every firefighter. We know they will be there when we need them. (And we've had some really big fires in the county since 1928.) Thanks to every one of them!

The details for the past two articles were gotten from the seventy-fifth anniversary report of the Ventura County Fire Department. Thanks to Assistant Chief Dick Wilson for compiling all the information and pictures and Bill Stocker for sharing his copy of the book with me.

Fillmore volunteer fire department

Decoration Day

Do any of you remember Decoration Day? This is the term many of us grew up with instead of Memorial Day. It was the time when people went to the cemetery and worked the graves and cleaned the cemetery area. A cemetery-working was lots of hard work, but it was fun to see old friends again and accomplish a public service at the same time.

Everyone brought their wheelbarrows, hoes, and rakes; arrived early with a picnic lunch; and just got to work. Before the days of tractors and gasoline lawnmowers, it was a big job to do by hand. The ten acres of native grass probably had not been cut and cleaned since the previous year. A horse-drawn hay mower was used around the edge where there were no graves. The rest was done by elbow grease. Frequently, graves needed some soil hauled in to level them. With rain all year in the Midwest, the grass grew so tall it was hard often to find graves.

Family and friends spoke quick greetings and went to work. One year, when my mother was a teen, about 1920, they decided to burn off the cemetery and be done with hoeing the tall grass. That fire soon got away from them and almost into the adjoining pasture before people got it under control by beating it out with wet tow sacks. That group was very careful about doing things the quick way after that. (But it sure took care of lots of old weeds and grass underbrush. We understand that from the local fire last year.)

By noon, everyone was more than ready for an hour of eating, resting, and visiting. They caught up on local news, gossip, and family happenings while they shared their food. My family is buried at McAlister Cemetery with a twenty by twenty open-shade roof used for funerals and gatherings. My grandfather helped build it in the early 1900s, and it still stands and is used. My brother and nephew put on a new roof in 2000, so it should last another thirty years. Country families buried their loved ones at the nearest cemetery or churchyard. They all worked together to keep the area presentable. On Decoration Day, it really looked nice after the annual work was completed. All through the year, our family helped maintain the family plots on a fairly regular basis, but by Decoration Day, everything needed to be spruced up before flowers were placed by each headstone or sandstone rock marking a grave. As children, we were taught to walk around graves, avoid stepping on them, and to be respectful at all times.

One year, my grandmother went to Galveston and also visited where she grew up just north of Houston. When she returned, she brought a big box of seashells home with her. On the next Decoration Day, she let her grandchildren carefully place them on the grave of their great-grandmother. Yes, we decorated graves too.

My husband and I have now placed appropriate granite stones at each of our families' unmarked graves. Our cousins banded together to purchase them so our ancestors will be remembered for future generations. You realize how important it is to leave a permanent record for posterity when you work with genealogy. The old Indian Territory still has many of these small country cemeteries in use.

In 1895, a local group organized the Bardsdale Cemetery. Some of the shareholders were C. C. Elkins. J. D. LeBard, Martin Stoll, R. F. Robertson, C. J. Michel, and R. J. Ealy. When two-year-old Lillian Elkins died in November 1895, she was one of the first to be buried there. (Remember, in 1895, everyone still expected Bardsdale to become a town. It was platted with streets, a church, a school, space for stores, and a post office; and ten-acre lots were being sold.) In 1914, it became the Bardsdale Cemetery district, operating under the Health and Safety Code of the State of California, and continues under that title. In 1985, the cemetery board set up an endowment, and each burial pays into that fund to provide everlasting maintenance of the graves.

Any public entity is fortunate when their board finds an employee that loves the job and is willing to give time and effort beyond the normal concerns. The Brockus family filled that place for the Bardsdale Cemetery. For two generations, they maintained the cemetery with pride of ownership that they would give to their homes. We were fortunate to have such dedicated individuals working for the district. The old-timers still fondly remember them.

As far as I know, the Bardsdale Cemetery has always been mowed and well-kept by paid employees. It was not necessary to have a cemetery-working and to clear out the weeds on Decoration Day. By being frugal, the board had tax money to do that. (The current board continues the tradition of a well-kept cemetery.)

We are fortunate to have a lovely burial place with a formal ceremony each Memorial Day. The service this year will be on Monday, May 31, at 11:00 a.m. Local youth groups put flags on each veteran's grave and collect them a few days after the ceremony. Fresh flowers appear at many other sites. It is a beautiful way to honor the dead. Some still call it Decoration Day, and some call it Memorial Day—it is still a time to decorate graves and remember our loved ones.

Christmas Decorations

By the time we get into high school, we start remembering a special Christmas that occurred when we were just a little kid. As you age, new memories continue to be stored in our souls, until by the age of seventy-five, there are a whole bunch of them. Younger generations get pretty tired of hearing about all the good old days, and I don't blame them, but their elders can't resist passing on information to them.

I didn't arrive in Fillmore until 1947, so I am way behind on the early day celebrations and decorations in town. (If you know about pre-1947, please give me a call so I can add your story to my collection.)

During my first Christmas in Fillmore, there was a BIG Christmas tree in the middle of the intersection at each end of Central Avenue. A large section of cement pipe, probably from the Munoz pipe yard, was filled with sand to be the tree holder. They were the biggest lighted trees I had ever seen, and it was so beautiful. This was the decoration for downtown for several years. I can't find anyone who remembers Christmas decorations prior to those trees. The auto traffic was light, and people were careful so the trees were not a hazard until—yep!

Near Christmas Eve, one of our well-known local imbibers drove down Central. He probably saw two trees at the Sespe Avenue intersection, couldn't decide which one he needed to go around, and hit that tree head-on. The next year, the city, or maybe the chamber of commerce, changed the downtown decorations.

Several six-foot fir trees were bought and planted in large pots. They were placed on Central. There were probably ten or fifteen trees on each side of the street. Many elementary classes adopted a tree and spent lots of time making decorations for their tree. Styrofoam peanuts, aluminum pie plates, spools, and many assorted items were made into decorations. Lights were added to reflect the shining ornaments. With the bulbs within reach, the temptation was too much for the high school crowd. So many lights were stolen that the open sockets were declared a hazard for young children, and after two years, lights were no longer used.

The trees continued to grow in their pots, and after about five years, it was decided to transplant them in the new Shiells Park near Sespe Creek. They continued to look pretty and provided shade for several years. After the Los Serenos flood, a dike was built that reduced the size of the park by about half, and some of the trees were bulldozed although a couple can still be seen in the creek bed. I think two may still be in the park.

Fillmore needed new decorations. The local Soroptimist club took on the project of making enough money to purchase strings of lighted garlands to be hung across the street in about five places. Several service clubs joined in, and within a year, the $10,000 purchase price was accumulated, and the garlands arrived. The city crews were always responsible for hanging them. For some reason, those men thought the garlands should be stretched tightly across the street with no swag at all. Those were about the tackiest things I ever saw. Those decorations were a big flop with me. Each year, they looked worse after rats found them in storage. Oh well, we all tried.

The Soroptimist also bought and installed two tall poles near the highway on Central Avenue for a large Christmas light display and Welcome to Fillmore sign. When the lights burned out, they were never replaced. Now banners are hung from the poles.

Before the city hall park was renovated, the old one had a huge evergreen tree just across from the Santa Clara bank. There was a narrow strip of land there, and it was the perfect place for our big community tree each year. Lights were hung near the top, and in the evening after the Christmas parade, there was a special ceremony to turn them on. The tree was beautiful, and I still miss it. This event was often accompanied with a merchants' night with tickets for a drawing and the start of Christmas shopping for many people. A lovely German couple owned the Sweet Shop, and he often would appear on the street as Santa to surprise the kids as parents made purchases.

After the garlands were retired, the current holiday wreaths were purchased. They are certainly more modern, seem to be weathering nicely, and are pretty; but it took us over fifty years to get to them. So much for history!

MERRY CHRISTMAS TO ALL, and TO ALL A GOOD NIGHT!

Peppertrees

One of my favorite trees is the California pepper. (After the oak, of course.) It makes a mess in the yard and on the sidewalk, but it is so light and airy. Several years ago, when one of the ranches was trying to clear away burned trees after a brush fire, the Department of Fish and Wildlife told them that Brazilian peppertrees could be cut down but not California peppers. There is a very minor difference, and it does not seem that the California pepper is a native tree, but anyhow, those were not to be cut.

I guess the best thing about peppertrees is the fact they will grow with almost no water and in any kind of soil. If you plant them, they will grow. Now that is my kind of tree. The berries are sometimes used and mixed with other peppers for seasoning. Requiring little care, peppertrees were a favorite in the early days for both main streets and highways.

Moorpark still has peppertrees beside the railroad tracks for several blocks. Since they are getting old and unsafe, they are replanting them to save the ambience around their depot. One rancher along the Simi freeway has planted a long row. They are popular again.

Fillmore also had peppertrees along Main Street parallel to the railroad tracks and then along Central Avenue. One of those trees survives near the Fillmore Historical Museum. Another one is behind the Heritage Valley tourist office. Both these trees are beauties and should be painted by one of our local artists. The old highway, just west of town, still has a few of the original peppertrees. They were very popular long ago. I have learned to watch and try to spot others that are very old. There were several across from the library, and they were in such bad condition the city cut them down ten years ago. Several people protested. The trees looked fine to me, but when they cut into the huge trunks, they were rotten and hollow inside and certainly poised a threat to people when we got east winds. They needed to be cut, but I still felt sad about losing them. Sespe Avenue across from the old school also had a long row. The barbecue at festival time was held under their shade. They were removed when the packinghouse expanded. Some of the pictures of Central at the historical museum show the early day peppertrees that lined both sides of the business part of town.

Recently, we took a Sunday drive up Holser Canyon below Piru Dam. At this time of year, it is not a pretty area, but it was new to us, and we enjoyed a little exploring. We found cattle, horses, and lots of old barbed-wire fences with rusting farm equipment and limited access to private property. Several times in the distance, down narrow, unkempt trails, back in little protected canyons, we could spot big peppertrees. We felt sure those trees marked old house sites. The little homes are long gone in this isolated part of the county, but the peppertrees still grow and provide shade for cattle and horses during the summer.

The city has started new plantings of peppertrees in the area of some of the new subdivisions. They look nice, should grow well, and be a real asset to town. Maybe soon, the peppertrees will be as pretty as the sycamores that Sarah Hansen and her volunteers planted along the bike path. It only takes a few years for trees to add to the beautification of our town—even the early day settlers knew that!

Trees, Trees

How often do you look around you at the ancient trees? The Eagle black walnut at Rancho Camulos has been famous for years. That tree is more than 150 years old, measures over twenty-six feet around the base, and is still healthy. The three-fourth acre of shade has seen many fiestas, work parties, and barbecues.

Judge Elkins planted a long row of palm trees along the road from his home near the golf course to the small community of Fillmore. They didn't give him much shade when he walked to town, but he enjoyed the fine view. A few still remain to sway eighty-five feet above the ground.

Julius Baldeschwieler planted a row of fan palms across the road from his home and an orange orchard on Ventura Street after the turn of the century. He liked the looks of them. Many years later, his son, Harold Balden, bought the house on the northwest corner of First and Saratoga Streets and raked leaves from two huge sycamores growing in that yard. The last one was cut down about two years ago, but it was a beauty. In the early days, it was a favorite place to pit apricots. My, how times change.

Pole Creek originally ran sort of southwest down Fourth Street to Kensington Drive and then on to connect with Sespe Creek. They probably joined about where the railroad bridge is located near Grand Avenue. I haven't found any records or tales about the exact location, but I KNOW Pole Creek was relocated long ago. You can look at the cement channel on Fourth Street and tell that the ninety-degree turn is not natural. I think you can probably follow the old channel by looking at the old sycamores in town, starting with the one at the end of Fourth in the front yard of the two-story Fairbanks home. Then you follow it down to First Street and the old Balden property and across to Kensington near Jack Schleimer's home. My research tells me the Kensington tree originally shaded a sheep pen near the water for a local man. The rest of the sycamores that traced the path of the creek have all been cut, so you have to use your imagination from there. (Many locals felt the same way in 2016 when we came to town and found the city had cut down our beloved palm trees during the night and didn't even leave the sawdust on the sidewalk to show what had taken place.)

When the city wanted to cut down the peppertrees on Central and replace them with palms, the local constable protected the one in front of his hotel with a shotgun. As soon as possible, the city sent him on an official trip to find a robber; and while he was gone, they cut down his tree. I guess there is more than one way to skin a cat!

Early day pictures of Central Avenue show it was planted with peppertrees. They even shaded horses and buggies on Main and Sespe Avenue. The ones near Sespe School were the location of the May Festival barbecue as late as 1948. When the bank, the Gurrola building, and the packinghouse expanded on Sespe Avenue, the trees there were cut down. The old peppertrees across from the library on Central Avenue were unsafe because of rot and had to be removed about ten years ago. We still have a couple of the originals near the museum on Main Street, and perhaps they can be preserved or replanted in the future. The last of the downtown eucalyptus became our Chumash Indian statue on the southeast corner of Sespe and A Streets. We are fortunate to save a piece of it as a memorial.

The Northeast corner of Central and Sespe had a beautiful big oak tree on in the early day. The local Mexican American band played concerts there on Saturday nights during the depression to entertain people. In a few years the Masonic Lodge bought the lot and built a three story meeting place for their organization and oak tree was removed. After the Masonic building was destroyed by the 1994 earthquake, Soroptimist erected an old fashioned gazebo on the site. It was very pretty but the lot sold and the gazebo was moved to the historical museum complex. That lot is still unimproved but I can still imagine that big native oak tree providing shade before 1900.

You can learn a lot by looking at our trees. Isn't history fun!

Building in Fillmore

The citizens of Fillmore have pulled together to build some very nice community improvements through the years. The first that I remember was about 1948. I had just married and was living on First Street in a tiny house owned by Grandma Hinckley. Around the corner from us, the Shiells family owned a large lemon orchard. They donated about two acres of their land to form the Fillmore-Piru Veterans Memorial District. Local people raised funds to construct the memorial building and youth building dedicated to the use of our community. A plaque inside lists the names of our veterans killed in the service to their country. The new district boundaries coincided with the high school boundaries, so the buildings could be used by the people and organizations of Fillmore and Piru. They have served a real need for activities since that time. An elected board is responsible for running the district. Several years ago, due to increased cost of insurance for the buildings, an agreement was made to combine with the city of Fillmore to run the district. At the present time, the only purpose of the memorial district has been to maintain the buildings for public use. The objective of the district is to honor our veterans by providing these buildings for community use.

About 1970, the Soroptimist Club started a fund to build a gazebo in the city park near the railroad depot. With lots of help from other groups and fundraisers, this group of women accomplished their goal. Their husbands provided hands-on assistance, and it was built with lots of pride. When the city decided to improve the park, the gazebo was moved to the vacant Masonic lot on Central Avenue. For several years, it has served as a meeting place for awards. Kids enjoy playing there. They can be seen hanging from the railings or skipping around the interior. Tourists find it enchanting at the end of their walk from the railroad along our main street. It has been a fine addition to town. Now that the lot has been sold for commercial development, the gazebo will have to be moved again. Everyone is hoping it can be relocated to a permanent place in the new park and continue to add to the ambiance of the town.

In 1965, the Lions and Rotary Clubs formed the Fillmore Boy Scout Foundation. Their aim was to build the Scout house on Texaco property at the end of Sespe Avenue near Pole Creek. When that log building was completed, this group of enterprising men had spent $6,000 for the precut logs and another $5,000 for parts and supplies to finish it. Carpenters, plumbers, electricians, and general handymen donated all the labor. Everyone in town donated their money and efforts to get this 2,200-square-foot building ready as a meeting place for the two Scout troops and Cub groups. Several of the men signed a personal note for a loan to pay the final balance due, but it was quickly paid off. The citizens of Fillmore and Piru supported the effort wholeheartedly. The building has recently been refurbished and the forty-year-old structure looks like new. It continues to serve Boy Scouts and Girl Scouts in this area. This last effort had time and material once again donated by local businesses. Funds from the Paul Haase Memorial account paid for necessary out-of-pocket expenses.

The Fillmore-Piru community can be proud of the support and effort they have given to building things for the benefit of everyone. It is people helping people! I guess that is what makes living here so special to us.

Presbyterian Church

About the time Southern Pacific came through town and started Fillmore, people around here got really interested in organizing churches. With the railroad bringing in more settlers, Sespe Land and Water Company selling lots, and businesses opening up, there was a need for churches too.

The *Fillmore American* newspaper reported some interesting items in 1928 when the Presbyterian Church celebrated their fortieth anniversary. They had a long article about the founding of the church. It was originally organized in July 1888 with a meeting of people at Kenney Grove under the live oak trees. Rev. Seward, a Sunday school missionary, organized the group that included charter members as follows: Mr. and Mrs. Robert Dunn, Mr. and Mrs. O. J. Goodenough, Ms. Maud Goodenough, Mrs. L. M. Kenney, Mrs. Inez Arundell, Mr. Ralph Jepson, Mr. Joseph Rue, Mrs. Nancy Lorton, Mrs. J. C. Allee, Mr. and Mrs. S. V. Tietsort, Mr. and Mrs. Norman Kellogg, and Ms. Occa Kellogg.

After instruction of the members and election of elders, the service was concluded with the giving of the Apostolic Benediction by the pastor of the German Methodist Episcopal Church at Bardsdale.

The first church building was erected the following year by O. J. Goodenough, an architect. The building stood on the corner of Sespe Avenue and Clay Street, and much of the construction work was donated. Sespe Land and Water Company deeded nine lots to the church upon the condition that a building costing not less than $1,500 be erected there.

Presbyterian Ladies Aid group

While the men were putting in sweat labor, the women were busy with socials and suppers to secure sufficient funds to buy the final building materials and purchase chairs for the congregation's use. When Sunday school opened, they had fifty-four members in attendance. Rev. Drummond McCunn was the first pastor and stayed with the fledgling group until 1893. Four generations of the Goodenough family served on the session.

The building was expanded in 1911 but continued growth in Fillmore, and the church found it necessary to make plans for a larger building. By 1928, they had outgrown the facility. A new brick building was constructed on the corner of Central and First Streets. It was larger and more modern with a beautiful stained-glass rose window behind the choir. It cost approximately $70,000. In April 1943, Mrs. Maud Goodenough Holley, the last surviving member or the original group, symbolically burned the church's mortgage.

The city owned a small park adjacent to the church on the south and sold it to them for additional Sunday-school rooms. Two one-story units were constructed in 1955 for Sunday school. In 1962, the Carrie K. Price estate bequest a generous sum of money to the church, and it was used to build a two-story addition with a chapel and rooms to expand the facility.

A pipe organ was dedicated in December 1960. It had been a part of the CBS Radio Studios in Hollywood, and after it was rebuilt, the 1,070 pipes were installed in the church. It is one of the finest in Southern California. In 1926, Tillie Harmonson was pianist for the church; in 1929, Edith Thompson was named church pianist/organist until she retired in 1984. Charlene Howard McGuire has spent many hours playing the organ with several others close behind here. Music has always been an important part of their worship. The youth choir in the early 1970s attracted many youths to participate.

The church celebrated its diamond jubilee in 1963. Many people in Fillmore still recognize names of pastors at the Presbyterian Church— Taylor, Orr, Arbuckle, Gammon, Miller, Korver, Youngquist, and Myerscough. These men moved on to other assignments, but the core of the church remained in Fillmore. Faithful elders and workers are known by families—Musgrave, Goodenough, Mayhew, Felsenthal, Holley, Mitchell, Dudley, Deeter, Kelman, Banks, Dewey, McGregor, Boardman, Young, Taylor, King, Phillips, Hackney, Mumme, and many others.

Times change. Disagreements happen. Congregations split. But the love of God survives all! (The escrow on the church building should be closed this year, 2019, and the building put to other use as the congregation has moved.)

Gasoline Service Stations

When my genealogy magazine arrived this week, under "History Matters," it shows "TRENDS THAT SHAPED YOUR ANCESTORS' LIVES!" Well, that was interesting, but I soon discovered that I could remember about two-thirds of the things they were talking about, so maybe I am my own ancestor! Perhaps that should make me feel old, but I try to avoid that when possible.

Now let me tell you a little bit about what was included in that informative article about cars, gasoline, and "filling them up."

In 1888, Bertha Benz insisted on driving her husband's newly constructed Patent-Motorwagen auto from Mannheim to Pforzheim, Germany, to prove to him his invention was marketable. The thing ran on *ether* stocked by every pharmacy. This was just a side business for a drugstore and handy for the owner of an auto.

Henry Ford put the finishing touches on his new Quadricycle in 1896 to start the new industry in the United States. He had worked over two years to get this thing running on four bicycle tires with a three-gallon tank holding gasoline. It had two forward speeds and no reverse and looked more like an old-fashioned buggy without a horse. Gasoline was a by-product at the refineries where they made kerosene for lamps and a few other things. It didn't take long for Henry Ford to improve on the Quadricycle, and the next thing was a Ford Model T.

The automobile idea took off, and by 1900, the US had four thousand cars scaring the horses on every American road. Henry figured out the assembly line idea and used it to bring down the cost of manufacturing his new Model T, and everyone wanted one. All they needed to do to fill up the tank was take a bucket to the general store, hardware dealer, drugstore, or local refinery to get some gasoline. In a few places, salesmen sold gas from pushcarts equipped with hoses.

When the US manufactured twenty-five thousand cars in 1905, Sylvanus Bowser figured out a pump to transfer gas from a barrel into a car's tank. He already had a similar one to pump kerosene, so it was easy to make it work for gasoline. His hometown, Fort Wayne, Indiana, named a street after him; and fuel pumps in New Zealand and Australia are still known as bowsers. His invention started a new filling-station business.

The barrel and pump continued to be located right on the sidewalk and started causing traffic jams even after Standard Oil opened a pump at the curb in 1907. Company-owned curbside stations continued until the Supreme Court dissolved Standard Oil's monopoly in 1911. After that, anyone could sell gasoline if they wanted to start a business, and THEY DID!

The country had over half a million cars on the road, and in 1913, the first real drive-in service station opened in Pittsburgh. Baum Boulevard was already called automobile row with several car dealerships lining the street, and now they could fill up the tank on every car too. This new station sold gasoline and offered free air and water and sold the country's first commercial road maps. (I guess they got a jump on the Auto Club that time.) The idea of a separate building and off-the-street location to fill up the gas tank quickly caught on, and you know the rest of the story. Pittsburgh has now placed a historic marker on that corner to commemorate the first drive-in filling station, which would be one hundred years old this year. The day they opened, they sold thirty gallons of gas at twenty-seven cents a gallon.

The early day station just sold gas. There was little market for other automotive service. Fords were designed for easy owner maintenance. Every Ford had a grease cup so the driver could lube his own car. As other brands came on the market, they all got more complicated and needed more maintenance. Soon greasing palaces were added to gas stations. Sinclair opened the first three stations equipped with lubrication equipment in 1926.

Mr. Erskine told me that when he came to California about 1913, when they wanted to go for a Sunday drive, he would take his car engine apart in the morning, clean it good, and reassemble it so he would not have any trouble when they hit the road after lunch. I don't remember what kind of car he drove, but it must have been a simple engine.

The US census in 1929 counted over 121,000 filling stations—they were called that until 1948 when they enumerated them as service stations. When the Depression HIT, the business attracted newly unemployed people to open stations or to work in one. By this time, large pumps had replaced the old barrels. These were manually filled by a worker pushing and pulling a long handle on the side, and this pulled the gasoline from an underground tank into the long glass cylinder at the top. This cylinder was marked with gallon measurements, like a kitchen measuring cup. He measured the gas you wanted and then used the hose to put it into your tank by gravity. It was all pretty simple. (The California Oil Museum in Santa Paula has one on display if you would like to see it.) The pumps were tall and round. The bottom section was metal with the long glass cylinder top ready to measure the gasoline.

I remember my father pulling into a filling station about 1932 or 1933, and there would be three men instantly there to take care of us. One man manually pumped the gasoline from the underground tank to measure it and fill our car. It was fun to watch the red liquid splash into the top and then go down as it went into our car. As this was being taken care of, another man washed the windshield and used a whisk broom to sweep out the inside. With few paved roads and lots of mud in New Mexico, the floorboards were always a mess, and he took care of cleaning under the feet of both the driver and passenger. The third man checked under the hood to be sure the water and oil levels were not low. In about ten minutes, we were in and out and ready to go. That gasoline was fifteen cents for regular and a real bargain with the service thrown in to bring you back when you need to fill the tank again. (I think a barrel of crude was selling for about ten cents then as the production was way ahead of the market consumption. Gasoline was mostly used as fuel for cars, so crude oil was way ahead of the game. Eventually, my father and another man shared a job in the oil fields, so each worked two weeks and had two weeks off, but both were able to buy food. I don't know if it was government regulation or just the companies who started the proration until they brought up the price of crude. It worked, and in a few months, Dad was back working full time again.)

Oil companies remained involved in the design of both company and independent stations. Frank Lloyd Wright even did some designing for them. Many of us remember the big box with a flat roof and two bays, one with a lift and one with a drain for washing cars. Restrooms were accessed from the outside.

Self-service stations were not invented until 1947 when one showed up in Los Angeles. They were not very popular as most people wanted to be waited on with the extra service. The 1973, the Arab oil embargo changed our thinking about that. After waiting in line for an hour to get gas, we were glad to pump it ourselves. Now it is hard to find a station that is not self-service. Well, times do change, women have learned how to "fill her up" and wash the windshield and remember to check the tires before taking off on a shopping trip. Dad uses a credit card to pay for the amount he needs for his pickup, and the kids pools their pocket money to get enough to get around for the evening. Oh yes, we should be calling them filling stations again as the only service is what you provide for yourself!

The Depression

I enjoy putting historical facts in this column, but this week, I have hit a dead-end. I wanted to write about the Depression during the 1930s and how this section of the country dealt with it, but I have no information. If some of you will share your personal stories about their era with me, I will use them at a later time and perhaps incorporate them into a new community history book. The Depression is not covered in the books I have in my library, so for research, I need YOU. I would appreciate it if you would share your memories with me.

This idea for a column started when I was reading a historical magazine this week. A lady was remembering all the things they made out of flour and feed sacks in Kentucky during the Depression. Flour and livestock feed were about the only things a rural family bought in Kentucky or Oklahoma and many other parts of the country. You were lucky to be able to grow your food, but there was little to sell for cash to buy anything at the store. Families in the country had to make do with what they had.

I was living with my grandparents on a small Oklahoma farm during the worst of the Depression. Fortunately, their 110 acres was not in the dust bowl section of the state, so we escaped that experience, but we sure learned to get along with almost nothing. The feed sacks were about the only extra in our lives. The companies selling livestock feed used an assortment of calico prints on the sacks, and if you bought several hundred pounds of feed and matched the sacks, there was enough cloth to make a dress. I think every little girl in Prairie Valley School had one or two flour-sack dresses. There was no stigma to wearing them. I don't remember about shirts for the boys, but they probably wore them too.

The plain white sacks were used for everything else. We used them for dish towels, slips and panties, quilt linings, and anything needed in the household. I adjusted to everything made from feed sacks except the sheets. When four large sacks were stitched together in a double-size sheet, there was a seam down the middle and one cross ways. Woe is me when the cousins visited and we slept three or four little girls to a bed because one of us got that seam down the middle, and you could feel it on the coldest night snuggled under a down comforter. All three of us felt that one going across. I never got used to those seams in the sheets. I don't remember when times got better and we were able to buy sheets, but I will always remember those Depression-day linens on the farm. Every time I smoothed the sheets on our bed today, I enjoy the feel of the sheets without seams and remember how fortunate we are now. Did any of you California natives use feed-sack sheets?

I am sure that Oklahoma families who arrived in Fillmore before the war brought quilts with them that had printed feed-sack squares incorporated into the colorful blocks and a plain feed-sack lining. They held the cotton batting between with tiny stitches that only an experienced quilter was able to do with pride. I know the Wren family has several special quilts, and I suspect the Carpenters, Suttles, Taylors, Tuckers, Ballards, Jacksons, and Butlers have them also. Grandmothers made them from any scrap of fabric that was still usable. Nothing was wasted, and each quilt block has its own memories.

With no government aid to take care of you or unemployment insurance, it was the original do-it-yourself project to feed and clothe a family, and everyone helped each other. The Depression was hard, but we learned from it and survived. Yes, the Lord helps those who help themselves. Any job was better than no job, whether it was exactly what you thought you might want to do for the rest of your life. You worked at it until something better came along. No wonder the young people of today do not understand the attitude of their grandparents. Times have certainly changed.

No, I do not want to go back to those day, but the lessons learned have helped me for over ninety years. Each generation is formed by the circumstances of their times, and I am proud of my generation.

Chapter 7

ENTERTAINMENT

Californios

I enjoy folk music, and it comes in all styles. Bluegrass is a favorite, and it is supposed to be truly an American original along with blues. Now I have discovered another—the music of Los Californios. It sounds like no other!

When Spain and Mexico ruled this part of the country, we were known as Alta California. After it became a territory of the United States, the *Alta* was dropped, and now we are just *California*. During the mission and rancho days, ranchos were far apart. When there was a party, fiesta, wedding, or christening, people might take two days to get to the event. Needless to say, when they got there, they stayed several days or a week before they loaded up carts or mounted horseback to go home. This time was spent with music, dancing, food, and a smattering of sleep between activities.

The Californios developed their style of music with a combination of tunes from Spain, Mexico, and the United States. With guitars, violins, mandolins, and accordions, it had a different sound that was pleasing to the ear. After the Americans came in great numbers, the culture and heritage of the Californios began fading away.

Charles Lummis came to Los Angeles about 1903. This rather strange character accepted a job at the *Los Angeles Times* and decided he would walk all the way from the East Coast to Los Angeles—and he did! As long as he lived, he maintained this different approach to life. One of his favorite places in the entire world was Rancho Camulos. He was active in forming the Southwest Museum and pushed to preserve Indian and Hispanic culture that was quickly dying out. Rancho Camulos was the last remnant of the way things used to be, and he enjoyed every minute he spent there. Lummis probably hoped to be reincarnated as a Mexican don in his next life. He loved everything about the ranch and wanted to preserve it.

A chapter of the Archaeological Institute of America provided Lummis with funds to buy the new Edison cylinders and record music from several of the old ranchos. These recordings of Californios singing hundreds of their songs are now at the Southwest Museum in Highland Park. The dances were also described and survived in circles through several revival periods in California. Waltzes, contra line dances, jotas, and varsovianas were popular and beautiful.

Helen Hunt Jackson, author of *RAMONA*, said that Don Coronel was the best waltzer in Los Angeles. (We have a picture of him dancing on the veranda at Camulos.) This elderly man was the one who encouraged her to stop at Rancho Camulos to see the last of the real ranchos in California, and afterward she used the old adobe as the setting in *RAMONA*.

Nena and Susie del Valle taught their tradition dances and music to Charles Lummis, and he recorded over twenty-two pieces at Rancho Camulos. Dona Kamp from the Higuera family, recorded sixty-five songs for him. Lummis visited and recorded at every old rancho where the elders remembered the music and dance. Without him and his attraction to all things at the ranchos, all would be lost. The old Edison recordings preserved this wonderful heritage for all Californians. The Los Californios will be playing this music all afternoon at the Rancho Camulos Fiesta on Saturday, October 8—hope you will all come and enjoy early California with us.

Local Fun

Both kids and adults used to entertain themselves night and day with an assortment of games, activities, and idleness. Before the time of radio, TV, video games, or cell phones, we found all sort of things that were fun to do.

Before the highway was straightened out along Ventura Street, that street was a dead end with the community baseball field located between it and Santa Clara Street, which served as the highway through town. Every town had a team of kids and adults to challenge other communities. Fillmore had some outstanding teams.

Swallows Nest on Sespe Creek was used when anyone wanted to go swimming. The sale of new swimsuits was active early in the year. Kennie Fine's aunt bought suits for all her nieces and nephews and swore they would all learn to swim after one child drowned in the Sespe. Families often spent a warm Sunday afternoon with a picnic and swim time in the area. Church took up the morning and picnics in the afternoons.

Every man had his favorite hunting and fishing spots. Long-term hunting camps were set up back in the mountains and used over and over. Many families still have an old photo of their grandpa with a couple of nice bucks taken in the Sespe. The story is, when the Warrings discovered how good the hunting and fishing were around here, they decided right away to move here, and they called their place Buckhorn Ranch.

Fishing holes near the present hatchery or down by the highway bridge would yield a mess of trout anytime you wanted to throw in a line. When the opening day arrived on May 1, so many people came up from Los Angeles to fish that the locals almost camped out to save their favorite spot along the creek. With any luck at all, everyone got their limit on opening day. A fish spear was often used when a fish was needed for supper.

The movie theater on Fillmore Street was a favorite with kids any time they could do an errand and earn the ten-cent admission. During the silent-movie days, if there was no piano player to make the music, the big old music box was turned on, and it tinkled tunes for the afternoon. We are fortunate this beautiful old instrument can still be seen at the Fillmore Historical Museum. (And if you are good, they might even play it for you.)

Many large families had each of the kids playing a musical instrument. After dinner in the evening, it was time for all of them to tune up and play together. Oh, what a time that was! Many of them also played in the Fillmore community bands. If you liked music, if you wanted music, you made music! It was as simple as that!

Fillmore Mexican band with Frank Erskine as director

The elementary school and high school usually had an operetta every year—the Christmas program was the highlight of the season with assorted talents and the nativity as the closing. These activities brought out everyone who enjoyed singing too. The chorus practiced, and family groups often had their own gospel quartets or duets with a special friend and entertained everyone. Oh, what a joy to sing together.

When the May Festival committee started making plans, the kids all wanted to be part of the fun. They decorated wagons and bikes and pets and loved being part of the parade. Adults and older kids worked on elaborate floats or fancy costumes for riding groups. The town not only wanted to be entertained but many wanted to do the entertaining. Horseshoes, tug-of-war, and kids games kept people busy all day. Occasionally, the greased-pig contest or the greased pole-climb challenged the more adventurous boys. The orange-peeling contest was open to different age-groups with trophies for every winner.

All kids enjoyed camping and hiking. The Boy Scouts had the first troop in 1915. They were actually part of Henry Young's YMCA group but were soon incorporated in the Scouts. Girl Scouts were a part of Fillmore lore by 1937. Being active and camping was great fun for any group. Fresh air, hiking, and learning to cook were all part of being a kid.

On a long summer day, while you waited for the ice man to make a delivery down your street and you could sneak a tiny piece of ice, boys and girls flopped on the grass or under a tree and just played being idle. For real adventure and sheer pleasure, books were brought outside for an afternoon of reading. Their chores were done until Mom called again, and they did not need to do anything. If they got bored, they watched the clouds and picked out figures in them or looked closely at the ground to watch tiny bugs scurry under a leaf or climb into the center of a flower. They dreamed about what they wanted to do when they grew up. But there was no rush to grow up. They relaxed until a friend came by and invited them to go fly their kites in an open lot or play ball or dolls. In the evening, counting shooting stars was great. (Or catching fireflies if you were lucky enough to live in the Midwest.) If you had the chance to quietly listen to the grownups reminisce and tell family stories, you would add a bit to your knowledge of history and genealogy and wouldn't even realize it. It probably took years before you realized what those stories meant to you.

There were dozens of things to do for fun, but sometimes, you don't need to be entertained! Those were the good old days.

Baseball

How many of you remember the baseball team from the early 1900s when Harold Mayhew and his buddies were all crackerjack players? (I'm still looking for that old picture of the team.) The ball field for our community was between the current 126 and the railroad tracks. Ventura Street was a dead end, so there was plenty of room down that way for a baseball diamond between Frank Howard's place and Southern Pacific.

I wonder what the rules were then. A recent article in the paper told about some men in Northern California who are reviving the game with the original rules from the 1880s—they now have two teams who play by those old rules. They required the pitcher to deliver the ball underhand, without a windup. The game had one ref who stood behind the plate, and his decision was never challenged. He was suited up in a black coat and a top hat. It was a game for gentlemen. (That seems to have changed!)

When a batter came up to the plate, the ref asked him what kind of a strike he wanted, the batter told him, and that was the way it was called. If the man wanted a high inside ball for a strike, then that pitch was called a strike. Wonders of wonders. These guys now play in old-fashioned uniforms to go with the old-fashioned rules—if they ever play in Ventura County, you can bet we will go see that game.

Summer softball leagues for the returning veterans were popular after WWII—local businesses sponsored teams, and the young men had a great time. The four teams wore jerseys showing Jones Brothers, Munoz Pipe, and Frenchy LaToile on them. We cannot remember the fourth sponsor. The companies each provided uniforms and equipment for their teams. The fellows only had to bring their shoes to be ready to play. It was good advertising for local businesses and supported Fillmore recreation. The league used the high school facilities. The baseball field was located where we now have tennis courts and the abandoned swimming pool. There were a few bleacher seats and lots of fun. All the fellows were buddies, but when they got on the field, they played to win.

With a population of about six thousand, everyone knew everyone, so there was no chance to bring in a ringer who lived outside of Fillmore.

In our house, we often watch GIRLS playing basketball and baseball on TV and anything else between. We have discussed the passage of Title IX, which opened the way for girls to have the same chance to play sports as the boys have in school. I had just been voted to the local school board when it was passed, and I loved the equal opportunity in sports that Title IX brought. Our youngest daughter played basketball for two years and loved it. Track was about the only thing open for the girls prior to Title IX. Now it is hard to make the girls understand how much times have changed in their favor.

Gene enjoys watching the girls play as they are still playing the games more like the original intent. There is less pushing and shoving and ranting and raving. They play with more finesse. Gene frequently mentions their mastery of basic fundamental skills that make them interesting to watch. After a recent Women's College World Series and his admiration for some of the good old-fashioned hitting, pitching, and catching, I told him, "I think *you* used to play like a girl!"

I ducked. He didn't hit me! Perhaps I should leave well enough alone with that one! Yes, our marriage does have humor.

Alumni Football

When the local library is able to secure a microfiche reader, I will be able to give you more definite dates and details and not use so many *about*s in my column. Until then, here is the way I must start today.

About 1948, some of the younger alumni from Fillmore High thought it would be fun to have a football game between the kids and the old-timers. As I remember, the kids were the classes from 1942 to 1947. The old guys had graduated before 1942. (Now remember, my brain isn't very sharp, so these may not be the exact dates.)

Most of these men had been in the service for WWII, came home, and tried to settle down, but the good times from high school kept beckoning them. The idea of actually playing a full game of football on their home field again was just too much. A whole bunch jumped at the idea and signed up.

These guys had matured since their high school days, and uniforms had to be borrowed from Ventura Junior College to accommodate the new sizes. They still wanted to think like high school boys, but their bodies said, "No way!" The use of the field was secured for practice, and two weeks of regular drills were instituted. (Can you imagine about how READY they were to play an actual game with only two weeks of conditioning?)

Wives and mothers already had their say about these young men, fathers of small children and breadwinner for several, who had no better sense than to get out there and play for the thrill of victory again! We all thought the men belonged on a loony farm!

In spite of all, that game was played with officials, the scoreboard lighting up at the proper time, and no one was carried off the field unconscious; so it was successful. Gene remembers that K. B. Rogers, Don Cox, Bill Case, Bob Huestis, Don Goodenough, Dean Kenfield, Unk Carter, and Bill Thompson all played. Don McKendry did get a cut above one eye, and they told him it looked like doe meat. Being a deer hunter, Don got the message right away. Gene said on a kickoff, he and K. B. Rogers went down under the ball, and it looked like a mile back to their end of the field. He also said that Bob Huestis was the toughest man on the field—quite a compliment from a younger man.

The men all got bruises where they'd never had them before. As far as I know, none of them missed work on Monday. When the purples and blues turned to green and eventually back to various shades of brown skin, they suddenly decided it was so much fun they would do it again the next year. AND THEY DID! This continued for another two or three years. I am not sure who sponsored the event, maybe the chamber of commerce. Was the money used to buy a new scoreboard? I don't know, but the fellows had fun, the wives worried, and the little kids all loved going to an out-of-season football game. What more could a small town ask for? YAY, TEAM!

Boy Scouts

Gene and I cannot get away from Scouting. Anywhere we travel, it seems to FIND us. When I did a presentation at the Oklahoma Historical Society's annual meeting in 1999, I discovered several nearby museums to be explored. One was located in Pawhuska, Oklahoma. On our recent vacation, I couldn't wait for Gene to view my find.

The first Boy Scout troop in the United States was organized in Pawhuska in 1909. The new Episcopal priest there had been assigned from a church in England. Scouting was in full swing over there, and he brought the idea with him and started the first American troop under an English charter. The nineteen charter members were equipped with English uniforms and manuals.

The next year, these young men hiked to Bartlesville for a three-day outing. On Saturday, they helped organize a group of local boys there as the second troop. After church on Sunday, the kids started for home. A team and wagon hauled their supplies, and some of the boys rode horseback and some walked. On the return trip, the boys on horses were back in Pawhuska by dark, but the kids hiking had stopped and camped and completed their hike the next day.

In later years, the Pawhuska Kiwanis Club had a bronze life-size statue of a Boy Scout placed at the depot to commemorate the founding of Scouting for the US. This Boy Scout is dressed in the original uniform, with knickers, leggings, and campaign hat. A local Pawhuska artist, Bill Sowell, designed the statue. The Kiwanis Club sold twenty-four-inch miniatures for $1,150 each to raise funds for the full-size bronze at the museum. A plaque with the names of the original troop members is nearby. It didn't take much persuading from me to get Gene to put his arm around the shoulder of the first Scout in the United States.

In 1911, Bardsdale's Henry Young was the leader of a group of boys associated with the YMCA camping program. With Scouting in full swing, Henry and his boys were incorporated into the Boy Scouts of America when the Y changed their camping groups to that association. Henry stayed as the Scout leader for several years.

The local historical museum has a picture of these boys, and most of the kids have been identified. They were Howard Burson, Ronald Ritchie, Harleigh Baker, O. J. Winkler, Vernon Young, Melvin Hudson, Albert Haase, Russell Baker, Clarence Young, Everett Gibbout, Romaine Young, Lloyd Michel, Carl Moisling, Jim Ritchie, and Bert Mayhew. Many of you will recognize these names and know they always represented the finest of our local citizens.

Scouting was a great training ground for a successful adulthood then, and it is a great training ground for a successful adulthood now. No other youth program teaches and upholds the moral values of Boy Scouts: A Scout is TRUSTWORTHY, LOYAL, HELPFUL, FRIENDLY, COURTEOUS, KIND, OBEDIENT, CHEERFUL, THRIFTY, BRAVE, CLEAN, AND REVERENT. And as our beloved friend of Scouting, Paul Haase, frequently reminded us, the last Scout law should be "A Scout is always HUNGRY." These laws were embedded in the new sidewalks when the troop did the recent renovations at the Scout house to remind every boy at every meeting to do his best to meet them.

Scouting in Fillmore continues to have the active support of the community, and all the troops and packs in town appreciate that interest and concern.

Rod Peyton

Gene said Rod Peyton was the one who bought the old army trailer for Boy Scout Troop 406. One night, when we were putting gas in the car in Ventura, Gene was visiting with Rod, who was doing the same thing. Beside the little office, they had stored an old army trailer, and Gene kept looking at it while his brain was spinning. It would make a great cook trailer for the Scouts. I had been doing the cooking for the troop summer camp for a couple of years, and the old army tent was a mess. Gene wanted to improve things for me to make the work easier. After a little exchange of ideas with Rod about it, Rod just said okay and bought the trailer for Troop 406 on the spot! What a great gift to the Scouts.

Gene and the Scout fathers lowered the axle and made it into the Scout cook trailer that I used for about twelve years, and now others are using it. Rob also gave the first $1,000 to the FOUNDATION to start construction on the Scout house. This log building was constructed by the Lions and Rotary Clubs for the exclusive use of Boy Scouts in Fillmore. Texaco provided about two acres of land for a dollar a year lease, the clubs invested about $10,000 cash, and the rest was sweat labor by the men. The building is located at the east end of Sespe Street and is still in regular use.

Rod Peyton was a real friend of Scouting in Fillmore.

Chautauqua

Since no one called me about their family attending a Chautauqua after I mentioned in last week's column, I had to do some research for myself. (It is always faster and easier if friends can just repeat things to you.) I recall some of my elderly friends talking about Chautauquas in the 1920s, so I hope these memories are correct:

At that time, Ventura had a boardwalk along the sand about where the Pierpont houses were built. Many local families moved to the beach during the summer. Some had simple houses along the Rincon, and some took a tent and really camped out on the sand below the present harbor. It always sounded like so much fun to me.

Fillmore's Grandma Burson took her kids over for the summer, and they drove a wagon filled with their beach stuff. If they left Fillmore early in the morning, they could noon at the big Morteson Bay fig tree on old Highway 126. That old tree is still providing shade beside the road, and the ranch is called Fig Tree Ranch. They could get to Ventura before night. At one time, they had a large two-story house on the beach, so there was plenty of room. In later years, that house was moved back to Fillmore and used on the ranch property at the corner of 126 and C Streets. A grocery store is now at that location. (My brother lived there when he worked for the Burson Ranch in 1957. When it burned about fifteen years later, it made a fire to end all fires. It was old, single walled, and dry. It made great firewood.)

Well, back to my story about the Chautauquas! In the 1920s, we had few radios and no TV. Information was delivered to home by newspapers, magazines, and books. People were hungry for entertainment and educational speakers. Then along came the Chautauquas.

Several companies had a Chautauqua circuit. They booked locations and secured the people who entertained. Some Chautauquas went on for three days and some were a week. It was sort of like routing a circus. They had several places, and when one booking was completed, everything was moved to the next site. They covered most of the larger towns in the Midwest and West. The large tent accommodated several hundred people. It was set up, and elaborate sets for stage productions often filled it. Each day, there would be a different program. One night would be a lecture with a play, opera singers, or dancers. The next day, the speaker and entertainment would be another group. The Chautauqua had something interesting for all ages, and it costs from fifty cents to a dollar to attend. It provided culture to many towns. It provided good, clean entertainment too. Often the performers would do ninety performances in ninety nights in ninety different towns.

Usually, there would be both a matinee and evening performance, including music, a lecture, and some kind of variety entertainment. This might be a magician, comic reading, or a lecture by William Jennings Bryan or former president of the United States William Howard Taft. One circuit had an all-girl orchestra. Children's programs were organized with skits and musical events. It was THE event of the summer.

Edna Wilson claimed, "Chautauqua is one of the most potent single forces now at work for the advancement of national thought, entertainment and ideas." I bet the Burson family went every year when they were at the beach. One year, Ventura got HIGH TIDES that washed out the boardwalk, and many of the small houses were either damaged or moved to higher ground. This was probably when the old Burson beach house was brought to Fillmore. Their kids grew up. Then the Depression of the '30s arrived, and that put an end to the Chautauquas. Yes, times change. (And this keeps on happening till the present time.) It is still fun to find out about things from the good old days. And NOW YOU KNOW!

Basketball in 1926

Every day brings new historical information to me. Last week, a friend asked if I thought the Alumni Association would be interested in her father's letterman sweater from 1926—the year they won the CIF championship in basketball. A CIF Southern Section Championship? Well, I've never heard about that! That tidbit got me to the library to read old *Heralds* from 1926 so I could tell you some of the details about those good old days in Fillmore sports. The town had about a population of two thousand. The headlines in the *Herald* referred to the team as "first string quintet" and "casaba tossers." (Yes, in eighty years, terms have changed.)

In 1926, fabled Eugene Kennedy was a young coach for basketball in Fillmore. The teams were either heavyweights or lightweights rather than varsity and junior varsity as we now know them. A seven-man squad picture shows Ernest Mosbarger, guard; Russell Aldrich, subguard; Stephen Stroud, forward; John Coulson, center; Fred Johnson, guard; Ed McCarter, subforward; and Harry Imhoof, forward. This team picture shows the boys wearing two different colors of short uniform pants, but all had matching blue-and-white stripped sleeveless tops. There were no visible numbers, insignia, or school name, although those might have been on the back. Their high-top shoes were mostly black. They all had short, neat hair. The school did not waste a lot of money on fancy uniforms, but the boys were neat.

In this era, basketball was a defensive game. Boys shot with two hands. There was a center-court jump ball after every score. They played eight-minute quarters and no coaching during time-outs. The boys had to figure it out for themselves. It was a whole different defensive ball game from the way the kids play now.

Early in January, our boys beat Pasadena; the next week, they won the Van Nuys tournament. The roster consisted of Coulson, Mosbarger, Johnson, McCarter, Gilmore, Stroud, Harry Imhoof, Nolan Hays, Reed, and Snow. According to the *Fillmore Herald*, "Neutral spectators remarked repeatedly on the speed and team work of the Fillmore team. Their clean and fair playing and freedom from 'crabbing,' the support given the team and the real school spirit shown throughout." Each of the boys received a gold basketball as tournament winners, with a plaque for our high school. By February, the team had defeated both Oxnard and Ventura to become Ventura County League champs.

Van Nuys and Fillmore met in the finals for the CIF Southern Section championship. The game was held at the USC pavilion. Our boys had reached the big times. It was a hard-fought game, but Fillmore won! Van Nuys was stunned. The final game score was 10–6. Yes, you read it correctly. (Remember, I told you it was a defensive game in those days.) The final game score was 10–6! When the last shot was fired, Tiny Burson led a giant serpentine around the court for ten minutes, and all 350 Fillmore fans participated. Coach Kennedy took the boys to the *LA Times* building at the request of their sports department for pictures and more information about the little team that could— and DID!

The next stop was playing the Central Division champs, Lemoor. The game was held at Fillmore, and the hometown boys lost, 23–15. The *Herald* reported that the lightest boy on the Lemoor team weighed more than the heaviest man on the Fillmore team. Lemoor was able to just muscle their way to victory. The reporter said, "To our belief, Fillmore has done better with this team than any other team in California could, for our boys, thrown all over the court by Lemoore, instead of getting angry, showed the sportsmanship that has always been characteristic of Fillmore." The average weight for Lemoor was 190, and Fillmore was 150 pounds. The reporter did give Lemoor credit for their skill, and combined with their brawn, they won.

The next week, the *Herald* reported on a surprise birthday party for team member Fred Johnson. Stella Harthorn and her parents held the party at their home on the corner of Mountain View and Blaine and used an Easter theme. Those attending were Hattie Mae Strickland, Alfreda Coulson, Virginia Buzard, Merle Lowry, Violet Nelson, Stella and Evelyn Harthorn, Ernest Mosbarger, John Coulson, Nolan Hays, Harry Imhoof, Steve Stroud, Elgin Snow, and Albert Bartels.

After that, the only thing left was the spring athletic banquet to honor the team. It was held in the school cafeteria, with mothers doing the serving for the boys, their parents, their friends, and a limited number of guests. Ralph de Bolt was the toastmaster. Of course, Principal Ely spoke on the community backing and morale that were important factors in the success of the team. Each boy had a chance to speak along with several parents, who lauded the boys for their clean playing in every game. F. L. Fairbanks, president of the high school board, added his praise. Elmer Riggles led the boys in yells for the various speakers. It must have been quite an evening!

The event was finished off by Glenn Mosbarger. He presented each member of the team and the coach with a handsome watch and chain with appropriate remarks. The citizens of Fillmore donated the money to pay for the watches, and Montague Everill's jewelry store engraved each one. Yes, our town was PROUD of those boys who battled to become all-CIF Southern Section basketball champions in 1926.

(The Alumni Hall of Fame recently received the letterman sweater worn by Harry Imhoof, from his daughter Gloria Gritz and it is now on display.)

Old-Time Festival

Our May Festival is OVER—and we had it in spite of everything! The chamber of commerce stumbled over every roadblock anyone could put up; the city helped out with financial support, and a few faithful community members and the chamber got it together in a very short time. Few things were up to snuff, but they were done, and Fillmore needs to thank those who worked so hard at the last minute to get the job done.

Following the parade and lunch, I spent my Saturday afternoon at the library doing research. In those three hours, I discovered several things about festivals in the past, and I will share with you.

In 1931, it was called FILLMORE DAY. The emphasis was on supporting local businesses. It was the time when many local folks shipped oranges east to friends and relatives. During WWII, things were put on hold, but when the war was over, the community got back on track.

In researching 1946, I found several things about the festival that year. Although the war was officially over late in 1945, sugar was still rationed, many of the military were waiting to be discharged and sent home, and newly arrived veterans were trying to get enrolled in college or start a new business. The Red Cross was still raising money to continue their work, and our town had a big used-clothing collection to be sent overseas to help war-ravaged Europe and Asia. The society section of the *Herald* reported lots of weddings and stork showers, so our young people were catching up when the fellows got home.

The Junior Chamber was a very active young group, and they took over the Fillmore Frontier Festival and set the date for June 22. At a regular meeting in the fire station, they choose a general chairman, John Oxford, and put Dick Wilson in charge of publicity. A big parade with decorated floats and a community barbecue was envisioned. Glen Fansler and Walter Hall took over the cooking, and they served the food under the big peppetrees on Sespe Avenue across from the school.

The Fillmore theater had a continuous showing of a movie from 1:00 p.m. until midnight, and the only admission was showing your raffle ticket on an automobile to be given away about 10:00 p.m. I don't know who donated the car, but Vic Casner used a silver dollar to purchase the first one sold. That week started with a bang when three people bought a hundred dollars each. It was a great way to have fun, throw your name in the pot, and help our community.

Jack Beekman was in charge of the horse carnival on the football field in the afternoon. An amateur show with local talent started at seven. Part of that entertainment would be awarding a prize for men with the longest and fanciest beards. After a month of unshaven husbands, the ladies were happy to see the end of the contest. These things were staged on a bandstand set up in the center of Central Avenue, and Omar Myers was in charge.

Bob Hutchins was in charge of the street dance that started at nine. Ralph Stanley guided the concession stands for the day. It was all Fillmore, and the money would stay in town. The Junior Chamber used the proceeds for the purchase of emergency lifesaving equipment to be stationed in Fillmore-Piru. The equipment was on display in various business windows and ready to be installed in a light, fast panel truck. We would have it for immediate use in any emergency. Five local men were trained to operate the unit.

Of course, there was a queen of Fillmore contests. Several girls put their name in the pot, and the public voted on the winner. Each time you bought anything in town, you received tickets, and you used those to vote for your queen selection. Votes were tabulated and posted weekly in front of the Fillmore theater. The Rotary Club provided prizes to go to the queen and the runner-ups.

Among the special activities during the week was a hobby show. It included a display of souvenirs brought back from overseas by local veterans. Everyone was included in some way. Everyone participated. Everyone had fun. Oh, how we long for the good old days. (Wouldn't it be fun to add some of these things back to the festival in 2007?)

Festival 1

Another Fillmore Festival is over! We were out of town and missed it for the second time in over fifty years. We've always enjoyed it and participated in many different ways. This week, I want to tell you about the festival after WWII. When I moved to Fillmore in 1947 I loved the idea of this community celebration. The annual festival was a one-day event, and it was a whopper for fun and frolic. Merchants decorated their windows with antiques from the family or business so people learned about the old way to do things. It was a joy to walk Central Avenue and see all the different things every year. A small plaque was often awarded for the best display.

The week before the Saturday activities, businesspeople dressed up in western or early California costumes to get into the spirit of things. Mexican skirts and pioneer sunbonnets were eye-catchers everywhere. One year on festival day, every lady wearing a bonnet received a ticket for a drawing with the prize being a handmade quilt. One year, the beard contest brought out some beautiful specimens for judging. One year, a baby contest took center stage. There was always something new and fun to do.

The FFA sold tickets for a prize beef for a freezer. The kids added to their club treasury, and someone got delicious eating for a year. Often the chamber had a drawing for a new car. The competition to sell the most tickets was hot and heavy.

The main block of Central Avenue was closed off for the day, and the stands assembled there. Booths were all locally run with food and games enclosed in simple stands and palm fronds to cover the top. The local palms were well trimmed at least once a year to provide a roof over a booth. As the event grew, it was necessary to change the location, so several areas near downtown have been used.

Everyone wanted to be in the parade. The special kids section saw many decorated bicycles and wagons. Pets were dressed to walk along with little owners. One year, I borrowed a big wicker baby buggy and baby and walked with the PTA kids. It was great fun for all of us. Every business expected to have an entry—they ranged from stagecoaches to elaborate floats or something simple like Speed Stewart in a motorized bathtub. (You would have to know Speed to fully appreciate this float. He was always a good sport.). Politicians could ride in the parade, but they were not allowed to carry signs stating more than their name or do any politicking. Often Pole Creek Sally or a balloon vender worked the crowd before the parade started at exactly 10:00 a.m., Boy Scouts from Troop 406 showed off their uniforms as they manned the barricades along the parade route.

The queen and her court had a float with enough paper flowers to cover the sides, top, and bottom. It was always pretty. She had been chosen by a rather simple interview by local judges—evening gowns and bathing suits had no part of it. It was very special to be nominated by a high school club to be their representative in the queen contest. These girls helped sell tickets for the drawing later in the evening.

Originally, the pit barbecue was held at noon under the big peppertrees across the street from Sespe School, and everyone waited for that tasty dinner. When the packinghouse bought the property, the dinner was moved to the park. About this time, the old WWI cannon was put into use. The mayor fired it off exactly at noon, and the eating commenced. The year they put in too much powder and blew out windows across the street was the year the old-timers all talk about.

The old park provided lots of room for Maypoles, kids' games, and orange-peeling contests. These kept the younger set entertained after lunch. The games were organized by age-group, so young and old had fun. I think the favorite was the pie-eating competition. Wow! What a mess that was. One year, a greased pole-climbing contest kept the young men occupied. Often teams were organized for tug-of-war. We had everything except speeches on festival day, and no one missed those.

The carnival was the only thing from out of town that was allowed to participate. They were strictly policed and provided only rides and a floss wagon that sold items not available from local booths. They were not permitted to have any gambling or game booths. The carnival posters were used to promote the event throughout the county without expense. The idea was to make money and keep it in town for the local organizations. The token fee paid by these groups covered the minimum expense of the festival committee. No alcohol was sold, so families could enjoy all the activities. The volunteers did lots of work and loved every minute of it.

The festival was held once a year. It was for one day. It made money for every volunteer and church group in town. It was fun! It was simple! It is long remembered by some of us. Oh, for the good old days.

Festival 2

I hope that past honored citizens enjoyed being grand marshal of the festival parade as much as Gene and I did many years ago. Until old age slowed us down, we were always very active with the festival.

I still remember my first May Festival in 1948. I made a tiered skirt and white peasant blouse to wear that day. My knowledge of Mexican clothing was very limited, and I had nothing Western, so my choice seemed to blend in with both. The barbecue was held under the big peppertrees across from Sespe School—that location is now part of the lemon packinghouse (avocado packing plant in 2019). I am sure those old trees saw many festival dinners through the years. In a couple of years, the noon food was moved to the park near the depot where they could fire off the old cannon to start the food line moving. The small booths erected on each side of Central Avenue with tops covered by recently cut palm branches fascinated me. The parade just marched down the middle of the street and did not disturb anything. Everything, except for the few carnival rides, was locally owned and operated, with all the money staying in our community. Games were simple and fun for the kids, and food was homemade and wonderful for the adults. It was an unbeatable combination.

I went to work at Ramon Building and Loan, and they supported all the community things and often had a float in the parade. One year, we did a '20s float with several of the thin gals in authentic flapper dresses from Mrs. Gertrude Schleimer; one year, we all rode in a stagecoach. I sat on the back tailgate holding a live chicken in a basket on our way down Central. Another time, we had a flatbed truck made into a schoolroom with Frank Erskine as our teacher in an early day black skullcap. He held a long rod in case any of us got out of hand during the parade and needed a lickin'. I will always remember the year Gene drove a tractor that pulled a little trailer with a harem tent and performing belly dancer. It was great fun to develop ideas and put them together to entertain folks along the route.

Ham that I am, I loved being in the parade. I got to lead the PTA children's section one year. The kids were in every sort of costume, and many had their pets along to show off. There were bikes and tricycles decorated by kids and mothers. It is surprising what you could do with some crepe paper cut into ribbons to make bows and weave through trike wheels. I donned an old-fashioned dress, found a wonderful BIG wicker baby buggy in Piru, borrowed the six-month-old Dunst baby, and I was ready! It was the best of fun for me. I felt like the pied piper with about fifty kids behind me.

Eventually, time caught up with us, and Gene and I were awarded the honor of being grand marshal of the parade in 1978. That was a grand event for us. We've usually involved our family in our activities, so we felt they should be part of our parade celebration. The chamber found a big open carriage with draft horses to pull us in the parade. As I remember, they came from the Cummings ranch in Santa Paula. I got everyone dressed in appropriate festival dress, and we all loaded up. The men had white shirts with an armband and straw bowler hats. I called Disneyland and ordered gorgeous beribboned and feathered hats for us ladies to wear. What a great surprise when those arrived and matched our long dresses. The wagon was the type used to take people from the depot to the hotel at the turn of the century, and we enjoyed the ride through town.

At the end of the parade, we were escorted to the noon barbecue and seated in the guest of honor section and waited on for the entire meal. Oh, what fun for all of us! Everyone made us feel so special all day.

We've been associated with several other grand marshals through the years and worked on carriages for them. We got an open buggy for Frank Erskine and decorated it with fresh flowers and crepe paper. He had a wing collar from Champ Cochran's store and looked as elegant as possible for the day. An old top hat completed his costume. I remembered all the things that made us feel so special and tried to duplicate that feeling for him. I think it was the high point of his retirement years.

One year, the Shiells family was selected. With four members—Jim, Helen, Bill, and Les—we needed a larger vehicle for them. It was the surrey with the fringe on top that carried all of them down Central. As a family, they had contributed so much to our community, and it was fun to honor them. They supported Fillmore for many years with land donation for the memorial building, funding for every charity in town, and all the civic clubs.

Many other families and individuals have been honored since my first festival in 1947. They are all part of history. I hope each of them enjoyed their day as much as the Wren family did. Thanks to the community who cared enough to honor every grand marshal.

Cannon

Fillmore has its very own CANNON. And where did it come from? I imagined it was a Civil War or western relic because I know nothing about any kind of gun or firearm. What a surprise when I discovered that it was actually a German piece dating from WWI. The local veterans' service club got it from our government and only paid the freight. It was placed in the corner of the original railroad park near the depot for many years.

Gary Haley lived in the Rudkin apartments across the street and used it for his personal playground. It has stood the test of time with almost every kid who ever walked, ran, or ate in the park. It was a traditional favorite for all of them. The barrel was smooth as silk from all the pants sliding along it. With a little imagination, kids would have a great time and not have to move more than twenty feet.

For many years, the mayor of Fillmore fired it to start the barbecue at noon on festival day. The Fillmore Historical Museum has a wonderful picture of Mayor Fred Bryce in a top hat and swallowtail coat as he lit the fuse. He found a costume for the occasion and looked about as official as you could find. Each year, the load of powder with no ball made a lot of noise but usually did no damage. After it was fired, everyone was ready to eat pit barbecue. However, one year, the powder was a bit more than needed, and the noise broke some windows in the immediate neighborhood. Well, you can't be right all the time.

When the park was improved, the cannon was moved to the newly landscaped corner on the highway. The city added grass and shrubs, and it looked really nice—for a short time. After some disagreement between the city and the owner of the property, everything was torn out and returned to the original bare ground. The cannon went into retirement with the wheels about to fall off, I think. We missed that odd piece of Fillmore history.

The next thing we heard, the local VFW had our cannon repaired and put on the corner of the Fillmore-Piru Veterans Memorial Building front lawn. It had been repainted; the wheels were in good shape and probably replaced. Regardless, it now looks nice, has a nice new home, and it gives all of us something old to remember. Thank you VFW. (The kids still miss having it at the park for playing, however.)

Sespe Swimming

Swimming in the Sespe

With the summer weather really showing its stuff the last few days, most of us have longed for a shady place and a swimmin' hole to cool off. (We still live without air-conditioning.) Sespe Creek used to provide both for us. If you have lived in Fillmore for very long, you've heard about Swallows Nest, Kentuk, and other good spots in the creek where you could swim and picnic and enjoy the summer. In Kennie Fine's book, he talked about the creek and the pleasures it provided as late as the 1940s

Kennie remembered a time when most Saturdays, during warm weather, the neighborhood kids put a cold biscuit and a piece of leftover breakfast bacon in their pocket and headed up the Sespe to spend the day. They knew that Young's had the perfect swimming hole on the creek. It was a couple of miles from town, and most of them walked. (Very little juvenile obesity then.) That hole of water was twelve to fifteen feet deep, so the boys dove off the rocks. Once, a kid from the city drowned. The next day, Kennie's aunt Lora Kenney took the kids and her family to town to buy swimsuits so they could all learn to swim. She insisted, "You have to learn at least to dog paddle, as none of my family is going to drown in our backyard."

Swallows Nest also had a nice sandy beach and good, deep hole. Families often piled into a wagon for the trip, and everyone—young and old—had a cooling day in the creek. Neither hole is there now after the County Flood Control did some work on the Sespe.

As the rivers weren't all dammed in those days, the Santa Clara River and Sespe Creek often ran all year round. I have seen a picture of a rowboat on the Santa Clara River. (Can you top that for a tall tale?)

There is nothing like having access to a natural body of water for swimming. The local museum has a photo of Edith Moore and several other girls as bathing beauties on the rocks at Devil's Gate in the early days.

Our own kids learned to swim at Kentuk, a nice hole just below the little irrigation diversion dam. Our four-year-old enjoyed the freedom of the creek in a life jacket and saved her parents from early gray hair. The older two learned to swim that summer. It was great family fun in the 1950s when the original school pool was closed for two years. (Did you know that Fillmore High School was the first in the county to have a swimming pool?)

Times change! The roads on both sides of the Sespe are closed to everyone except the property owners, so there is no access to the creek. Now the Sespe seldom has very much water for swimming, but kids can still play in the creek near the old bridges early in the season after a wet year. Our own grandsons did that a few years ago.

For another summer, we have neither the Sespe Creek nor a local swimming pool for the kids—I hope that will change soon. This end of the valley needs a stand-alone parks and recreation district with their own taxing power to provide a swimming pool and other rec services for all the population. Their only responsibility would be parks and recreation.

The city of Fillmore is interested in attaching this to an existing district where the primary purpose is *not* parks and recreation. Let's make it a separate entity that will provide needed facilities and activities for this end of the Santa Clara Valley. It may take more work, but let's DO IT RIGHT!

Our city has all kinds of special landscaping and lighting districts, and now I'd like for the council to be the leaders in forming a separate PARKS AND RECREATION DISTRICT. A new council will be able to direct our city employees to start work on putting in place a new district and carry it through to a vote. We need it! We want it! Let's get it!

We can recall the old days, but we can improve on the new ones. Let's DO IT RIGHT with a whole new district dedicated to PARKS AND RECREATION. We need a new swimmin' hole.

Fats and slats for fun

Fourth of July

Another Fourth of July in Fillmore has come to a safe and sane conclusion. The volunteer groups are counting their money and hoping they made enough to pay all the city permits and have enough profit to support the activities of each individual organization. From our part of town, there were so many other skyrockets that we were not sure when the public display at the football field concluded. Certainly, this was the worst year for illegal fireworks in my memory. It is only a matter of time until we have a serious fire or injury and lose our privilege to shoot off the safe and sane items in front of our homes. It will be the out-of-bounds actions of a few that will penalize all of us, so what else is new! But that isn't what I want to tell you about this week.

In the old days, the Fillmore Fourth was celebrated at Kenney Grove. That beautiful stand of native oaks was the perfect place for fun and picnics. It was only a couple of miles from town and accessible to everyone. If you did not want to hitch up the wagon for your family, you could ride the morning train from town to the Brownstone flag stop (Grand Avenue) or go a little farther and get off at the Keith stop (Rancho Sespe). It was an easy walk to Kenney Grove from either. (I suspect the train would make an unscheduled stop as near as possible to the picnic area. People were accommodating then.)

A day at the park was fun for all. Every family brought their own picnic lunch for noon, unless a pit barbecue was planned. The kids were entertained with an assortment of games, from sack races to egg toss, and probably received a ribbon if they were the winner. The afternoon would be filled with oratory from local politicians, for an election issue needed opinions before it was time to vote. Without any TV and radios, the only communication was through newspapers or in person. People were interested in local, county, and state issues; so speeches and debates were important. Without political issues, the speaker would deliver a good, rousing patriotic address that made people want to wave the flag and remember how good it was to be an American. At least one speaker would always remind the folks about the reason for celebrating Independence Day.

Kids would be playing with their firecrackers all day, so not a single baby got their afternoon nap undisturbed. A baseball game got everyone sweaty and dusty, but lemonade helped the thirst for those who did have a private bottle behind the wagon seat. Fireworks started later in the evening, either at the park or after they had gone home. Dusk started families back to town. Without electricity at the park, they did not want to wait too late to gather the kids and picnic basket and head home. If you had cows and chickens, there were still chores to be done by lantern light if you waited too long. The horses needed to be fed and brushed in their stalls and the night work done. The party was over, but the daily work still had to be completed. Each Fourth of July was long remembered. By the next day, small boys would start saving pennies to buy firecrackers for the next year and make plans to practice with their best friend for the three-legged race. Oh, what a time for kids.

About 1962, Fillmore had an old-fashioned Fourth at Kenney Grove Park. The chamber sponsored it with many organizations participating. Gene was active with the chamber, so we became involved. A barbecue was arranged. Scout Troop 406 organized kids' games—tire rolling, potato relay, and other things to entertain the various age-groups—and it was a fun day. Watching five-year-olds trying to roll a tire was worth the price of admission. The Scouts sold lemonade for five cents and still made a small profit for the camping fund. Everyone in town who wanted to be a part of it was included. Yes, our kids were filthy with dust at the end of the day, but it all washed off. Who would want to go to a park that was covered with grass? The dust was part of the fun. The old oaks shaded long rows of table in view of the baseball diamond where it was comfortable during the game. It was another day of fun. (Does anyone remember if we had a speaker? Surely we did!)

Most of my readers are older people. I hope you will remember to ask your own grandchildren or the kids next door why we celebrate the Fourth—I'd bet most of them do not know it is Independence Day for the Unites States.

Volunteers

My old college dictionary defines a *VOLUNTEER* as one who enters into or offers himself for a service of his own freewill. Volunteers have built our country since the first settlers arrived from the East Coast. I like to think that us westerners volunteer more than others, but I am probably wrong. I had never crossed the Mississippi River to the East until last summer, so I have a very midwestern/western mentality.

Our part of the Santa Clara Valley has always been full of volunteers. The old-timers called it being neighborly. I'd bet every one of you have family stories told by grandparents that go back to 1900. They remembered helping build a school or church, rebuilding a barn or house when it burned, marking the safest ford across the Santa Clara, plowing a field or harvesting a crop when the owner was suddenly taken ill, or helping deliver a baby and nursing the ill. That is what a good neighbor did! You helped each other when the need arose. And anyone who happened to be at the house at mealtime was expected to sit down and eat with the family. The meal might be just bread and gravy, but you were welcome to share it.

Rancho Camulos was known for its hospitality. When the trail went from Castiac down the valley to San Buenaventura, Camulos was the only place to stop for food and rest between the San Fernando mission and Buenaventura mission. Don Ygnacio del Valle always welcomed travelers. They brought news and a change of pace to the rancho. They stayed as long as they needed before continuing their journey. Ygnacio was being neighborly in a much-needed way. Everyone was used to helping others.

After Camulos was sold to the Rubel family, this hospitality and volunteerism continued for many years. After the St. Francis Dam broke in 1928, the Camulos men, led by August Rubel, were among the first to start searching for survivors and caring for those who made it. They were farther upstream, so they got the first start on rescue efforts. After that wall of water passed along the valley to the ocean, everyone came out to help. Disasters seem to bring out the best in our citizens. Restoration was a long and tedious task, but people did what was necessary. Volunteers!

During the Depression of the '30s, our towns had more volunteers to help those in desperate need. The churches and chamber of commerce did fundraisers for entertainment, but the money was used for gas to get stranded travelers to the next town and buy food for locals. When the price of oranges was high, it was easier to raise money than it was in a year when the bottom dropped out, but money was raised and used to advantage of the unfortunate.

After the CCC and WPA were organized, jobs and a small paycheck at the end of the month were provided for anyone who needed work. Our community secured some much-needed general improvements from these working men. Some of the rock ditches in Bardsdale were put in by the WPA, and they are still in good shape. All over the country, you will find armories, rock school buildings, and small bridges with *WPA* inscribed on the abutment. Roads and trails up the Sespe were cut and improved by the young men of the CCC. These men were doing meaningful work in return for a small salary. (I've heard Fillmore could have gotten a sewer plant built by the WPA, but the local Republic majority would have no part of such a Democratic project. We had to wait until 1955 and pay for it ourselves.) The WPA and CCC men were mostly volunteers.

In my own memory, we've had the Los Serenos flood in '78 and the 1994 earthquake that brought our communities together. Last year's fire also got our attention and a chance to be neighborly. Once again, it was volunteers who came out of the woodwork to help the officials, do the cleanup, and get things back to normal for this end of the valley. Yes, it was our neighbors pitching in and helping us!

The location of Fillmore puts us in a precarious situation with rivers and creeks on three sides to block and wash out roads. Our city administration, doctors, and some emergency personnel live out of town; so we will be on our own to get the job done when needed. THE THEORY IS, with helicopters and modern equipment, they will get here to bail us out—well, don't you believe it! They may be in the same boat as we are, and small towns will have to figure out a way to help themselves, but hey, I'd bet on Fillmore and Piru anytime! Been there, done that! If we keep up the good-neighbor policy started by our grandparents, we can do it. Neighbors helping neighbors—just like the good old days. Those grandpas from 1900 would be proud of us.

Fillmore's Bunion Derby

Many of you have read Kenneth Fine's book of memories about growing up in Fillmore. (It is still for sale at Patterson Hardware and the museum.) In that book, he talked about participating in the Bunion Derby from Santa Paula to Fillmore for the Fourth of July 1927. (I think Kenneth was off a year, and it was 1928.) It was sponsored by the packinghouse for their employees, with a monetary prize for the winner. The idea was to have a footrace from one town to the other, and the winner got a prize of fifteen dollars.

Kenneth had always like to run, and this cross-country race seemed like a good idea, so he entered. And he won, but he did not collect the prize money. The details in the book are delightful. I had one person call me and ask why it was called the Bunion Derby, and I explained about feet and running, etc.

This summer, I found a book titled *The Great American Bunion Derby* written by Molly Griffis. That title got my attention immediately. Needless to say, it was purchased posthaste and read even faster. Now I know the rest of the story:

Mr. C. C. Pyle put together a race from Los Angeles to New York in 1928 and called it the First Annual International Trans-Continental Foot Race. He secured sponsors and made all the arrangements for food, water, and cots and sleeping tents for the runners along the way. The $25,000 first prize brought out more than two hundred men between the ages of sixteen and sixty-three from all over the world.

Each entry was required to pay a twenty-five-dollar fee for the fun of running three thousand miles and also put up a hundred dollars to guarantee he had money to get back home when he dropped out or finished in New York. Each runner would be clocked for daily time with the total used to determine the winner when they got to New York. The runners were expected to run all day and then sell programs in the evening to pitch the carnival and sideshow that went along with them to the little towns. Some towns even put out a bit of front money to get C. C. Pyle to bring the race down their main street.

Andy Payne graduated high school from Foyil, Oklahoma, and often ran to school and got there before his siblings arrived on horseback. His Indian heritage made him a born runner for the sheer joy of running when he wasn't practicing with the school track team. He hitchhiked to California after graduation to make his fortune in the Golden State, but he failed to find the fabled gold and did anything he could to support himself. When twenty-year-old Andy saw the ad for the coast-to-coast run, he was eager to give it a try.

The entry fee was a problem, so Andy hitched a ride back to Oklahoma to raise the funds to get into that race. He had no luck convincing the locals to donate to his cause, so his father took out another mortgage on the farm so Andy could follow his dream. With $125 in his pocket, Andy went back to Los Angeles to enter the longest race in United States history.

In January 1928, Andy was working odd jobs and starting to condition his body and mind for the challenge. When the training camp opened at Ascot Speedway, where the race would start, he was there in a flash to start training in earnest. His food and bed were provided, and he soon got used to the lumpy cot in a tent and slept fine each night. He made lots of friends from the assorted group of runners as each man arrived and set up his own training program. It was all pretty loose. When Tom Young came to the camp to enter the race and discovered how tough it was going to be, he withdrew as a contestant and became a trainer for Andy. They worked well together and became great friends.

Andy knew the importance of taking care of his feet, building his legs for the long race, and getting all the rest possible. After one lap around the Ascot Speedway one afternoon in March, they were on their way. Andy was disappointed to find his time far down the list when they were posted at the end of the first day. The second day brought rain and then the Cajon Pass. People were dropping out like flies, but Andy was moving up to a good solid third place. The reporters soon started calling the race the Bunion Derby, and that name stuck as feet gave out and more runners returned home.

Well, this is a good story. He got across the Mojave Desert without blisters or shin splints. The men were delighted when they crossed the Continental Divide. As they neared Oklahoma, the home folks were so proud of Andy they passed the hat to collect $1,000 for the first runner to cross into the state. Of course, Andy collected that. They continued to roll out the red carpet for him in Tulsa, and Andy held either first or second place for most of the race. The runners continued through an Oklahoma blue norther with the coldest of winds and freezing temperatures. Andy fought a bout of tonsillitis with fever for a couple of days and could barely move out of his bed, but he couldn't miss a day or he would be out of the race. The going was not easy, but Andy was running to pay off his father's double mortgage and have enough to get married, so he had to win. Quitting was not an option.

C. C. Pyle found moving camp each day for the runners was too hard and expensive, so he started giving each man $2.50 daily to pay for a bed and meals in the little towns. Now the boys had to run, sell programs for the sideshow at night, and find their own place to sleep and eat. Andy was starting to wonder if Mr. Pyle would have the money to pay the $25,000 prize in New York.

The publicity for this Bunion Derby followed the race coast-to-coast. When Will Rogers called Andy the Cherokee Kid, he was sure the name would stick. When he entered Madison Square Garden for the final lap of the race, he was fifteen and a half hours ahead of the second-place winner. Mr. Pyle was able to pay part of the prize money to the winners on the spot with the rest coming in a few months, but the full amounts were received. Andy paid Tom Young 10 percent of his winning for being his trainer and still had money from the Bunion Derby to clear all debt from the family farm and marry his sweetheart, Vivian. In June 1928, $25,000 was a huge sum, and this gave the young couple a good start in married life.

Andy Payne tried his hand at entertaining and newspaper writing before deciding to give politics a try a few years later. He was elected clerk of the Supreme Court in Oklahoma, later joined the army for WWII, and eventually returned to his clerking job where he worked for the next thirty-eight years. His runner's heart gave out, and he died in 1977. A sculpture of Andy in his running uniform is located at the Cherokee Heritage Center near Tahlequah, Oklahoma, and in his hometown of Foyil.

Only a month after Andy collected his prize money, in July 1928, Kenneth Fine was ineligible for the fifteen-dollar prize because his parents did not work at the packinghouse. The guys at the pool hall passed the hat and got enough for Kenneth to pay for his sodas and ice cream for a year, so he was satisfied with the win. He still had fun and was a part of the local Bunion Derby. His little book is the closest thing to a statue we have for Kenneth Fine, but he, too, is remembered in the hearts of locals. Hats off to all runners! Now you have a little bit more history about our community!

Golf

How many of you remember when Fillmore had two golf courses? It was about 1965, as I recall. Elkins Ranch Course was constructed, and Fillmore got a small par-3. Ken Hunter owned some no-good sandy land on the west side of Bardsdale Bridge along the Santa Clara River. It seemed to be the perfect place for a small par-3 golf course, so it was laid out there. Fillmore felt pretty special to have their own place to hit a ball and keep score. It looked very nice and was a great addition to the community. Soon lights were installed so a round of evening golf could be played after work when it was cooler. Everyone wanted to give it a try. (Our family quickly discovered hitting a tiny ball with a club was not their greatest talent.)

Now it just so happens that Arlie Hooper lived next door to this new establishment. Arlie was born in Bolivar, Missouri, and came to Fillmore when he was just a boy. He had been a caddie on many of the local fairways when he was growing up and loved the game. He and Ann married and had five children who attended school in Fillmore. As an adult, he played every chance he got. There was no point in letting irrigating get in the way of having some fun occasionally. He amassed a total of twelve holes in one before his death, so this guy was pretty good (And LUCKY too).

It was not long until Arlie was giving lessons to many of the locals and teaching them to enjoy the game as much as he did. As he gradually retired from his farming, he taught more and more. If a par-3 course can have a pro, then Arlie was it for Fillmore. He enjoyed every minute of it. He was comfortable with this work almost in his own yard, and it was near home for meals or naps. Who could ask for more? Arlie continued playing golf somewhere until about six months before he died at age eighty.

Before we could count a next generation at the par-3, Fillmore had the flood of 1969! As so often happens, the Santa Clara went on a rampage, cut out the bank on the south side, and TOOK the golf course. That was the end of our delightful Fillmore par-3.

Eventually, the land was sold to the Fillmore Unified School District for a school farm. It developed into a good place for the ag classes and FFA to practice tractor work, raising oranges, and taking care of their livestock projects. It has been the showplace for ag classes all over the county of Ventura.

Well, then we had another wet year and the flood of 2005. As so often happens, the Santa Clara went on a rampage, cut out the bank on the south side, and TOOK the school farm. Recovery work is still being done there, and the community hopes to keep the ag classes going for the school.

For various reasons, some of our city fathers think the Santa Clara River can be controlled, but obviously, history tells us otherwise. One of these wet years, that river will decide to go on the north side of the channel and do its work along there. Well, don't say we didn't mention the possibility—first the golf course, then the school farm, and who knows what else a few years down the line? But it sure was fun to have that par-3 in our backyard for a few years.

Chapter 8

OIL

California Start

How many of you have been involved in the oil industry around Fillmore or other parts of the world? When I moved here in 1947, there were two industries that kept the town going full speed: oil drilling and growing oranges! Both of those have changed in seventy years. My early days as an oil patch kid in New Mexico have left me with an abiding interest in the oil industry—I am so hooked on it that I do not find the odor from crude oil offensive! When I married, my husband was working in the local oil fields, and his mother taught me how wash his work clothes—now that laundry takes skill! In a few months, he turned into a farmer, and we left OIL behind, but it is still interesting.

Last week, I bought a book about the history of the Union Oil Company—it mentions locations around here and people that we've heard about and a few that my husband Gene knew. The description of how the early wells were drilled answered many questions for me.

Most of you know the oil industry started in Pennsylvania. They had oil seeps very similar to those found near Santa Paula. A 1755 map even has a spot called Petroleum on it. There was little demand for oil. The Seneca Indians called it *au nus* and used it for rheumatic complaints. General Ben Lincoln in the Revolutionary War said his troop "paused in the valley to bathe their feet and joints in oil they found floating on the creek." Another man said it burned well in lamps and might be good for street lighting, "if by some process it could be rendered odorless." (I guess the smell discouraged people, even in the very early days.)

When the Indians wanted to collect oil, they found a seep and dug a pit and let it fill naturally. Then they dipped out what they needed. The first commercial sale of this thick, sticky rock oil was by Samuel Kier, a Pittsburgh druggist. He bottled the stuff and sold it to heal just about anything that was wrong with people. He urged it for external or internal use. Sam became the first oil millionaire. His success brought others into the picture to try and figure out how they could use and sell the stuff that was just pouring out of little seeps.

A Yale professor, Ben Silliman Jr., analyzed samples and suggest a synthetic coal oil could easily be refined from it and used for lighting homes. And the oil industry was OFF. The Seneca Oil Company was formed, and they were ready to go to work. They were sure that if they dug a hole deeper in the ground, they would find the lake or river of oil, and that would be faster than letting it seep into a pit.

Uncle Billy Smith was a blacksmith and toolmaker, and he became the first oil driller. For centuries, water wells had been drilled by using a small flexible limb with one end and the middle laid across supports and something heavy hanging on the free end where you wanted the hole. By pulling down on the pole and letting the spring back-thrust the bit in the ground, you were able to punch a hole and make a well. Uncle Billy attached a heavy bit to do his drilling and rigged up slings so two men could pull down the limb, and when they let go, the bit bounced up and down and cut into the ground. It was simple, a proven way to make a hole, and worked. As the hole got deeper, Uncle Billy inserted stovepipe to keep the sides from caving in. On August 27, 1859, when Uncle Billy peered down into the sixty-nine-feet-deep hole, he saw a black substance floating only a few feet from the surface. Yep, they struck oil for the first time!

This original well never had flowing oil, but it was easily pumped. Soon the little valley was the scene of a wild scramble to lease land and start drilling. The oil sold for twenty dollars a barrel. Everyone would soon be rich. They quickly learned a faster method of drilling with a wooden derrick and better bits instead of the spring pole for punching the hole—cable-tool drilling was invented! Steam engines provided the manpower to lift the bit, but they still had to develop a market for their product.

Lyman Stewart had grown up in that area and knew every oil seep in the county. He was nineteen years old and working as an apprentice to his father, learning the tanning trade. He hated it. Lyman soon took his small savings of $125 and invested in a one-eighth interest lease and quickly lost every last cent. But it started his lifelong love of oil and developing it, and eventually he turned it into the Union Oil Company. Most of the time, through the years, he was on the verge of bankruptcy or borrowing money for the next enterprise. This is typical of big oil tycoons. It has usually been a big well after a whole bunch of money eating dusters. Lyman's life was an interesting one that went from Pennsylvania to California, but his eye for knowing where to look for oil eventually took Union Oil into a class of its own. Yes, he died in 1923 with money in his pocket.

Oil Fields

The oil industry hit Ventura County with a BANG early in the twentieth century. The Ventura Avenue field was in full bloom, Santa Paula Canyon was full of drilling rigs and wildcatters, and new companies were spudding in around Fillmore and Piru.

By the turn of the century, it was reported the Little Sespe district required more money to explore than the oil that was taken out. However, things soon changed. In 1911, the *Herald* listed many of the drilling sites up Sespe. There were names like Big Sespe Oil Company, Kentuck, Clampett Oil Company, Brownstone Oil, Four Forks, Dixie, Rose, White Star, and Turner Oil. If you are interested in the local oil industry, or worked in it, you probably recognize some of these old companies. The drilling extended from the mouth of the Sespe and Tar Creek across to Hopper Mountain. Some of the oil was very light gravity.

Frank Howard hauling oil equipment up the Sespe

Pictures in 1907 and 1909 show Frank Howard and other local teamsters hauling timber and equipment with four teams hitched to the wagons. The Sespe hills were steep, and it was difficult to get any machinery to a well site. The Merchants Petroleum wells were located on a steep side hill up Sespe and had a tram from the bottom of the creek to the well sites. Everything had to be put on the tram and taken up the side of the mountain. It was an unusual solution to a bad situation, but it worked. (Gene worked on some of these wells in 1947.)

The Torrey field south of Piru was then the best-paying field in the county for the amount of money expended in development. Some of the oilmen said, "Torrey gave Union Oil its start." Union Oil was formed in 1890. The original Torrey lease had fifty-nine shallow wells, drilled at a cost of about $3,400 each. The deepest was 1,600 feet. The wells were pumped by jack line, and the oil was piped to Santa Paula. By 1952, they were drilling up to two miles deep in the same field.

Edith Jarrett on a wooden derrick

According to Leland Lewis, the Torrey lease had two groups of houses for workers and a school for the kids. Each family owned their house and paid Union five dollars a year for a lease on the land under the dwelling. The houses sold from one worker to the next for about $500. When the Lewis family left the lease in 1940, they tore down their house and moved the lumber to their new home in Santa Paula, where it was used to build a barn.

By 1911, the Montebello oil field was in full swing on Shiells's property on the south side of the Santa Clara. The wells in the little canyons on their Guiberson Road homestead, Calumet, and Shiells Canyon produced very light gravity oil. Worker housing and a school were built along the narrow roads going to the new oil field. (The little Montebello schoolhouse is now used as an office for the William

Shiells Company.) A small grocery store provided daily necessities until families went to Fillmore each Saturday to restock the pantry. Ventura Oil Company did the drilling. Later, that company became Texaco. Until the crash of '29, as many as three hundred men worked at Montebello and Calumet. They also had a bunkhouse and a dining room for single men. When Texaco built a refinery in Fillmore in 1915, the oil was sent there for processing.

Montebello Oil lease

The new Texaco refinery was located on the north side of 126, near Pole Creek. It was the best place to work in our community. When you heard the siren of an unscheduled wail, you knew there was a fire or accident there, and everyone would be concerned. It was dangerous work. The small refinery operated until 1950, when it was closed down. Several employees transferred with the company to the Wilmington facility. Joe Scanlin was superintendent, and he turned off the gas to the furnaces on February 1. Fillmore lost their only industry, except for agriculture. The property has been cleaned up in the recent years. There is still a pumping station for the pipeline near 126. Texaco leases a small parcel of refinery land on the west side of Pole Creek to the Boy Scouts, and their log Scout house is located there.

Oil is still pumped from the local fields, but the glory days are gone—they are only a memory but make for interesting historical research.

Sespe oil field

Oil Torrey

The oil industry in Ventura County is interesting and dates from the mid-1800s. We had cable-tool wells drilled on Sulphur Mountain and in the Sespe about that time. Some of the rig sites up Sespe were so steep that equipment had to be hauled by tram from the floor of the creek to the wells. I have a picture from about 1965, and those old wooden derricks were still hanging on the side of the canyon. Frank Howard hauled many a load with several mule teams hitched to a wagon to pull over the steep grades. Books have been written about the small oil companies, the mergers and falling-outs among the men involved.

One of the most productive fields turned out to be Torrey Mountain on the south side of the Santa Clara River across from Piru. Several locals grew up on that mountain and had stories to tell about it and the oil fields. Edith Moore Jarrett told my favorite. When a Girl Scout troop interviewed her, one of her memories was growing up and always wearing a red dress. With wild mustard on the mountain, her mother wanted to be able to find her if she was playing outside their yard or nearby hillside, and a red dress helped. (Where were the cell phones when we needed them?)

Leland Lewis was also generous to tell me lots of things about the Torrey lease. He was born there in 1922 and didn't move until he was almost out of high school. With limited transportation in the early days, most oil companies wanted their workers to live near their work. Torrey had two camps. The one at the top of the mountain was called the Upper Lease. This was where Leland's family lived with one other family. Most of the employees lived at the Lower Lease, with eleven houses and the school at this site. In the early days, there was a bunkhouse and boarding house for the single men. Juan Fernandez's parents ran the cookhouse for several years.

Leland's father started as a roustabout, then became a pumper and worked up through the ranks. During the 1930s, he worked for five dollars a day and three days a week. During the Depression, it was a common practice to let two men share one job so everyone was able to squeak by and keep food on the table.

Crude oil sold for three dollars a barrel, and gasoline was ten cents a gallon. Most of the wells brought in gas along with the oil. The homes used this natural gas for lights, both inside and outside. One-inch pipes were put into the ground and connected to the gas line. They extended about eight or nine feet into the air. The gas was lit, and the torches provided plenty of light around the houses so the path to the outhouse was clearly illuminated. Burning off the natural gas in this way provided extra heat outside in winter and summer.

Pumpers were required to sleep at the powerhouse and often had to check the unit at midnight. If there was breakdown, they fixed it right then and there without overtime.

The wells were pumped by a jack line with three power plants to pull them. The oil went into tanks and then into a pipeline that went from Tapo Canyon to Santa Paula. The road up the mountain was unpaved and had only one lane with cutouts to pass if you met a car or truck. About 1938, they oiled the lower section with sump oil. If winter rains covered the road with mud, everyone helped shovel and clear it. Kids were expected to help in this project. The Lewis family had a car, so they wanted the road kept open.

The families bought flour and sugar in hundred-pound sacks. Wild game was frequently on the menu. The Lewis household had a milk cow. Leland was put in charge of milking the cow twice a day when he was about twelve, and he delivered milk to the neighbors every morning. Mrs. Lewis did all her own baking. When the Santa Clara River was dry in the summer, they bought groceries in Piru, but a wet winter required a trip to Fillmore to use the bridge across the Santa Clara. Leland's mother used the washboard for laundry and the number 3 tub did double duty for bathing.

Union Oil provided water for the two homes. They were limited to thirty barrels of water every two weeks. The company took the sulfur water and made it into steam and then condensed the steam back into pure water for home use. Hey, we do what we gotta do.

Ventura Avenue Oil

Oil fields and farming have always been a part of my life. I am so much attached to both that I do not find the smell of crude oil or manure offensive! They only bring back memories of my childhood.

When I married and arrived in Ventura County, I enjoyed a drive down the old Ventura Avenue with its oil-field smell and tool companies that I remembered seeing as a small child during the New Mexico oil boom in the 1930s. Most of these are gone now, but I enjoyed them years ago.

The Ventura Avenue field was known everywhere in the oil industry. When Lloyd No. 9A and Lloyd No. 16 each came in with a production of nearly five thousand barrels a day, the industry took notice.

Ralph B. Lloyd remembered his father checking on a brush fire on their property in the late 1880s in the Avenue section. He had to run for his life when the fire suddenly jumped hundreds of feet across bare ground. Naturally, escaping gas probably caused that leap. Mr. Lloyd rode to a steep drop and slid down to avoid the flames, but his horse burned to death.

(I've heard stories about torches on South Mountain that were naturally occurring gas leaks that accidentally ignited and burned for a long time.)

In 1899, Ralph Lloyd began to seriously investigate the possibility of oil on their land. When Joe Dabney joined him in 1913 in financing, the Ventura field was discovered. On January 20, 1914, Lloyd No. 1 was spudded and drilled to 2,558 feet before it went wild. That ruined the casing and any chance of bringing in the well. Shell Oil, General Petroleum, and Associated Oil Company became interested, and by 1920, the great Avenue field was becoming famous among oilmen.

The Ventura Avenue field had a peak production of about ninety thousand barrels A DAY! That field spread into canyons, mountain ridges, plains, and sea bottomlands in the county.

In 1890, Lyman Stewart and Wallace Hardison organized the Union Oil Company. These men were from Pennsylvania and joined with Thomas Bard to form Union Oil, now known throughout the world. W. W. Orcutt joined Union in 1898 and became the West's first outstanding oil geologist. Their original office building is now a museum in Santa Paula and worth spending an afternoon to learn about local oil and drilling the old-style way.

Chumash Indians used the asphaltum along Santa Paula Creek and the foot of Conejo Mountain to make their beautiful baskets watertight. It was a good trade item for them also. When the Americans found these natural oil seeps, they were sure they could drill for oil and find it. The first well on Sulphur Mountain was drilled in 1867, and the site is marked along the road to Ojai. They got a gusher when well No. 6 was drilled, but the oil was too heavy to pump.

As early as 1857, a whale oil merchant, George Gilbert, had built a refinery and produced oil to market from seepages. Oil was used for lamps but did not have the demand for other things—cars and many of the things that now need oil had not been invented. The price was not high; it was hard to produce and not a big success for several years. It was not until the twentieth century that the demand for oil and the development of better drilling and processing methods made it possible for oil in Ventura County to be a major industry.

(The Ventura Avenue oil field info taken from the Ventura County Genealogical Society journal.)

Conejo Oil

Many of us grew up with the sayings of our grandmothers ringing in our ears, and my Grandma Mary had lots of them. One of her favorites was "Necessity is the mother of invention."

Gene and I have always enjoyed figuring out a way to do something when we had neither the tools nor expertise to accomplish the task. Boy Scout summer camp at Horseshoe Lake near Mammoth often presented us with a problem that needed Yankee ingenuity to solve. The kids were not very interested, but the adults loved it. I don't remember we ever failed on those challenges.

When my journal from the Ventura County Genealogical Society arrived last week, it had an interesting story about a small oil field at the foot of Conejo Grade. That story was certainly the necessity that brought out an unusual invention. I had never found anything written about oil in that part of the county, but sure enough, they found some there. Don Treadwell wrote the article, and my information comes from his report.

Mr. Treadwell did some research and found his facts from John May, a geologist with Tide Water Associated Oil Company about 1940. He reported the shallow field was about forty acres at the foot of the grade. Several natural oil springs in that location encouraged exploration by drilling. Union Oil dug in their well Calleguas 1 in 1892 and brought in the well between sixty and eighty feet. It is unusual to find any oil in volcanic rocks associated with Conejo Grade, but they did. The oil was in irregular concentrations from twenty to three hundred feet. The early field had fifty-three wells and pumped about twenty-five thousand barrels of oil over several years. The crude was low in gasoline, and the wells produced very little gas. It was not a very good field.

Union Oil was still pumping the wells in the 1950s with a donkey engine pulling a series of cables that operated each of the wells. I remember the same kind of setup in small Oklahoma fields near where I grew up. We have also seen them in the Bakersfield area, so they were in common use.

Robert Norris, professor of geology emeritus at the University of California-Santa Barbara, said the wells produced ninety-nine barrels of water for each barrel of oil in the 1960s. Ventura County would not let them dump the water into nearby Calleguas Creek, which eventually went to the ocean near Mugu. The man in charge of the pumping seemed to have been Mr. Burns, so the problem was HIS to solve.

This is how the journal reports the solution: "Burns devised a scheme to get the oil out and leave the water in the hold. He rigged a loop of endless chain over the hub of a low windmill. As the chain came up it rubbed what appeared to be an old leather shoe sole causing the oil to drip off into a bit of a rain gutter which led to a collection barrel. The plan worked and the water stayed in the hole." (There is even a picture of the windmill that produced the power. It was about fifteen feet high with a full-sized vane to turn the whole affair.)

The wells were so shallow you could look down the hole with a flashlight and see oil below. The casings were about ten inches in diameter. The oil was very high quality and suited for lubricating oil. Mr. Burns arranged with Shell Oil to have one of their trucks stop now and then to pick up his few barrels of oil.

Mr. Norris became interested after seeing this group of windmills when he went to visit his grandparents in San Fernando Valley. He always wondered about the funny low windmills being bunched together at the foot of the grade. Sometime in the mid-1960s, the field was closed and the ground reverted to market gardening. Eventually, it was purchased by developers, and now it is filled by a mobile home park, golf park, and new houses.

Now this is a true story about necessity being the mother of invention.

Gene Wren's Rig Experience

Gene told me about his worst RIG experience, and I have forgotten many of the details, but here is what I remember. I am not sure whether this happened when he was seventeen and working before he was drafted for WWII or if it happened after he returned from the army just before we married in 1947, but it made an impression on him.

The company Ray Price Oil Well Supplies (Reese and Price) pulled old wells and brought them up to speed. On one job, Gene was working on the high platform while they were taking out drilling pipes to replace the bit. He kicked the blocks, and somehow, he got tangled in the blocks, with one foot caught between the cables. He could only envision losing his foot, having it crushed or cut off, or dangling head down in the whole mess. While yelling at the driller to STOP, and with an extra spurt of adrenalin, he grabbed the cables and pulled them apart enough to release some of the pressure, and he was able to pull his foot out of his slip-on boot. He survived.

About a year later, he was working with Dave Ingles. Dave was born with one arm that had little beyond the elbow and no hand, but he was able to do just about everything a normal person could do at work except wrench rods. Gene and Dave were unloading drill pipes at a site up Santa Paula Canyon. They used heave timbers between the truck and the pipe rack to let each section of pipe roll to the rack for storage. When one of the timbers slipped, the end of the pipe bounced on the ground and then hit Dave's lower leg, shattering it. Gene was able to get Dave into the pickup and get him to the Ventura hospital for treatment. It was a long drive as Dave held his knee and let the broken leg dangle in the truck. After a couple of days, Gene and I went over to visit Dave in the hospital to check on his progress. The leg did heal, and Dave went back to work.

On the way home that night, we stopped for gasoline, and Harold Balden, local Fillmore citrus rancher, was also filling up his car. He asked Gene if he knew anyone interested in a ranch worker job he was trying to fill for the Balden brothers. Gene said YES. After two narrow escapes, newlywed Gene Wren was ready to get out of the oil fields and into farming, and he never looked back. (I found washing dirty clothes a lot easier than washing oily clothes too.)

Chapter 9

KIDS

Janet Fremlin

4-H & Scouts

Few of us who are working with kids ever realize how much we impact those lives. It takes something very special to let us know how many people some adults have affected. Charlie Mozley's retirement brought loads of letters from adults who now realize what he has done for them. Gene Wren's recent party to celebrate his fifty years with Boy Scout Troop 406 brought letters and former Scouts to party with him. Dick Mosbarger touched many, many kids in FFA. Almost every year, we have teachers and community volunteers in every capacity retire and receive accolades from people they have affected in many different ways. Some of us may just be the neighbor or adult friend next door who had a chance to talk with a student occasionally, but it all makes a difference in that young person's life. Have you thought about the person in your own life that really made a difference in how you felt, what you did, and how you did it?

I don't need to tell you how I feel about Scouting. It teaches moral values and good conduct to kids who may not have received it from parents and do not go to church on a regular basis. Both boys and girls benefit from these lessons incorporated with nature and the outdoors. It is an unbeatable combination for kids.

The FFA and 4-H are year-round programs that are incomparable! Where else do kids learn the responsibility of long-term projects, record keeping, and finance? They learn about judging and parliamentary procedure.

All these organizations teach leadership too. As adults, the kids will soon know all these things are important to be successful in life. In working with civic groups, you can almost tell the officers who have been a part of these youth groups by the way they organize and follow parliamentary procedure, follow through on necessary records, and work with other members. Kids don't realize all the things they are learning from the adults and principles of the organizations.

For Gene and me, Mr. Rudy Folsom was the one who started us on the road to learning at school and within the community. We were in the sixth and seventh grade. Mr. Folsom, a thirty-five-year-old one-quarter Choctaw man, was our teacher in a little country school with two teachers and less than thirty kids. He had been an oil-field worker who turned to teaching as his calling in life. He completed his master's degree in education from University of Oklahoma and arrived full of ideas at Prairie Valley School in Carter County, Oklahoma.

Now this was country living in the Depression of the late '30s. We were all poor but had shoes to wear to school. This man expected us to always do our best, achieve the highest level possible, and never give up on anything. He got things started for a free lunch program so his kids would be fed and able to learn. After that, he started 4-H in our little school, brought in community service, and promoted outside opportunities for each of us. He organized an academic achievement competition with other small schools in our area. We all loved that day of both academic and sports competition. Everyone ended up with ribbons at the end of the day. It was true FUN.

Mr. Folsom opened the door to the rest of the county, state, and world for us with 4-H. We were able to see how other people lived and the things available outside our community if we were interested. There were field days to improve planting crops and berries. Vegetables were canned at school to be entered in the fall fair. Flower seeds were distributed so kids could make their homes more attractive. Our club won the parliamentary procedure contest for small schools. Speeches had to be written and memorized. Record books were graded. Oh, what a challenging time for all of us.

After I married and moved to Fillmore, my annual visit to my Oklahoma family always provided a long afternoon with Mr. Folsom to catch up on our California activities. Gene and I wanted him to know how we continued to use the skills he gave to us as kids. Now we have Scouts returning to see us and tell us how those Scout skills have helped them. I am sure many 4-H and FFA leaders have the same pleasure from their kids.

I guess it is called giving to your fellow man. There is no greater pleasure than helping kids develop into healthy, clear-thinking, and well-rounded adults. Without caring adults, these things never happen.

Radio and Scouts

First Boy Scouts troop in Bardsdale

Our family has been involved in Scouting for over sixty years. When I hear someone say things about Boy Scouts when they really don't know beans about the program, it sort of gets me UPSET! Several weeks ago, I had the car radio tuned to a local station. One of the talk show hosts was spouting off about Boy Scouts! He didn't see any need for the program since we have Boys and Girls Clubs, kids were ashamed to wear uniforms, and the skills were totally useless in today's society, and who needs to know how to build a fire!

Well, let me tell you, if I could have gotten off the road and my cell phone dialed, he would have gotten a piece of my mind. I hope this man is not typical of middle-aged adults, but I am afraid he may be. I would like to answer some of his criticisms.

He said the Scouts have just come out with a new directive that open fires could not be used. He may be right, but this information has not been sent to our house. I suspect the National Council is urging fewer wood fires to help with both wood conservation and pollution, and that makes sense. However, people do need to know how to build fires and keep them contained and controlled for proper use.

He said kids were ashamed to wear Scout uniforms because he never saw them in uniform. Obviously, he does not attend Scout functions or activities where it is appropriate to appear in full uniform. There are times to wear your uniform and times not to wear it. The local troops conform to Scouting rules.

He said people did not need to know about tying knots. He had an acquaintance tie an elaborate knot to hold items in his pickup and then just pulled the end of the rope and it all came undone, insinuating the knot was no good! This dummy did not know his friend was using a truckers' knot, which can be adjusted as tight as needed and still only needs a pull on the free end of the rope to release the whole thing when you are ready to remove it. Such ignorance! The basic Scout knots are used by people every day, from putting ribbons on a gift package to connecting strings on the patio shades or tying down the brush going to the dump in the back of the pickup. This guy probably just uses duct tape for everything.

He said we have other clubs for kids and did not need the Scouting programs. Well, who else beside the YMCA, 4-H, and Scouts teach moral values and duty to God and country? Boys and Girls Clubs are great for entertaining kids and helping with babysitting and homework, but usually they are not *teaching* organizations. Boy Scouts is a teaching organization!

This numbskull overlooked the fact that Scouting starts kids on the road to leadership and organization. Ask anyone in the military, and they will tell you it is the Eagle Scout who is appointed as first platoon leader from a group of new recruits. He already knows the basics of leadership. In Scouting, boys and girls learn to plan, organize groups, follow through, and get the job done.

When push comes to shove in a disaster or emergency, it will be people with a Scouting background who will know how to build fires for cooking and heat, organize rescue efforts, apply first aid, rig up shelters, provide pure water, and contact the authorities to arrange for additional help! I want them on my team every time—and I'd bet the nut with the big mouth would be there to accept their help too.

Xmas Toys

At a time when many of us will have grandkids and great-grandkids visiting during the Christmas holidays, we need things to entertain them before it is time to open gifts. Put away the TV and video games and give the kids something new to them. The old-fashioned things will stand the test of time, so consider some of these:

- Assorted cardboard boxes to make a house, train, or just climb inside.
- A card table with a sheet over it to make a wonderful secret clubhouse.
- A new flyswatter for a little one to wave and hit at any innocent bug or fly. (This was a favorite with our adopted great-granddaughter for her second birthday last month.)
- Wooden spools to stack, thread on a shoestring, or make into a train pull toy.
- A large button on a string—you wind it up and then pull the ends to make it buzz.
- Raggedy Ann and Andy dolls with a story about them are probably stored in your closet.
- A button box with items to be sorted by size or color and then counted.
- A handful of change to count or play store and make change.
- An old catalog and scissors to cut out your own paper-doll family.
- Small wood scraps for blocks or to make a boat or car.

- Pine cones that can be made into a fort for a set of toy soldiers.
- Wiffle balls to throw or hit on the patio.
- A dozen marbles, jacks, or pickup sticks for inside play if weather is bad.
- A set of dominoes can be used for games or just lined up to push and watch them tumble.
- Jigsaw puzzles appropriate for the age-group.
- A kite for a run in the park when energy builds up at home. (Available at the kite shop at the Harbor in Ventura. They do not have any sticks and easily fly with a slight wind.)
- A swing in your backyard will do wonders or a long knotted rope from a high limb the older boys can climb.
- A saucer filled with dish soap and a spool to blow bubbles.
- They might enjoy learning how to sew a button to a piece of cloth and then make a design on cloth with buttons. (This was a great hit with one of my grandsons.)
- If you have any leftover toys from their parents, pull them out for playtime.

If you really get desperate, try making sugar cookies in special shapes or instant pudding for dessert. If cookies are baked ahead of time, you can have a decorating party. (Call me if you want an easy recipe for making the sugar cookies. It came from my grandmother and dates back to 1895.)

Many of these things will be new to the current generation. You can weave some of your own experiences into them for a good family story. Many kids enjoy knowing some of the things we did growing up. It is up to the elders to pass along stories of family events and memories if we want kids to feel the pull of our lives and their ancestors. We must be the storytellers in our family. Oral history is important.

Check your house, and many of these play things will be waiting for you to pull out. Be prepared for something old and something new when the grandkids come, and these ideas are both—the name of the game is HAVING FUN! It is all part of continuing each family's history.

Chapter 10

KEEPING HOUSE

1905: The Good Old Days

Last month, the Rancho Camulos Californio Fiesta celebrated the First Families of Santa Clara Valley. We wanted to honor all the old families whose roots go back at least one hundred years in the east end of the valley. We had fifty-six families and hope to add more as we find them, so if your family qualifies to be a First Family, please give me a call so we can add you to our list. All this genealogy information will be kept on file at Camulos and available to anyone who wants to read it.

However, that is not the point of my column this week. Recently, I found a list of how things were in 1905, and I want to pass some of those things along to you. From these things, you can see how far we've progressed in over one hundred years.

Here are some of the US statistics for 1905:

- The average life expectancy was forty-seven years.
- Only 14 percent of the homes had a bathtub.
- Only 8 percent had a telephone.
- A three-minute call from Denver to New York City costs eleven dollars.
- There were only eight thousand cars in the US with 144 miles of paved roads.

- Maximum speed limit in town was 10 mph.
- California had 1.4 million people.
- The average wage in the US was twenty-two cents per hour.
- The average worker made between $200 and $400 a year.
- More than 95 percent of births took place at home.
- Ninety percent of doctors had no college education but only attended medical school.
- Sugar costs four cents a pound; eggs were fourteen cents a dozen, and coffee, fifteen cents a pound.
- Most women washed their hair once a month and used egg yolks for shampoo.
- Five leading causes of death were pneumonia, tuberculosis, diarrhea, heart disease, and stroke. (Cancer was not listed as it was a "shameful" disease.)
- The American flag had forty-five stars as Arizona, Oklahoma, New Mexico, Hawaii, and Alaska had not been admitted to the Union.
- The population of Las Vegas, Nevada, was thirty.
- Iced tea had not been invented.
- There was no Mother's Day or Father's Day.
- Two out of ten adults could not read or write.
- Only 6 percent of Americans had graduated from high school.
- Eighteen percent of households in the US had at least one full-time servant or domestic help.
- There were about 230 reported murders in the entire US.

So, guys, these were the "good old days!" Would any of us choose to go back to those times? I doubt it! It would be wonderful to look into the future and peek at what the next one hundred years will bring to us—I can't even imagine the changes the next century will bring. The future generations will laugh at our simple lives, the cost of things, and what we are doing in the same way we now laugh at the past! Maybe we should just be happy with what we have and enjoy each day that is allotted to us. The things we are doing today are making the history of tomorrow.

Furniture

Do you ever think about how furniture has changed in the last two hundred years? In 1802, the families back East had beautiful things—most of them made by hand by real craftsmen. As families moved to the western limits of the country, they hauled along the barest necessities and learned to make do when they built a cabin for shelter.

As the western frontier expanded and the great migration began, women learned to pack a wagon and often tried to include one treasured piece of furniture along with the trunks and linens and kitchen items. They hung on to these things until they reached Salt Lake and started across the great desert. As the oxen or mules pulling the wagon got weaker from lack of food and water, the wagons had to be lightened. Items were thrown out along the way. Soon the trails were littered with everything you can imagine, and any heavy furniture item was the first to be left beside the trail. It was necessity!

My pioneer family came to Indian Territory with all the possession and household goods for three families in two small wagons—about four by twelve feet each. Now that isn't very much room, so you know they did not have very much. When they settled and found jobs, they started to accumulate furniture. Until then, a trunk held any nice dress clothes they owned, a few other things were stacked on a shelf above the bed, and things for the kids were stored in a wooden crate in the corner. They received two cane-bottom chairs from my great-grandfather for their wedding gift to go with a homemade table. Kids could sit on logs cut high enough they were able to reach the table. Short pieces of logs were put under the legs of a homemade bed so it would be tall enough to slide another bed underneath as children arrived and they could not all sleep in one bed.

By the time my mother married in the mid-1920s, people were buying real furniture—she had a dinette table and four chairs and a bedroom suite with bed, vanity, and chest of drawers. The top of this chest had doors on it that opened, and all the linens were kept there. The three lower drawers gave each of us a place for all our clothes. It worked very nicely.

The '40s brought new-styled furniture and lighter-colored wood if you wanted a modern house. We had everything needed for a one-bedroom home and acquired more chests and beds as our family increased. Then we needed storage for books, toys, and tools. As we bought more stuff, we needed a place to put it.

Now in the new millennium, many of us are looking back over the things acquired by grandparents and parents and wishing it had been saved and passed on. A few families do have old things, but many lost them or threw them out as they relocated.

Babies

While adults adjust to summer heat, imagine what it was like in pioneer days with babies and toddlers. In reading women's diaries and stories from my family, I know it was hard and often fatal on small children.

People did not know water carried disease. They did not know about typhoid fever coming from contaminated water. Babies often died from summer complaint. I think this was mostly diarrhea added to extreme heat, fever, and bad water. It was so common that some women refused to name a child until they were a year old because they felt there would be less attachment to a baby without a name if they died that first year.

Mosquitoes, flies, and bugs carried germs for fevers and disease beyond our imaginations. Pioneer cabins were small, had little ventilation, and had no screens. My own grandmother was born in a swampy area near Houston in October 1874. Out of the eight children born in her family, only five lived to adulthood. Mosquitoes bred everywhere. All kinds of fevers prevailed with yellow fever causing the most deaths near the Gulf. Some years it was so bad the area was quarantined. My grandmother was born in the fall, so she had a better chance of survival than a baby born in the spring.

My grandmother and her surviving siblings all lived into their late eighties and nineties. I have an aunt who will be one hundred in

November, so those strong genes continue to give many of us long life spans. But remember, in those days, the weak died young and only the strong survived to have families. It is a cruel fact, but true.

Diaper rash and heat rash must have been terrible. With the air swarming with flies and mosquitoes, babies were covered with long stockings and long sleeves to protect them from bites—they were hot, but mothers hated to see flies crawling on their little ones. Older children had the job of waving flies away from the baby, asleep or awake. Cloth diapers not immediately changed when damp produced diaper rash most of us would never believe. Parched flour was the only thing to help dry it up. Babies cried and cried, and it is no wonder. Often, water for laundry and bathing children had to be hauled long distances on foot. Life was difficult.

My great-grandmother was lucky to have a husband, although he was not in good health. Her two sisters' husbands both died from fevers and left eight children in the two families. They combined with my great-grandparents and all struggled to survive together. When women had no way of making a living and no husband, it was imperative they have some masculine protection. My great-grandfather became the supporter and protector for his own family with five children as well as two sisters-in-law and their additional eight children. They slowly moved farther from the Gulf each year when they found a place to sharecrop another fifty or seventy-five miles inland. Eventually, they were farming in the western part of Texas and hoping the drier climate would improve his health.

When they started for Indian Territory in 1893, he died the first night on the trail. The three widows and thirteen children continued alone. How did my great-grandmother manage diapers for her eighteen-month-old baby? It was a cold and rainy winter journey, and that was worse than the summer heat they had in Texas. My grandmother was the oldest of the kids, and at eighteen, she drove one of the two wagons with other added responsibilities during that thirty-day trip. She told me the stories before she died, and I wrote down many of them for the family. They all made it to Indian Territory! They survived. They were tough people.

One TV pioneer history about the overland trail said it was a trail of diaper rash. I can believe that! It is the daily things about pioneer life that intrigue me—summer heat, being pregnant, limited food, almost no medicine, and taking care of small babies were all part of that era. In 2018, we expect to be clean and comfortable at least 95 percent of the time. It hasn't always been like that, so count your blessings!

Laundry

Sometimes we really get caught up into historical research and forget about the plain, ordinary things that made up life in the good old days. This week, I want to talk about the hardest household chore: Monday washday! Every member of the family did not have fourteen changes of clothing to be done as in 2005. However, with eight or ten people in the household, even one change per person each week added up to a huge pile of laundry.

Native people in many societies still use a river for washing clothes. Fortunately, I have missed that experience, but I grew up with the next step in advancement: the washpot. To start the process, wood had to be cut and split to build the fire around the large cast iron washpot. If it had been used for other things like collecting rain or rendering lard, it had to be scrubbed clean and any rust removed.

Water had to be hauled by bucket or barrel from the spring or well. If that was nearby, wonderful! My grandmother hauled water from a spring that was a quarter of a mile from the house for twenty-two years. My grandfather tried to get at least two barrels of water hauled for her before washday, but sometimes, he couldn't because of other work, and she did it herself. They had a wonderful big spring on Hickory Creek and a sled to haul the barrels by mule power, but it was still hard work. The water had to be lifted from the spring by bucket and poured into the fifty-five-gallon barrels until they were full. That was a lot of muscle work to get the water and bring it back to the washpot. When you got the wood and water ready, you could start on the laundry.

In our part of the country, washing was done outside during winter and summer. A fire was built around the big pot of water. When it was HOT, the least soiled things were put in to boil. (Baby clothes were usually washed in a boiler on the kitchen stove every couple of days. No one had enough clothing and diapers to keep a baby fresh and clean for a week.) In our family, sheets were done first, then towels, underwear, colored clothes, and socks with work clothes—in that order. (No wonder print dresses faded so quickly.)

Each sorted group was boiled and punched around with a long stick to loosen the dirt. The same stick lifted them out of the hot water, and you let them drip back into pot. Then they were put into a large tub of soapy water where you rubbed them on a rub board to remove any resisting spots or stains. When they were clean, you wrung them out by hand and put them into a tub of fresh rinse water to remove the soap. Then you wrung them out by hand again and rinsed them a second time with bluing in the rinse water to make the white things sparkle. Then you wrung them again.

Many things needed to be starched. You had already made the starch from the powder and boiling water. The starch made fabric look nicer after ironing, but it also kept the ring around the collar easier to rub out. Things were put into the starch and wrung out again.

Then it was time to hang them on the clothesline, if you were lucky enough to have a wire clothesline. Many farm ladies hung clothes from bushes or a rope from a tree to the corner of the house. My grandfather always provided a good clothesline for Grandma. If the line sagged, a forked limb would prop it up in the middle until it could be tightened. In Oklahoma, we always had wind to pop the sheets on the line. You were in big trouble if the clothespins did not hold and those sheets dragged in the dirt! That really made more work, and you avoided it at all costs, so our sheets were usually thrown over the line instead of being hung by the corners. Hopefully, the heavy overalls were dry by night when you removed things and took them inside to fold. In the winter or rainy days, damp clothes were taken inside and dried around the house. That was a real chore if they were frozen. Most things needed to be ironed, so they went into one pile, and you carefully folded and put away everything else.

Lunch had to be cooked and served and dishes cleaned up on laundry day the same as any other day. Supper still had to be provided for a hungry family, cows milked, and produce harvested from the garden to go on the table. Every girl in the family learned how to wash and helped with the weekly chore. She also learned to be careful with her school dresses and take care of them so they did not need to be washed after only one wear. As soon as they got home from school, all the kids changed into their work clothes and saved that school dress or shirt to wear another day.

I am sure that living in Fillmore was different from living on the farm, but laundry was laundry regardless, and it required time and lots of hard work. Women were JUDGED by how their wash looked and took pride in having clothes without stains and white things that sparkled. (My, haven't our ideas changed in sixty years?)

More next week about ironing clothes!

Ironing

Last week, I talked about the hard work of washing family laundry. I guess that ironing the next day was almost as bad. Once again, that was hard work. (I guess everything was hard work back in the good old days.) So I guess most of us are happy to live in the days of electrical appliances.

Until the last couple of decades, all fabric needed to be iron. There was no wash-and-wear material. There was no polyester material. There were very few knit items. Everything was pure woven cotton that wrinkled like crazy, especially after it had been put through a hand wringer or twisted in opposite directions by hand to remove water. The wind did not remove wrinkles either. (Our family did not iron sheets and dishtowels, but everything else had to be ironed.)

The things that had to be ironed were sprinkled with water, rolled tightly and packed into a pillowcase, box, or basket to wait for the iron the next day. The old cast iron sad irons weighed about three pounds. You needed at least three to do the job. Before breakfast was finished, the sad irons were put on the woodstove to start heating. Once again, you needed extra wood to keep the fire going all day, and hopefully, the men had cut it.

We had an ironing board, but some people improvised by ironing on their table. We visited a lady in the 1940s that ironed starched white dress shirts on her tabletop and did a beautiful job, so it could be done. Every kitchen had a set of heavy potholders that were used to hold the very hot handle of the iron. You picked up one and started, and in about five minutes, it had cooled so much it was not doing you any good. So it was returned to the stove to start heating again, and you took another iron to work with. You rotated the three irons all day. And I guarantee everything was beautiful and crisp when you finished all of it. Well, YOU weren't very crisp, but the clothes looked nice. You were just dead tired, but supper still had to be cooked, the cows milked, and the kitchen cleaned for the last time before you went to bed.

I loved it when we moved to town and could use our electric iron again—what a treat! All the clothes still had to be ironed, but it was much easier.

By the time I married, pants stretchers were in vogue. These aluminum frames were inserted into each leg of the wet jeans. They were adjustable so you could fit them into the pants crease, pull them tight, and stretch the denim. Wonder of wonders! Those pants dried with nary a wrinkle in the legs. When you took the stretchers out, only the top of the pants had to be pressed if you weren't too particular. My husband quickly learned to like his work pants with almost no ironing. Most of us also had curtain stretchers. It's another large rectangle of aluminum that was adjustable, and a curtain could be attached around the edge on pins and held there until dry—again, no ironing!

When automatic washers came on the scene, women learned that spinning did not put nearly as many wrinkles in clothes. Then when we got driers and the new wash-and-wear and polyblend fabrics or knits, our ironing was cut to almost nothing. Oh, how times have changed.

An aunt had given me a huge old-fashioned damask tablecloth. I remembered my mother had spent hours ironing it when I was a child. It was a family treasure but seldom used because it was an all-day job to iron it. When our oldest daughter married, I felt family tradition required it be used on the reception table. I used that cloth and dreaded the thought of the ironing it would require. It was washed and put into the drier, and I'll be darned, it barely needed to be steam-pressed. I discovered that most of the ironing was caused by the method of wringing out the clothes and not the material. I learn something new every day.

A couple of year ago, I was shopping, and a young lady about eighteen was looking at silk blouses. In making conversation, I told her I was sure she could wash it, but she would need to iron it before it got too dry to make it look nice. She looked at me with a straight face and said, "What is ironing?" We've come a long way, baby.

Rah, rah, for every electric appliance in the house!

Independent Women

Recently, a cousin sent me a newspaper article about a woman who left her abusive husband in 1905. After he went back to the saloon for the night, she took the wagon and team and her five kids and left. The children were three to sixteen years old. The family started near the Oregon border and headed to her brother's in Temecula. She left in a hurry and took very little. She had fifteen cents in her pocket and a small gold nugget—and she made it!

The journey was not easy. Once, they helped themselves to hay for the horses. Once, a ham bone was taken from a storage place at a house with no one home. Without an abandoned field of sweet potatoes near Sacramento, they probably would have starved along the way. It took them six weeks to travel those seven hundred miles during December and January. It rained and was cold. The Grapevine was closed by snow, so they detoured to Tehachapi.

One horse lost a shoe. One got loose and got into their stock feed. They had no wagon sheet. The rain got everything wet. Their coats were inadequate. It was hard! Yes, they had some sympathetic help along the way, but it was still a long ways for a mother and children to travel alone. (Later, the father came by train to take them home, but she refused to go and later got a divorce.)

Some things never change, and abusive relationships still head the list. I think the only thing worse than spousal abuse is sexual abuse of children. We are all aware of that as it is frequently talked about in the newspapers and magazines. That abuse is now out in the open, and many agencies work to get rid of it. Long ago, it was seldom acknowledged.

After my maternal great-grandfather died on the way to Indian Territory with his family in 1893, his wife soon remarried. She had her five children in a new country, but trying to feed them was difficult. Her health was poor, but she and her oldest son worked clearing land to provide food. My grandmother was the oldest of the five kids, and she worked six miles from home at a hotel during the week. Saturday night after work, she took her two dollars weekly pay to the store and bought staples to take home so the younger kids had food the next week. She walked those six miles alone, without a light, in the middle of winter to deliver that food. It was a terrible struggle.

When my great-grandmother remarried, she got a ringer. He brought two teenage daughters with him to add to the family and was not a good provider. He spent most of his time trading, so he was often gone from home. He was also a sexual abuser of girls—both his own daughters and the two little sisters of my grandmother.

My mother and her sisters occasionally mentioned this fact quietly as I was growing up, but it was not an openly discussed family item—it was more like the family secret! A couple of years before my mother died, she told me most of what she knew about the situation. I was making one of my annual visits to Oklahoma and we were enjoying exchanging stories and discussing family. Soon she told me that the four girls in her family were very careful to stay out of arms reach when they visited their step-grandfather. He enjoyed reaching under their skirts when possible, so they knew not to get close to him. Mother had no love for the old rascal.

It seemed to be common family knowledge that he had molested his own daughters and, later, his two young stepdaughters. These girls all married when they were about sixteen and left home. (I wonder why!) My generation has often wondered why our great-grandmother put up with it. Well, times were different. Although she was very independent for her time and had a good first marriage, she was not able to disengage from her second husband. Oh, how I would like to talk with her for a fuller discourse on how she thought and why she accepted his abuse of her children. Some things we will never know.

It is sad that these things still occur. I know stories about other men who are not very clean and virtuous. You can't tell from the outside how some people act in private. After being married to a kind, considerate, upright man for fifty-eight years, it is hard for me to believe men still act this way.

Women still allow men to abuse them and their children. All we can do is try to help them when they are ready to get out of the situation—and most will never leave their husbands. Some things I just don't understand!

Linen Closet

I love reading and doing research into history for both Indian Territory (Oklahoma before it was a state) and early California before it became a state. This week, I realized that I have my family history in my linen closet. I'd bet many of you do too.

Recently, the lady who helps me weekly with cleaning dug into the bottom of my stack of pillowcases and came up with a pair of white ones with lace on them. Oh my, I haven't used those in years! As I was ironing them today, my mind brought up my own family history again.

These pillowcases were made from coarse flour sacks. Nothing was ever thrown away in my family, and the Great Depression added to that. During the time we lived with our grandparents on the farm, our flour was often bought in hundred-pound sacks. These sacks were our source of fabric for many things.

The printed design was washed out with a good boiling in a big pot outside when the weekly laundry was done. The sacks were soon pure white and used for everything. Of course, the first item was dishtowels. After the dishes were washed and scalded with a teakettle of boiling water, they needed to be quickly dried and put away. Flour sacks were just the thing for wiping dishes.

My petticoats and panties for elementary school were made from flour sacks. I will have to admit, I was happy when I finished the eighth grade and received two pair of rayon panties as gifts, so gradually, the old flour-sack panties could be retired. (Those new panties cost twenty-five cents for each pair.) Oh, that fabric was coarse on a bottom! Even handmade lace around the legs did not relieve the scratching.

Our sheets were four flour sacks stitched together on a treadle sewing machine. There was no way you could sleep and stay off a seam. Years later, I reveled in a bed with real sheets and no seams! But we had clean sheets every week even during the worst of times!

Everyday aprons were made from flour sacks—they were sturdy and kept dresses clean so they could be worn for a whole week before changing on Sunday. Those aprons had pockets big enough to carry garden seeds, eggs, baby chicks, fresh carrots, or any small tool that might be needed in the cow barn or garden. Every woman wore an apron and changed it daily to look clean. (If you saw company coming, you had time to grab your nice apron and remove the everyday one.)

When it was time to put up a quilt and work on quilting a pretty top, the flour sacks were often the backing with lightweight cotton as the lining. Those quilts were what we used to keep warm in the winter, and when it was very cold, you needed several of them on a bed.

Many windows were covered with flour sack curtains, and the fancy embroidery across the bottom showed off the talents of the woman of the house.

As I ironed that pillowcase today, I remembered family history and the aunt who did the crochet lace around the bottom. I do not remember for sure, but I think she gave me the pillowcases as a wedding gift when I married in 1947.

When I put those freshly ironed pillowcases back in the linen closet next to the napkins, there was another memory. At the top of stack of napkins, I saw six napkins made of terry cloth. Three were green with one each in yellow, red, and blue. Those were a Christmas gift from my mother soon after we married. Mom was working at a nice department store for eleven-dollars-a-week salary and supporting herself, my grandmother, and my brother. Funds were TIGHT for gifts at Christmas. When the store had a sale on assorted clearance napkins, Mother was able to buy an unmatched set of six. Oh, how many times have we used those through the years! They do not show soil or grease spots; they did not need to be ironed, and I loved them. I have many full sets of matched napkins for every occasion now, but for everyday use, I still reach for those old terry cloth napkins. They were our favorite for taco suppers. (And some are getting very thin after sixty years.)

On the top shelf were some small tablecloths and brightly embroidered things I bought in Mexico when we went to Cabo fishing many years ago. Some have gone to Rancho Camulos to use for displays in the gift shop and table items, but a few are still in the linen closet as a reminder of our fun times together in Mexico.

The stack of table runners and napkin rings are left over from the many Soroptimist fashion shows and decorated tables that I did through the years. A layer of small tablecloths is a reminder of our family Fourth of July parties in the past years. When the fireworks stands closed down and our volunteer work was done, it was time for everyone to gather on our patio and share food and drink with the annual stories of how each group did to generate money for the many charities they represented. The old beach towels brought memories of the kids learning to swim at Kentuk on the Sespe when the original Fillmore High School plunge was closed for several years before bonds built a new one.

I even found some pillow covers that were left over from the girls' college days. I marked their things so they would not be mixed up with roommates in the dorm. And I know I found one pillow with my name on it from my own college days! Throwing away things is like throwing out my family memories.

Oh my! All this because I had to iron a pair of pillowcases! (Flour sacks are not wrinkle-free fabric.) I hope you enjoy your family history as much as I enjoy mine.

Air-Conditioning

As Americans, we've been spoiled beyond belief for physical comforts. For many of us, it is unusual to ever break a sweat. We have air-conditioning in our cars, home, businesses, and schools. If you work outside in the sun and heat, you will be back to the air-conditioning as soon as your workday is over. Many people think they could not live without it!

Well, HELLO! How many of you remember what life was like before AC? (You are probably well over seventy if you do or live in one of the Los Serenos homes built in 1955 without central AC and heating.)

This is how it used to be: you expected heat in the summer and got used to it as it gradually built up from May to September. Around the Santa Clara Valley, it stayed hot until October, with the dry East wind adding to the discomfort.

When we lived on the farm in Oklahoma, it was the kids' job to take cool well water to the field when the adults were working away from the house. The grownups took water with them in the morning, but by 10:00 a.m., it would be getting hot. My grandparents always appreciated a canteen of cool water we had just pumped from the well. Oh, how good it was! In the middle of the afternoon, we repeated the procedure for them. If it was a day of preserving garden vegetables or fruit, we often prepared stuff in the shade of a big mulberry tree near the well. If Grandpa had brought in watermelon for our ten o'clock break, they were stored in wet gunnysacks to hold in the morning coolness. They were just right when we cut them. And, oh, how good they were. We hoped for a breeze to help with the shade in keeping us comfortable.

When it was time to fill the canning jars and start the pressure cookers to preserve the veggies, the old wood cookstove was going full blast, and nothing could cool down that little kitchen before midnight.

It was the original hot box but necessary, so everyone had plenty to eat in the winter. The women sweat through every stitch on their bodies while the men were doing the same thing out in the sun, baling hay or plowing corn. It was nothing new for the adults—they did it every summer. The kids did not fuss when we had to carry the newly canned jars of food to the old dirt cellar. We enjoyed that cool blast of air when the door was opened for us to go down the steps to the dark, damp hole. The earthy smell was wonderful.

After the dishes from the evening meal were washed and put away, it was time for a cooling bath. You'd be surprised how good one bucket of cool well water feels about dusk. And you can get very clean with a small amount of water when necessary. My grandparents had recently moved to this small 110 acre farm and soon installed a windmill and ran a cold-water pipe to the kitchen and another to the back corner of the smokehouse where they made an outdoor shower. They were about seventy then. Cold running water was a luxury beyond expectations for both of them. Grandpa put a rustic privacy screen around the outside shower, and we were ready for business. Everyone used it. For summer cooling before bed, nothing is better than a shower to get rid of the sweat and reduce body temperature. The adults appreciated that shower even more than the kids.

Small single-wall houses without insulation just got hotter and hotter as summer progressed. We had a big, square heavy-duty worktable in the backyard. In the winter, it was used to block out meat for smoking when Grandpa butchered hogs, but in the summer, it was the perfect place for a bed. He and Grandma moved that table under a big pecan tree in the backyard to catch any evening breeze. Then they put their springs and mattress on top for most of the summer. It was high, so the first year, Grandpa built a set of steps so they could get into bed. It was a wonderful place to sleep and was as cool as they could find. A top sheet caught any falling leaves or bugs, and they never rolled off, so it was a perfect sleeping arrangement.

During the summer, we usually had a family of cousins who came for three months—beside my grandparents, there were two mothers with nine kids and another aunt, so it was a large extended family to accommodate. As soon as the kids were not afraid of the dark, they could sleep outside too. We each had a folding canvas cot, one sheet, and a pillow. We set our cot anywhere in the front yard we wanted under the black walnut trees. Oh, how wonderful it was to sleep outside and catch that night breeze. The house was on a small hill with meadows around it, and we could see the lights from town in the distance, an occasional car on a road five miles away, and shooting stars. Crickets and cicada chirped, and the whip-poor-wills called every evening. When the moon was full, it was so bright it almost kept us awake. If it bothered us, we just slept with our heads at the other end of the cot for a few nights. There was nothing better than sleeping outside in the summer.

On the farm, we had no electricity, but the iceman made a delivery each week so the big old icebox kept milk and butter cool. Occasionally, we made ice cream if we had enough cash for the extra ice. We didn't buy much meat but had all the fresh garden items and seasonal fruit you wanted with the last of the sugar-cured pork—every kid expected to eat at least four ears of fresh corn at noon.

One summer, my aunt bought a Servel propane refrigerator, and what a treat that was for everyone. The kids despaired of it every making any ice. No wonder! We kept checking to see if it was frozen, so it never had a chance to even cool the inside of the refrigerator! Oh well, we learned, and by morning, there was a tray of ice frozen. That Servel kept the homemade root beer and bottled grape juice just right for us. We were rationed to one cool bottle a day, so it lasted most of the summer.

In Oklahoma, it was hot and humid in the summer. We learned to use nature's cooling with shade, well water, and the south breeze and just endure the rest of it. We had it every year, so it was expected. Everyone knew it would be over soon and we would start preparing for the winter cold—it wasn't so bad.

People around here used the same shade, cool water, and breeze to make life bearable. Fortunately, we can usually expect the nights to cool off, and with the ocean breeze to waft through the windows, houses cooled at night. And as I said last week, the swimming holes at Sespe Creek gave us an extra option. People endured and few died from heat. Yep! We are a spoiled bunch.

Summer Heat

This will be my last historical tidbit for the *Herald*. I am cutting my ties with the paper and moving on. My first project will be to get my old columns organized and put it into a couple of little books that will be for sale. If I get inspired, I may put together some new stuff in a separate little book—I still have lots of research stories to write. And the history of the Santa Clara Valley is still on the back burner, so perhaps I will have time to move along on that. I need to write the First Families stuff so others can know about them—there is plenty for me to do to entertain myself. And the RANCHO CAMULOS MUSEUM will stay high on my work list. Thanks to each of you for the past support—it has been fun, and I appreciate your comments. Please keep in touch and let me know if you come up with a great story that needs to be saved for our grandkids.

As we sweat and swear at the heat, we should remember how our grandparents grew up and accepted weather as it occurred and changed with the seasons. They had only natural air to cool them, and often water was scarce in the summer. They had no screens for the houses and had to contend with flies, bugs, and mosquitoes. We can't imagine trying to keep a baby well and comfortable under such conditions.

Since we still live without air-conditioning, our family quickly learned to adjust also. Through the years, we have added tons of insulation to our house in the walls and attic. Last year, we installed double-pane windows. We have a whole house fan to pull out the hot air at night and bring in the evening cool through open windows. Drapes are insulated. Early each morning, the windows are closed to save the cool air inside and then opened at night to start the cooling process all over again. I think I worked up a sweat just trying to stay cool. Oh well, that is life. I can always stop and sit in front of one of the fans and think about it.

In the long ago, kids played outside under the shade of a tree when it got hot; they often ran through the sprinkler in the front yard by midafternoon; the older kids headed up the Sespe to swim at Swallows

Nest. If you had your own well, fresh cool water from the pump was wonderful after you worked the pump handle up and down for five minutes. When the iceman made his weekly delivery, the kids might be able to talk him out of a little piece of ice to chew on. Everyone knew the coolest place in the house was a dark corner on the linoleum rug with the breeze wafting through. The floor was almost as good as being under a tree.

Sleeping at night was another thing! Kids in our family all put a folding cot under the black walnut trees in the front yard and staked out their space. It was wonderful to look up at night at the velvet black sky in the country, away from lights, and count stars or view the Milky Way. On lucky nights we could see shooting stars. On a night with a full moon we often had to turn our cots so the moonlight did not keep us awake. It was a great way to sleep in the summer. (And I still enjoy sleeping outside.) Most beds had two mattresses on them. The top one could easily be moved to the front porch for the grownups. Many old houses had large screened porches, and I'd bet they were filled with beds in the summer. Just check out the old houses in Bardsdale the next time you drive through that area and see the big porches that could accommodate sleeping for large families. People learned to accept the heat and still rest at night.

My grandfather never took off his winter long johns until haying season near the Fourth of July. I am sorry I never found out the reasoning, but that is the way it was. He drank gallons of scalding coffee year-round.

If you really want to know what it was like to live with HEAT, read some of the stories of army wives living in Yuma, Arizona, about 1880. I don't know how they managed babies in such extreme conditions—it must have been terrible. At one post, the women all went to the muddy river each morning and got wet in their clothes to cool off. Any little thing helped with the heat that cooled down to about 103 at night. When one lady moved her cot outside for sleeping, she found a rattlesnake by her shoes the next morning—guess we have it pretty good after all—just be prepared for the Edison bill next month.

Beds

How often do we think about the furniture we use daily? Not very! This week, BEDS seem to be in my thoughts most of the time. I guess that camping trip with the Boy Scouts a couple of weeks ago and my new improved camping bed got me started on that track. Gene rigged me up a set of legs for my foam sleeping pad so I could get up in the morning—the ground is a little low for me now to get to my feet, and I appreciated the extra elevation each morning.

Beds have been made out of everything under the sun! If you lived in the mountains, pine trees, small branches, or bunches of pine needles were used under a blanket to make a soft bed. If you were the hired hand, you probably slept in the barn or the haymow, but that fresh, sweet-smelling hay made a good bed. The early pioneers used big sacks stuffed with hay, straw, or corn shucks as mattresses. The contents could be freshened a couple of times a years as required. On frequent moves, they could be emptied out and were easier to carry along in the wagon. Of course, Grandma always had a feather bed that she toted around with her when she visited anyone to stay awhile. I guess it was a sign of old age when any lady had her own feather bed. She also had a good place to sleep in any house.

My grandparents were living in a tiny log cabin about 1900 with four preschoolers when a brother-in-law arrived on the doorstep with his four preschoolers in tow. Their mother had died, and he could not take care of them alone, so they came to Aunt Mary's to live for a couple of years. Grandma let the little girls sleep on the trundle bed, and the little boys had a pallet under the table at night. There was not enough floor room to make a bed. These kids all had measles one winter too—and we think life is hard! A pallet was a pretty good bed under the circumstances. It was warm near the cookstove too.

From straw ticks, we graduated to coil springs under a firm cotton mattress that soon molded to fit the bodies sleeping in that bed. It was really good sleeping, unless you were the third kid who had to sleep on that hump in the middle when company came. Most families had two mattresses on many beds so one could be put on the floor when visiting family arrived. In summer, it was easy to pull this extra mattress out to the porch for cooler sleeping for the adults. The kids were introduced to a pallet that consisted of a quilt spread on the floor or porch, and they loved it. You can't believe how many kids can sleep on one quilt!

By the time I grew up, townsfolk had innerspring mattress with box springs. That was pretty elegant to me, but I could not tell any difference in sleeping. After we married, we soon acquired an innerspring mattress for a short time. In a few years, when foam mattresses were available, we ordered a double-bed size that was extra long to accommodate Gene's height. Pat Wilson had a furniture store, and he ordered it special for us. (Now try to find sheets that would fit that!) We went through several of these foam mattresses. Once they started fitting our bodies, we were ready for a new one.

After years of back problems for Gene, we recently decided it was time to go bed-shopping again. This time, we hit the jackpot! We accidentally discovered the new Swedish foam that is used by astronauts during space flights. It took all the butter-and-egg money and everything from the sock, but we bought a mattress made from that super foam. This stuff should have been invented soon after the corn-shuck mattress, as it is the perfect thing for sleeping. It molds to your body, and there is never a pressure point. You never awaken from pain in the hip telling you it is time to turn over. As soon as you move, the foam pops up level, and you make yourself a new nest. We love it. (After it was installed, we did have to replace the peanut butter–jar lids I use as castors under the bed legs, but I had plenty on hand to do that.)

As we aged, Gene and I needed better sleeping arrangements when we were camping with the Scouts. We had long ago stopped trying to sleep on the ground; every air mattress developed a leak so went flat during the night and bounced when we turned over, so we needed something else. After a little discussion, I went to the Bell Mattress Factory in Ventura and had them put heavy outside covers on two twin-size foam mattresses, and we were back in business. Our kids were grown, and we only needed to pack for the two of us, so everything was put into the camper shell on the pickup, and the new beds were slipped over the top of everything. What a comfort for two aging adults!

It is all a nice change for us from sleeping on a pallet as kids. Children may still be called upon to take a quilt to the porch in the summertime and enjoy the night air where they can see the stars and where moonlight keeps them awake. It is all part of being a kid.

Well, times change! Our bodies change! Our beds change! It is just good sense to made changes! A good night's rest is essential, and I hope each of you has a good bed. Happy snoozing and snoring.

Bikes

Young people today do not believe you when you say things like "Women couldn't vote," "Women couldn't own property," or "Women couldn't marry without the permission of a father, husband, or brother."

My research found court documents from the early 1800s that were filed by a lady who bought a horse and buggy, milked her own cows, and delivered the milk. She had it officially recorded that her father had given her the cows when she married, the items all belonged to her, she did the work, and she kept the money! It would be interesting to know more about this hussy who was so independent that she was not turning over the income to her husband. Can we guess what kind of man she married? Very few women were willing to go against the tide and declare their independence in this way, but a few brave souls gave it a try.

The women in my own family have been fiercely independent as far back as I can find—about 1850. When my great-grandmother and her sister-in-law were left at the cabin for a few days while their husbands went hunting, the young mothers immediately got into a fuss. My great-grandmother just picked up her baby, wagon sheet, and iron pot and moved out. She set up camp on a nearby creek and managed very well alone until her husband brought home fresh venison a few days later. The men had been working on a second cabin for her little family, and I suspect that tiny house was finished without further ado!

These women were the exception to the rule, but their actions were the tip of the iceberg for women securing the rights we all now enjoy.

About 1890, the bicycle was invented. Like many new ideas, it got off to a slow start, but within a few years, it had opened the door for women's lib. The bike provided easy transportation. Anyone could jump on their bike and be off quicker than you could catch the horse, harness him, and bring out the buggy. All over Ventura County, bike clubs were formed to ride for pleasure. Large groups had regular meetings and rode ten to twenty miles at a time. Races were often organized too. And, glory be, women were included!

The long dresses in fashion at the turn of the century were not good for riding bikes. The skirts caught in the wheels and around the riders' feet, so something had to be done quickly. Hey, the ladies started wearing bloomers and split skirts. Old pattern books showed biking suits of wool serge, bloomer skirts with fashionable fitted jackets, and hats without flowers or feathers. Ladies magazines had interesting articles about proper clothing, manners while riding a bicycle, and the courtesies of the road. They were cautioned to be careful and not scare the horses pulling buggies and wagons along the way.

The girls were happy to slip out of their corsets and be more comfortable when they rode. Without the constriction of tightly laced corsets from bust to lower hips, they were able to pump vigorously and ride and keep up with the men. And that fresh air felt good in their lungs and gave their cheeks a ruddy glow. What freedom!

Once the girls discovered the fun of bike riding, there was no holding them back! The next thing you knew, they were group hiking in the mountains with the boys too. Sometimes they had to wear their skirts until they were out of sight of the lodge, but then they removed the skirts and left them hanging on a bush and continued the day in their new black wool bloomers. The skirts were retrieved again on the way home. A few diaries tell of girls crossing the plains in a group of covered wagons and riding astride in bloomers, but their horses didn't seem to mind, and the other women probably envied them. Necessity may be the mother of invention, but once the females discovered the comfort of living without corsets and wearing clothing more suitable to the occasion, there was no stopping them.

Every town had a bike shop for sales and repairs. Tom Walsh opened his shop on Central Avenue to keep the Fillmore locals happy. A picture at the museum shows young Tom in front of the shop near a peppertree. I have yet to find a picture of any Fillmore girls on a bike, but I'd bet we have some. (Call me if you have one—I need it for my collection.)

It is hard to imagine that the invention of the bicycle helped open the door for women to start the trek toward equality in this country, but it happened. It is a part of history, and I am proud to be a part of it.

The bike craze only lasted about fifteen years. About the time it was going good, Henry Ford came out with his automobile, and that was even more fun than riding a bike. It is another piece of the puzzle making women independent today.

Old-Time Remedies

After a few years of testing new pills and remedies they are declared SAFE by the government and put on the market. After twenty years of using them, people are starting to get severe side effects—well, that is our modern world. We are better off not messing with Mother Nature, but we all do when there is illness.

The interesting thing to me is the fact that many of the old-time home cures are SAFE! Well, at least no one has ever said they got sicker from using them. Most of them were things that our grandmothers had in their kitchen and pulled out when needed.

We still all laugh about the Jewish mothers who arrived with chicken soup when anyone was ill. Now we have discovered there is something in chicken soup that helps relieve symptoms of a cold.

From personal experience, as both a patient and a nurse, those hated mustard plasters worked on chest colds. Now laugh if you want to, but they worked at our house and saved several asthma attacks from developing.

Yes, yes, tea for burns! A few years ago, an acid in tea was proven to promote the healing of burns. Sticking a hand in a bucket of cold spring water kept many a blister from ever forming. (But don't try the old "smear it with butter" routine! That is a real NO NO.)

Last week, we viewed a TV program with a bunch of natural helps for personal use. They advised rinsing your hair with diluted vinegar after a shampoo. Oh, golly gee! I learned that from Grandma Mary a long time ago. Our family always used it to make our naturally dark-brown hair shine. (Well, mine used to be brown, and I have a long switch I saved when I cut my hair short in 1949 to prove it.)

We used kerosene to soak a toe that had been royally stumped in a summer romp in the meadow. We knew to be careful with any cuts we got in the horse lot and keep injuries clean. If you stepped on a rusty nail, a pan with kerosene was used to soak that foot. None of us every had a tetanus shot, but we learned to be careful. (After Gene and I had a family and did lots of camping with the Scouts, we ALL got a tetanus shot every May, so I did not have to worry if we were on the backside of nowhere and needed one. I am sure Dr. Musgrave would remember the five of us standing in a line in his office, waiting our turn.)

Generations of children in my family suffered from croup! Wood was put on the coals in the cook store, and a teakettle was set on it to start boiling. As soon as there was a good steam, the ill child was held over the steam, and a towel or light blanket was draped over the whole affair to secure the most steam for the child. While the child improved, the mother was a total mess after the ordeal. Her wet stringy hair and red face testified to the treatment. I was delighted when the new cold steam vaporizers were put on the market, and I used those with my children. Oh, those were nights to be remembered.

I still use the original hot saltwater to gargle for a sore throat. Gene's mother used a few drops of coal oil on a spoon of sugar for coughs. Damp soda or lemon juice bleached brown skin spots—well, there were a lot of simple ways to do things.

Now I have to admit that some of them were pretty drastic. My grandfather boiled black draught leaves and drank that for a purgative. It was awful stuff but did the job for him. He also pulled his own teeth when necessary by prying them out with a nail. (It is a wonder he did not get blood poisoning, but maybe his chewing tobacco acted as a disinfectant.) Until his stroke at seventy-two, he had never been to a doctor or dentist.

Although we grew up knowing never to eat fish and drink sweet milk together, we didn't know anyone who had died from doing that either, so guess some of the old tales were not very accurate. Are you still careful to wait an hour before going swimming? No doubt that is the longest hour in the whole summer for any kid! Old habits die hard!

Shoes

Rain, rain, go away,
Come again another day!

I guess we did not chant that enough last week. The recent weather has certainly reminded us about wet years in this end of the county. I wrote about that last week when I did not realize how current that column would be!

I wanted to talk about SHOES this week. This was an important item of clothing in the early days. If the weather was nice, kids often did not wear their shoes to school. They were used to going barefooted at home and at school too. Old school group pictures often show kids in their best clothes but with bare feet. Their shoes or boots were saved for cold weather or church. I've read stories about families where the child who had a pair of shoes to wear in the winter was the one that went to school that year. It was not unusual for a family to walk to church in their bare feet and carry their shoes until they were within sight of the building. A girl whose parents could afford lightweight kid slippers for dances was very lucky. Those shoes were always saved for important occasions.

On the Oregon Trail, footwear was critical. Few pioneer families realized how quickly boots wore out walking ten or twelve miles every day in all kinds of weather. By the time they reached Oregon, many were literally barefooted or covered their feet with rags or Indian moccasins, if they were lucky. Indians on a raiding party always carried several extra pairs of moccasins with them. They were ahead of the pioneers on being prepared with coverings for their feet.

A local story says that Judge Elkins often carried his shoes from home and did not put them on until he got to town (Fillmore). He lived near the present golf course and enjoyed walking along the sandy road and across the Santa Clara to work. Maybe he hated getting sand in his shoes or getting them wet. For whatever reason, he walked in a full suit, tie, and bare feet and carried his shoes to put them on after he got near his office or store.

When we were growing up, we always had at least one pair of good leather school shoes. My mother was a stickler about keeping them polished and looking nice. My dress might be patched or a little small, but my shoes were polished. Mother usually did this herself for both my brother and me. (After all, if I were studying, she would help me.) Dyanshine covered the scuffs and then paste polish was applied. After it dried a few minutes, it was buffed until it really shined. That not only made our shoes look nice, but it also preserved the leather through dust and mud. It was hoped one pair of shoes would last us for the school term.

One year, the most popular shoes for seventh-grade girls were high, lace-up white boots with a faux fur collar around the top. Although we lived in the country, I got a pair that year! Yes, they required white polish every night. They were the only pair I ever had, but I treasured them until my feet got too big, summer came, or they wore out. (I don't remember which.) I still need to remember those boots when I fuss about kids wanting the most popular clothing item each year and pouting if they can't have it.

A picture of my mother about 1921 shows her wearing a pair of lace-up boots that went to her knees. It must have taken her at least ten minutes to put them on each day. There were no zippers in the sides, just laces up the front. She was about fourteen, and I am sure she loved those boots. A picture of my mother-in-law shows her wearing boots about ten inches high, and the tops were white canvas with leather for the shoe section and soles. They matched her middy blouse nicely. In every generation, girls will be girls!

When I started wearing my pioneer costumes and being in parades, I borrowed a pair of real old-fashioned lace boots from the Hawthorn family. They were made from the softest kidskin with a square heel about one inch high. They were brown and laced up about ten inches. These antiques fit me perfectly and were the most comfortable of any shoes I ever wore! Oh, how I adored those boots. I borrowed them several times. I was sad when I lost the use of them after a family member died and things were sorted and stuff changed around. I would still buy them if I could find them. In those days, any real lady had a small foot, so I wonder who the original owner with such big feet was, but they were perfect size 9 for me.

When we started our family in 1949, we lived very simply but could afford for our children to have a pair of school shoes and a pair of shoes for church. The church pair was saved so the kids always had a nice pair for special occasions. Those were often outgrown and handed down to another family in near-perfect condition. The school shoes for our son were usually bought from Ipswitch Shoe Store. They had heavy school oxfords for boys with a sharkskin toe (Buster Browns) that was guaranteed not to wear through. Well, needless to say, several times they replaced those shoes for our family. NOTHING held up under our son, but Jack Ipswith made good on their guarantee.

Cotillion suits and party dresses required dress shoes to complement the outfit. By the time the kids were in high school, tennies for PE had become the shoe for everyday wear. Soon they were improved with heavy rubber soles and even leather tops. Now they have evolved until the kids drag them around and laces are never tied. Oh, how times change!

Today, kids often have only one pair of shoes. They wear those old white tennie for everything. When that one pair wears out, it is replaced with another very similar pair. These athletic shoes are called cross-trainers, walking shoes, or basketball shoes. Now you can buy them white with purple stripes, black with red trim, blue with yellow stripes, and every other combination of colors. But they are still tennis shoes in my eyes. The first time I saw two little boys in full dress suits wearing white canvas basketball shoes, I didn't believe my eyes! What is the world coming to! (I guess we are lucky Fillmore kids have a pair of shoes to wear to school.)

Sewing

I hope my readers will forgive me this week. I have little historical interest to write for you. The only thing I love more than writing is sewing. I am in the middle of making a christening dress using French sewing, and that is a new skill for me. In fact, it is so new that I am taking much longer than necessary to complete. This tiny dress has fancy puffing and yards and yards of lace attached with entredeux. I am excited to realize that I am not too old to learn something new, so it is worthwhile in several ways. (Now if I can learn how to make ribbon roses for trim, I will be successful.)

The original French sewing was all done by hand; however, the modern way uses a sewing machine to speed up the process. Recently, we visited the National History Museum, which is part of the Smithsonian, in Washington DC. They had several early day sewing machines on display. We've come a long way since then. Antiques always help us realize how much we've accomplished to make life easier. In making costumes, you research the way sewing was done in the past. Patterns and basic construction have changed drastically. Many people are interested in clothing worn by the well-to-do people in town. I am interested in clothing worn by the farmers and small shopkeepers—the everyday people in small towns and villages.

My great-grandmother had a widowed sister with three children. She made her living by sewing before the turn of the twentieth century. I am sure she brought her sewing machine in the wagon when they came to Indian Territory in 1893. She sewed for all the family and made a gray wool wedding dress when my grandmother married in1895.

Boys wore dresses until they were about four. True, they had little collars and pleats with belts, but they were still dresses. Until a little boy was potty-trained, those dresses were very functional as well. Little girls all wore a simple apron that could be changed when it became soiled, and the dress was worn for the rest of the week. Clothing was usually changed after the weekly bath on Saturday. Everyone was clean for church on Sunday and ready to start the week. Some kids were fortunate enough to have two changes of clothing. When they got home from school, their good clothing was removed, and they put on their older set to wear while doing chores.

I have a day dress made from an authentic pattern. It is my one concession to the upper class. This dress was worn in the morning before a lady put on her corset and got dressed to receive callers. The top of this dress has a separate lining in front that is fitted similar to a modern bra. The bodice was softly gathered and held with a belt. The lady of the house could be very comfortable when she arose before calling for a daughter or maid to help her get into a corset, corset cover, camisole, pantaloons, petticoat, and a dress. One of the ladies from Ventura acts the part of Senora del Valle when we do a living history at Camulos. She is authentic in every respect. She also needs help getting into her dress, and it takes her over an hour to put on the clothing. (Most of us would not take that amount of time in this modern age.)

Often you will find a wide hem around the skirt of long dresses. This is a separate piece of bias fabric about four inches wide that is stitched around the bottom on the inside. A lady's shoes would soon wear out the hem on the inside of a dress, and this technique would allow for the hem to be removed, repaired, or replaced; and the dress is used for many more months.

A well-to-do family usually had a seamstress come twice a year. This lady would live with the family for several weeks while she did all the necessary sewing for the next six months. The women and girls in the family learned to do some of the fancy embroidery and trim for lingerie and baby items. Mothers insisted the daughters be prepared when they married.

I've enjoyed sewing since I learned to treadle a machine. My first 4-H project was making a dress. I learned to follow the pattern guide and detailed instructions—skills that still serve me well. We modeled our items for judging just like they do today. I lost out on first place because I used fabric that cost twenty cents a yard instead of the eighteen cents calico. Oh well, back to my cotton Swiss batiste, which costs over twenty dollars a yard, and French lace for that christening dress. I still enjoy nice material, and that baby christening dress is waiting for me to add another seam.

Cooking

Food was usually cooked from scratch. Many women had gardens and preserved food from that all summer so it was ready for a quick lunch during the day. With limited refrigeration, meat was bought almost as needed, but that ten pounds of ice would keep milk fresh a little longer. Most families had three meals a day. If you lived in town or near school, the kids came home for lunch, and most fathers had a hot lunch at the kitchen table. The big meal was often the evening dinner with EVERYONE at the table to eat together. It was a time for parents to catch up on what the kids did that day and then exchange ideas with one another. The kids did school homework or helped finish up the household chores for the day, and everyone went to bed early—this saved on oil for the lamps or electricity, and they all needed their rest. Parents were tired, and kids needed to be fresh to learn at school the next day. Many families lived with "early to bed, early to rise makes a man healthy, wealthy, and wise." Making her own bread and starting each meal with basic ingredients was a big job, and the lady of the house was ready for any extra rest she could arrange. Cooking was her responsibility.

One of the early restaurants in Fillmore was the Orange Leaf Café. It was on the east side of Central near the corner bank. They served good meals and also had a great penny candy counter for the kids who might have the funds to buy an extra treat. If you wanted to really be kind and thoughtful to a wife and mother, you took her to the Orange Leaf for lunch or dinner. Times have not change much in that regard.

Orange Leaf Café

Local Shopping

I am starting my pre-Christmas shopping. The service and selection I found at a local ladies clothing store, which also has home decorator items, reminded me of the good old days when everything I needed could be found along Central Avenue. After putting my selected items on hold last week, the next day, I arrived with a box for shipping; and they helped me pack things and get them ready to make a quick stop at the post office. It was a delightful way to shop—no waiting, no proving identify, no parking a mile from the front door, and no long walks from one end of the mall to the other. Everyone should try the local stores for their holiday shopping.

Long ago, from 1930 to 1980, we had everything we needed right here in Fillmore. It was easy to pop into Martha's on the way for coffee from the office and tell her I wanted four pairs of little-girl panties in size 8 and pick them up ten minutes later on the way back to my desk.

When Gene needed new underwear, Champs had a complete selection of Munsingwear and carried the size I needed. Champ had suits, shirts, slacks, shoes, and work clothes. Whether it was orchard wear or a fancy evening with the local dance club, you could find the appropriate attire for the man in your life. Margie carried the nicest selection of stylish things for the women in town before Smith's changed from a five-and-dime to ladies' clothing. Between Martha's, Smith's and Margie's, Fillmore women could find whatever their hearts desired.

Stockers and Smiths originally had all the knickknacks you needed at home. Sprouse-Reitz eventually took over that market, and I still miss the old-fashioned five-and-dime. Fillmore had three hardware stores: Briggs, Dunn's on Main Street, and Patterson's. The latter is the only one still in business. (They celebrated one hundred years in business in 2019)I love going in to buy rope and finding it measured from a hole in the floor or running my hands through an open bin of nails. (The rope storage area below the floor was originally a cement box for storing dynamite.) You still don't have to know what you need as with a little description, they could diagnose the problem and will sell you the right items to fix the problem and probably tell you how to put the pieces together.

The best selection of furniture was available from two or three establishments. I remember Crawford's started out on Main Street but grew enough to move to Central Avenue. They occupied a building where we now have a vacant lot next to the post office. Speed Stewart ran Ballard Furniture, selling top-of-the-line items. My fondest memory was Speed in the local parade ensconced in a bathtub on the traditional decorated trailer sponsored by his own establishment. He was always good for a laugh.

And the drugstores! Cloughs was an old-line pharmacy and eventually sold to the Dunst family, who still have a small shop near the doctors' offices on the highway. Eberly Drug was the place to go because they had Jessie Jones and her fountain with the marble counter. Behind it were all kinds of handles to push and pull for the desired drinks while you sat on a stool. Who could ask for more? Both stores were the soul of discretion and could privately take care of any necessary personal item. (This was before the days of EVERYTHING being discussed on the evening TV program.) Both stores helped me through trying times.

Striffler Gift Shop had all kinds of fancy china and wonderful gift ideas for any occasion. I still have a collection of iron trivets that I bought there. We could afford one a month, and eventually, they almost covered the old kitchen wall.

By November, Western Auto was filling their window with toys—trikes, dolls, bikes, blocks, and trains. They filled many layaways for our family. By Christmas, it was all paid for; and on Christmas Eve, one of us made a quick trip to the store to pick up our items and be ready for Santa to arrange things under the tree for the next morning. For adult gift-giving, Mr. Goble and Mr. Landberg each had a full selection of jewelry in their stores. The first jewelry my husband-to-be sent me came from one of their shops. They also had sterling flatware and some fancy porcelain doodads for local ladies.

Early in the '60s, Central had several places for a good lunch. There was always Mr. Ipswitch and his pool hall that was restricted to guys only but a few brazen girls might sneak inside to eat. When Jessie Jones moved from serving food and cokes at the drugstore counter, she opened another little shop across the street. Her food there was always good and reasonably priced, and she kept us all up-to-date on local happenings. Carl Schiffel and his wife ran The Sweet Shop and had the best potato salad in town. We didn't eat out very often, but we loved their menu. Carl did his Santa impersonation a few weeks before Christmas and gave all the kids in town a casual chance to talk with him as he strolled along Central. Their son, Rudy, graduated from Fillmore High. In the very early days, the Orange Leaf Café included a homemade candy shop and ice cream store. When apricots were ripe and being pitted to dry in Bardsdale, the cafe owner often took ice cream to sell to the workers at the sheds. And they all loved that!

When we remember all the businesses that Fillmore had in the past, don't forget the barbershops. Olen Core had a tiny traditional shop next to the movie house. Men visited him on a regular basis and were alarmed when the price of a haircut went from $3.00 to $3.50. Mr. McKinney had a shop on the west side of the street. He gave our son his first haircut, and I felt like a Norman Rockwell painting as people watched from the sidewalk. His big windows were a perfect frame for viewing a crying ten-month-old getting his hair cut and wanting no part of Mac and his scissors. It is another memory I will always treasure. Occasionally, you would see a lady in one of the barbershops getting her hair cut—not styled! Just cut! Gossip said there was a lady barber in Santa Paula, but our family did not go there. Men went to men for a haircut, and women went to women. That is the way it was! Fillmore had no early day girlie men.

We had three car agencies: William L. Morris, Frank Rudkin, and Mr. Baker. Just about every brand was available from a local dealer. Oscar DeFever's service station on Central was handy and gave excellent service. Several other gas stations were located on the highway through town. (After the highway crossed Pole Creek on the east side of town, State Highway 126 went down Santa Clara Street, turned right on A Street, and then left on Telegraph Road.) Before we married, we often bought gas at the service station on the corner of A and Santa Clara. The deteriorating remains of the station are still there.

Besides the dress and children's clothing shops, we had at least two shoe stores. They carried different brands, so we had a good selection. They both had great sales in January and July. We were all sad when Pavin-Toppings and Ipswitch Shoe Store closed out.

Anyone who sews will remember Tillie Harmonson and her fabric shop. Tillie owned the apartments near the alley on Kensington Street. Her family had been around Fillmore forever. When she became a single, elderly adult, she opened a fabric store. She had her apartment full of bolts of material—you could buy corduroy in July and organdy in December. Her bed was stacked with fabric. She had a board covering the bathtub, and it was stacked with fabric. The kitchen table was stacked with fabric. I enjoyed visiting and buying from her but always wondered where she slept, bathed, and ate. I never did find out. She was a really nice lady.

There were four food markets on Central—the two on the west side of the street are still in business. A third was located where the Fillmore Flower Shop now operates. I loved that building because the front was all bifold doors that left the entire front open to the street. Mr. Coleman ran the meat market, and I think Mr. Anderson had the food section. Glen Fansler ran the Red and White Market on the ground floor of the Masonic building. Eventually, Safeway opened in the large building next to the DeFever gas station. The beloved Inadomi family had a store on Main Street until they were forced into an internment camp during WWII. There was a good selection of grocery stores. Main Street also had two other little neighborhood markets but I do not know who owned those.

We had two or three banks and, of course, Ramona Building and Loan. Fillmore's first bank building is now occupied by the antique store across from the park on the southeast corner of Central and Santa Clara Street. (In 2018, it was a real estate office.) The original brownstone pillars from the front entrance have been saved and now support a sign at the Fillmore Museum. Ramona Building and Loan was a locally owned and operated company and was the place to go when you wanted to save your money or build a house. They paid 4 percent on your savings and charged 6.6 percent on a building loan. Mr. Erskine, the manager for many years, thought 2.6 percent should provide operating expense and still pay a dividend to the stockholders, and it usually did. He would be shocked now at the cost of a bank doing business.

We had two lumberyards, several machine shops, and one real manufacturing industry—Corl and Fleming. They were the local boys who made good! They could fabricate about anything you could dream up if it was made from metal. They manufactured the first fertilizer spreader that worked off a three-point hitch with a power takeoff on a tractor. Every rancher wanted one, and it was very successful. (Last year, we discovered one still in use on an Acton peach ranch.)

Oh, it was fun to go to town and be able to buy anything your family needed. Early in our marriage, we lived on First Street, and I walked to town with my new baby in a big old-fashioned buggy. When I finished grocery shopping, I often had the buggy full and carried the baby home in my arms. Very few families had more than one car, and

Father needed that to go to work, so Mother often provided her own transportation by walking. Memories, memories!

When we go out of town, I realize just what Fillmore has to offer: very little traffic, easy parking near the store of your choice, a short line at the post office, and friendly faces willing to help every customer. No wonder when people visit Fillmore, they want to buy a house and live here. We have it all and don't even know it. Try shopping at home! I think you will like it, and the city will love having the extra sales tax for their budget.

Chapter 11

WILD WEST

Henley and Brownstone Quarry

The OLD WEST was on its last leg in Fillmore by 1915. The final closing of that era was the shooting of John George Henley in broad daylight, in front of the Orange Leaf Café on Central Avenue.

About the time the railroad was completed down the valley in 1888, mining was started up Sespe Creek. No, not gold! But it was almost as good! Brownstone rock! The mountains north of Fillmore still hold an incredible amount of wonderful building stone. The sandstone is pinkish-brown and great for any building requirements. State and federal geologists considered it the best construction-quality sandstone in the West. Four large pieces were selected to be part of a composite mineral arch erected by the state of California at the Louisiana Purchase Exposition at St. Louis in 1900. It was really good stuff! An international jury awarded it a bronze medal for its outstanding qualities. It even survived in the 1906 earthquake and fire in San Francisco.

Somewhere along the way, George Henley secured rights to a large tract of land up Sespe Canyon. He was in his midfifties with a wife and young daughter, and he wanted to build his dream home in the canyon near Pine Creek with the brownstone. The quarry was making money, and it was the perfect time to start construction. The steps and some of the foundation are probably still visible if you look closely. Before the house was completed, the flood of 1914 washed out the road. This made it impractical to try and live up the canyon. The house site was abandoned. The road was never replaced, and the old foundations and steps make for interesting conversation for hikers.

Once Henley secured rights to mine, he started in earnest to quarry the stone. Big chunks and boulders were hauled by wagon down Grand Avenue and piled near the railroad. His large crew of workmen cut the stone into the required size. When the special orders were completed, they were loaded onto the train for shipment. As late as 1950, you could still see the old Brownstone rail stop marked by the familiar white cross-arms on a tall post.

When the Fillmore State Bank opened their new building at the southeast corner of Central and Santa Clara in 1914, it was the finest building in Fillmore. The first-floor exterior was faced with Henley's Sespe brownstone. The brick-faced second floor became the original Masonic hall, with the bank occupying the ground floor. The elegance of the corner doorway was set off by two large Ionic pillar of Sespe brownstone, which supported a large slab of stone with BANK letters attached. Things were prosperous, and in a few years, the bank needed larger quarters. They moved into a new structure just across the railroad tracks on Central at the corner of Main Street. This building is now occupied by Santa Clara Bank.

The original building with the Sespe brownstone columns was sold and used for a radio shop, café and liquor store, and various things and is now an antique store. (In 2017, it was a real estate office.) The building was remodeled. The bricks and brownstone were removed, and the building was stuccoed and painted. The brownstone went to Bardsdale and became part of a wall. Earl Campbell bought the two elegant Ionic columns to use as an ornamental gateway on his Grand Avenue Sespe ranch. These things weighed 1,500 pounds each and proved to Earl that he had bit off more than he could chew. He always liked the idea but was never able to get them put in place. After her father died, Elizabeth Campbell Thomas donated them to the Fillmore Historical Museum. They were put beside the steps of the depot when it was relocated to the north side of Main Street and later moved again and installed near the museum's office in the bunkhouse.

If you look at some of the older homes in Fillmore, you will find foundations and steps made from our very own Sespe brownstone, so it was used locally as the town grew. Currently, the strip of grass and landscaping on A Street in North Fillmore has a big piece to catch the eye as you drive past. But construction materials change, and rock buildings went out of style. The old quarry has been closed for many years.

George Henley owned the Sespe brownstone quarry and controlled the land on the west side of Sespe Creek from the mouth of the canyon past Devil's Gate. He was very possessive of his property rights and, from all accounts, hard to get along with. (Things haven't changed much for that land.)

Before 1900, Mason Bradfield became involved in the oil fields farther up the canyon. He needed to cross Henley's land to get to his leases and well sites. It evidently became a constant conflict between the two men and developed into a real problem. Bradfield wanted to get his crew and equipment to work up Sespe Canyon, and Henley didn't want anyone going through his property. It was a wild feud for several years.

According to local Chuck Hanna, Bradfield had his own lease several miles up the Sespe and even built cabins there. Later, they were known by locals as the green cabins. The Sespe has always been a difficult area to traverse. It is a narrow canyon. The creek bed is full of boulders that are often as big as a house, and water sometimes runs bank to bank. There were no roads on the west side of the creek after the flood of 1914 washed out the short stretch of road to Henley's new house site. Bradfield planned to build a flume from his lease to Fillmore. They would mix the heavy oil with creek water and float it down the canyon. Once he got it here, the oil could be separated from the water and shipped. It was a usable idea, but never developed as far as I know.

One fateful day in 1915, Henley came to town on business and was walking down the street near the Orange Leaf Café on the east side of Central Avenue (the pool hall is located in about the same place now). Bradfield had taken all he was going to from Henley and decided to put a stop to the whole mess. He had his gun with him. When he saw Henley, he drew down on him and started firing. When Henley was struck, he staggered down the street, bellowing in pain, with Bradfield still trying to gun him down.

Constable Owen Miller came out of his Central Hotel to investigate the ruckus! He saw what was going on and waited until he was sure Bradfield had emptied his gun. Then Constable Miller went down the block and took Bradfield's gun from him. Doc Manning was out on a house call, so bystanders loaded Henley into a spring wagon to find medical aid.

The handwritten Fillmore justice court records show Criminal Docket No. 1 dated July 2, 1915. Mason Bradfield appeared before Judge Merton Barnes on a charge of assault with intent to commit murder. Bradfield raised the $10,000 bail and hired two young Ventura attorneys, Gardner and Orr, to defend him. This is the same Earle Stanley Gardner who later became a famous author of hundreds of best-selling novels based on trials and court cases.

After Bradfield got out of jail, Constable Miller gave him back his gun and said, according to people in town, "Next time, do a better job." (This was not a murder but would have been if Bradfield had been a better shot.) Thanks to Edith Jarrett's *Old Timers Tales* for much of this information.

Chuck Hanna said that Henley and Albert Riesgo were with Reed Elkins when Reed was later shot and killed during a drinking party.

Joe Dye

In searching for more details on the Bradfield-Henley shooting, I keep getting sidetracked into other details. Now I find that Bradfield had killed a man about twenty-five years earlier, so shooting Henley was not a new thing for him. His killing of Joe Dye got my attention, so I will let Bradfield off the hook this week and tell you about Dye instead.

Joe Dye was born in Kentucky in 1831 and made his first trip to California during the Gold Rush and drifted around the southwest as a mule-team driver, miner, and Indian chaser. He was a dedicated secessionist and joined the Mason Henry Gang as Civil War was ending. They committed robbery and murder and anything else they found fun. Dye was a great tracker and shooter and dropped out of the gang before Los Angeles marshal, William Warren, hired him to patrol the gambling halls, saloons, and bordellos of the city's Chinatown in 1867.

Joe was so successful that he was soon appointed special police officer and joined five other officers for the city of Los Angeles. In 1870, Marshal Warren and a deputy took off to return a Chinese prostitute to Los Angeles. She had been kidnapped and taken to San Diego. Dye stayed behind and used the telegraph to notify others to be on the lookout for this woman. Warren wanted to collect the hundred-dollar reward after they caught the woman and return to Los Angeles. During the trial, Warren and Dye got into a dispute about the reward money and carried it outside after the trial. Dye ended up pulling his gun (as usual) and shot Warren, who also pulled his gun and fired several times. Between the two of them, they wounded several others on the street. Warren died the next day, and Dye was arrested.

A jury acquitted Dye and felt he had fired in self-defense after several witnesses testified Warren pulled his gun first. It was an unpopular verdict, but Dye remained on the force for a short time. Vigilante justice soon made Dye decide it would be well if he MOVED, so he came to Ventura County and went into the oil business up the Sespe.

Dye continued drifting between Sespe and Los Angeles and keeping everyone nervous while he stirred up trouble, started fights, and pointed his loaded pistol in the faces of enemies.

Dye married, had a daughter, and found his wife stepping out with his oil partner, H. J. Crow. The two lovers sent notes back and forth through a Santa Paula merchant, Herman Haines. When Dye intercepted one of these messages, he just shot the messenger, killing Haines. The wife ran away, and Dye put his daughter into an orphanage in Los Angeles. The first jury found Dye guilty of murder, but on appeal, he was acquitted. He returned to the oil claim on the Sespe and took his nephew, Mason Bradfield, into the company as a partner. When Bradfield would not go along with an illegal oil scheme, Dye beat him up, stalked him, and was back to his old ways. Dye reverted to his former habits of conducting a campaign of death threats and intimidation against Bradfield and his partners.

Mason Bradfield got tired of the intimidation. When he knew Dye was going to Los Angeles on business, he quietly went along on his own business. He secured a second-floor room at the New Arlington Hotel on the southeast corner of Commercial and Los Angeles Streets. The window had a good view, and a double-barrel shotgun across his lap was a comfort to Bradfield. On May 14, 1891, as Dye walked along the street, Bradfield discharged both barrels and killed him.

The jury for this murder trial found Bradfield not guilty and believed the killing to be self-defense. The Santa Paula paper said that Dye's death "gave relief to Ventura County." Hundreds came to the funeral, and some said they just wanted to make sure a very bad man was really dead.

YES, THIS IS HOW THE WEST WAS WON!

(If you are interested in lots more details, get a copy of *CALIFORNIA BADMEN* by Secrest—he has a whole chapter on Dye. It is all interesting if you enjoy history, and it is part of Fillmore history. Thanks to John Heilman for the internet help and research.)

Stage Robbers

We often talk about the good old days when things were all wonderful and great according to our memories. Well, Harry Kenney's little book tells about the stagecoach robbers around here. The stage came through the valley about twice a week, and once in a while, it would be robbed. It nearly always carried money from San Francisco. There were no banks here in the early days, and the money was shipped by stage in express boxes.

Harry says, "On one of these trips a man robbed the stage right next to the Sespe Ranch house. They caught him up near Newhall, but he did not have any of the money with him. He had gotten away with $16,000, but they could not find the money so they shot him. Before he died, he said that he had buried the loot beside an oak tree near the mouth of the Sespe River. Of course there were lots of oak trees around that country, and up until 1910 it was nothing to go out on a Monday morning and find a tree that had been dug around. People were still hunting for that money. I have learned since then there was an Indian that was wise to the thing, and he got the money long years ago."

Not long after that, another fellow robbed the stage down east of Atmore Ranch. The road crossed the river there, and it was all overgrown with willows. He hid in those willows and stopped the stage and robbed it. Everyone took up their guns and went looking for him. They kept after him from both directions so he could not get out of the valley, but they just couldn't catch him. It seemed he was a stranger to the valley and did not know about the road through Grimes Canyon.

A couple of men riding along the road east of Piru saw horse tracks leading off into some willows, so they tied their horses and went to investigate. They found the man asleep and captured him. He was turned over to the sheriff. The posse and prisoner stopped in Santa Paula for supper on the way back to Ventura. The robber was not hungry, so they handcuffed the man and put him in a room of the hotel while they went down to eat. When it was time for them all to head on down the road, they discovered the robber had climbed out the window and dropped down to the street. The posse could not find him but made a big to-do about him getting away. The next morning, his handcuffs were found hanging in the willows, and they looked no further.

That was part of the game. They never intended to take him, they just let him go, and a citizen went out and caught him and hung him. There was no fuss about it at all. Everyone knew what had become of him, and they never found him. That broke up stagecoach robbing in Ventura County. (There was not a civil rights lawyer in sight.)

Law enforcement in those days was a good deal different than it is now. When a sheriff went out after a man and told him to halt and he did not halt, the sheriff halted him right there—funeral. Yes, we have advanced in our way of thinking!

Horse Thieves

I have one more story from Harry Kenney that you should hear. This one is about horse thieves around here.

In 1875, the railroad was being built from San Francisco to Los Angeles, and they had headquarters in Bakersfield. They had started going over the Tehachapi Mountains and needed more horses. A couple of fellows got an idea in their head that Ventura County had some good horses just waiting to be taken.

Everyone around Sespe had two or three head of horses that they turned out on the range. When they needed them to work, they rounded them up and brought them in to work. The Bakersfield fellows thought that here was the place to fill the need of Southern Pacific. They established a kind of horse market in Bakersfield and came down through the mountains to the Santa Clara Valley. There was an old trail they could use, and later it was called Horse Thief Trail. It turned off about Gorman Station and came down east of Piru Creek and out near Fillmore. It skirted around the mountain and came to a place about a half a mile from the road on the old Leavens and Goodenough place. The Bakersfield boys made their headquarters there.

Just about dark one night, they were hiding in the brush getting ready to go down to sleep at the ranch. Their plan for the next day was to go out and round up a bunch of horses, catch them, and start for Bakersfield the next night. They always traveled on a moonlit night. On this particular evening, a man happened to be passing along the road and spied the men. He went on down to Santa Paula, telegraphed the sheriff in Ventura, and messed up the plans. The sheriff came out that night and picked up two other men in Sespe to help him as deputies. He gave them double-barreled shotguns and loads of buckshot, and they went to get the horse thieves.

The lawmen stopped up the road about a quarter of a mile from the ranch house, and the sheriff went to the door and knocked. He sent his two deputies back to the barn to catch the fellows if they ran out the back way. When the sheriff asked if these two men were there, the man that lived there said no; they were not there, and they had not been there. The old man stalled for time to let the others get away. They got out, but neither of them reached the barn. The two deputies were stretched out in the darkness behind some old gangplows, and when the thieves ran for the barn, they downed them both.

Several years later, when Harry saw some old graves just east of the Goodenough place, his father told him the story. The horse thieves were buried right along the road. They never had any more trouble with men stealing horses in this part of Ventura County. They got the message quick.

I guess old-timers have enjoyed telling tall tales to kids as long as there have been old men and boys. Harry Kenney went with his father to buy a sheep to slaughter from I. D. Lord. Lord Creek and Lord Canyon were named for him. He lived over near where the Hardison Ranch is located. Harry was about five or six years old and had never seen Mr. Lord without a hat. On this occasion, Mr. Lord removed his hat, and Harry discovered the man didn't have a hair on his head. He didn't even have eyebrows. Harry asked him where his hair was, and I. D. Lord told him the following story:

> Oh yes, I used to have hair when I was a young man, but when I was about thirty years old, my hair began to turn gray, and some old woman told me that if I would kill a bear and take the grease of the bear and greased my head, my hair would never turn gray. I went and killed a bear and greased my head and kept it well-greased for about a month, and my hair all came out. The trouble was that I killed the bear at the wrong time of the year—the bear was shedding.

(Actually, Mr. Lord was born that way.) My grandfather would have loved this story. He had several to pull the leg of his own grandkids when they reached the right age, and we all loved them.

Bear Howard
by Tim Hagel

As you recall from our last story, Ventura County Sheriff Stone had caught and shot the Fillmore horse thieves, only to lose his office after two sensational jail breaks.

In September of 1877, forty-six year-old Sheriff Miller was elected and took over the office from Stone. He was a popular democratic frontier cowboy. Miller had even crossed the United States twice on horseback and wagon. He was a force to be reckoned with. Miller was determined to avoid Stone's mistakes.

By May 1878, Sheriff Miller set out to make good on his promises to catch all the escapees that vanished during Stone's administration.

Number 1 on the sheriff's ten most-wanted list was local murderer Jeff Howard. Jeff was a popular homesteader in Rose Valley. He had the county's finest year-round pasture that was the envy of all. Howard Creek and his homestead ranch are still the jewels of Rose Valley.

It seemed that Jeff earned his BI number when he was tired of sheepherders squatting on his homestead. In June of 1877, the county was in a terrible drought, and over five thousand head of cattle and sheep died of starvation in the Ojai, Fillmore, Thousand Oaks, Moorpark, and Camarillo areas. Sheep had just been introduced by Basque and Portuguese immigrants and were not readily accepted by locals.

Jeff Howard openly talked to ranchers in Nordhoff and Ojai about his disdain for sheep and the sheepherders. To make a long story short, he ambushed and killed sheepherder Alphonso Urtasan in Rose Valley and was duly arrested by Sheriff Stone. Needless to say, he escaped jail the night before he was going to be sentenced (likely hung). Jeff immediately fled the county.

Take a trip up to Rose Valley and see for yourself his ranch and acres of green pasture that occupies the first three miles of Rose Valley Road. The Howard Creek US Forest trail is a scenic day hike that cuts through Rocky Creek Canyon where Jeff Howard shot and murdered the sheepherder. Today, the area is a great place for family hikes and is full of Ventura County history.

Back to Sheriff Miller, he sent out telegrams and wanted posters across the West. No doubt his frontier experience helped him determine where murderer Jeff Howard was likely to hide.

In May 1879, Sheriff Miller caught a stage to Arizona where a local lawman turned over Jeff Howard, whom he had found living in the mountain country. Sheriff Miller brought back his prize. Before the sheriff could relish his increased popularity, just one week later, Jeff Howard had vanished.

Jeff left behind one crowbar, two knives, and a set of shackles. Later accounts determined that Jeff had fled on foot up Aliso Canyon to Sulfur Mountain, Upper Ojai, Rose Valley, and then made his way out of the Sespe through Mutau Flats and off through the Mojave, disappearing to the East.

By definition, Jeff was an early cross-country backpacker! The *Ventura Signal* used a lot of verbs to attack Sheriff Miller's escape boondoggle. He was quickly out of office.

The real story here in Backyard Expeditions is Jeff Howard. Think about it: Murderer, two-time escapee, and a homestead legend in Ventura County. For a century, the story ended there. Jeff Howard was never caught again. He simply vanished or died a terrible death in the Mojave.

While researching this rap sheet article on Sheriff Miller and his stage trip to Arizona, I stumbled across an archive of a historic list of Arizona pioneers and 1880s legends of Arizona. A name stood out: Jesse Howard. I thought about it. In 1879, how many Howards could there have been west of the Mississippi?

You got it! I used the excuse for a family trip, and we packed up the bags and went to Sedona, Arizona, to do more research and see for myself and confirm if this was our escapee, Jeff Howard. A historian's prize awaited me, and I was shocked at what I found.

Sheriffs Stone and Miller really would be surprised to find out that Jeff Howard fled to what is now called Flagstaff. He was one of the first pioneer homesteaders in the Arizona Mountains. Jeff changed his first name to Jesse Smith Howard and Charles Smith Howard and then just Bear Howard. He loved bear hunting and killed hundreds of bears for the western meat markets and Chinese immigrants in Prescott, Sedona, and Flagstaff.

Bear Howard married a local gal, and together with a hunting partner, they built one of the first cabins on Oak Creek below Flagstaff. Their cabin is still intact and is a major Arizona state pioneer landmark.

Bear Howard was six feet eight inches. He towered over other homesteaders. Bear Howard lived a frontiersmen legacy. Ventura County fugitive Jeff "Bear" Howard lived into his middle nineties, which was unheard of during our nineteenth and twentieth centuries. As a twist of fate, or just a flat-out metaphor for the crazy avenues of life, Bear Howard adopted an orphan bear cub and gave up hunting altogether. The bear lived in his cabin at his side, reported by the closest of friends, day by day until Bear Howard died peacefully in his sleep.

(Tim Hagel: I couldn't have completed this story without the tremendous work included from Patricia Clark (of Sheriff Clark) and the Arizona/Sedona Historical Societies.)

Horse Thief Trail
By Tim Hagel

(I have always been fascinated with the history of the Ventura County backcountry. Recently, I was honored to befriend a local historian named Marie Wren. She has sent me many stories of the Sespe from the Fillmore Historical Society.)

After hearing the story out of a pioneer diary, I gathered up a group of VCDSA friends and families and backpacked in the Sespe to retrace a part of the story.

You may want to take the same Sespe hike from Dough Flats to Alder Creek, also known in 1870s as the Horse Thief Trail.

Pioneer Harry Kenney (Kenney Grove) tells the story that, in 1875, the railroad was being built from San Francisco to Los Angeles. The railroad crews had started going over Tehachapi Mountains and needed more work horses. Two enterprising Bakersfield horse thieves thought that Ventura County was the place to fill the horse needs of Southern Pacific.

Everyone around the Sespe community had two or three horses that they turned out on the range. When they needed them to work, they simply rounded them up. Quickly, the rustlers established a horse market in Bakersfield and came through the mountains to the Santa Clara Valley. They used an old Indian trail later named in their honor as Horse Thief Trail. From Harry's account and historic maps and diaries, I was able to piece the trail together. In short, it meandered through Gorman Station and came east of Piru Creek to Mutau Flats, down to the Sespe Hot Springs, up Alder Creek, Cow Springs, Squaw Flats, through Angel's Pass, skirted around Hopper Mountain, and ended about a half a mile from the wagon road on the old Leavens and Goodenough place (Highway 126). An alternate trail also led from Angel's down Pole Creek to the Santa Clara Valley.

It became obvious that the rustlers likely enlisted the help of William Mutau, who was well-known as a horse rustler. Old man Mutau had a canyon on his homestead appropriately named Horse Thief Canyon. He used the canyon to rest and feed stolen horses bound for Tehachapi.

Harry Kenney's pioneer story continues:

One night, the rustlers were in the Sespe area and were hiding in the brush getting ready to go down to the Leavens Goodenough Ranch (Cavin Road at 126). It was assumed that their plan was to go out and round up a bunch of horses, catch them, use the advantage of a moonlit night to drive the stolen horses away on the horse thief trail system.

On that particular evening, a local Sespe man happened to be passing along the wagon road and spied the men. He quickly rode his horse down to Santa Paula and telegraphed the Sheriff in Ventura. The sheriff (John Stone) came out that night and picked up two other men in the Sespe, deputized them, and gave them buckshot-filled double-barreled shotguns.

The sheriff and his deputies stopped up the road about a quarter of a mile from the Goodenough ranch house where the rustlers were hiding. Sheriff Stone went to the front door and knocked. He sent his two new deputies back to the barn. The sheriff asked the old man about the rustlers. He said that they were not there.

Harry Kenney's account said it appeared to the sheriff (Stone) that the old man stalled for time to let the others get away. "The Sheriff was right, they got out the back door, but neither of them reached the barn."

The two deputies were stretched out in the darkness behind some old gangplows, and when the thieves ran for the barn, they downed them both.

Several years later, Harry Kenney saw some old graves just east of the Goodenough ranch. His father told him that the horse thieves were buried right along the road.

Using a modern Forest Service trail map, you can backpack along the old horse thief trail and retrace many of the steps from the Sespe horse thieves and William Mutau (later shot and killed at Mutau Flats). You won't see it labeled as such, but here is how to follow it:

Drive your car up Goodenough Road and then about seven miles of dirt road to Dough Flats. When you get out of your car, look back southeast to Hopper Mountain—you can still see Angel's Pass and remnants of the horse thief trail used to Fillmore.

Start your day hike or trip north from Dough Flats. You can make a fast day trip to Squaw Flats or Cow Springs or go on an overnight to Dripping Springs or Alder Creek.

You can also drive around through Lockwood Valley and park at Mutau Flats and then backpack the exact trail to the Sespe Hot Springs and Alder Creek.

While you are hiking, think of what it must have been like to be a deputy, using mules to bring justice to the Sespe wilderness.

Epilogue: An interesting side note is that Sheriff Stone was a saddlemaker prior to becoming sheriff, and he ultimately lost his third reelection over an escape of a Sespe sheepherder's murder suspect.

Chapter 12

PEOPLE

New Towns and Settlers

Before the Spanish explorers came down the Santa Clara Valley, the native people lived along the streams. Water is essential to life and life is better when it can easily be secure; thus, the Santa Clara River, Piru and Sespe Creek and Lords Creek all had villages nearby. The Tataviam and Chumash Indians welcomed the early Spanish explorers when they came down the valley and those men left diaries to record all the things they saw. The explorers camped near water also.

When the Mexicans petitioned the governor for land grants, every single one included good reliable sources for water. Once again, the Santa Clara River, Piru and Sespe Creek and Lords Creek were the centerpieces of the land grants.

As Americans followed their dreams of riches in the gold fields, they saw the possibilities of making new lives in the valley near the available water—the Santa Clara River, Piru and Sespe Creek and Lords Creek. These streams were the most desirable place for new settlers. And, those new settlers came.

Indian and Mexican families intermarried, made new homes for themselves in the adjacent area of the water source and farmed the land, ran cattle or started businesses. As the American arrived, they just became a part of the community. Families were often far apart, but more clusters of homes were near the streams.

Some of the earliest American settlers were Ari Hopper and Ben Warring. Ari loved to hunt! When he found great hunting in the area just west of Piru Creek, he moved from San Jose. From 1868 he called this area his home. Hopper Creek and Hopper Mountain were part of the inheritance he left to us. Ari was not content to be alone in this new hunting paradise, so he wrote to his friend, Ben Warring, and invited him to come and join in the hunt.

Ben Warring and his twelve-year-old son, Hugh, soon arrived. Ben bought out a homesteader near Ari and the Buckhorn Ranch evolved from that purchase. The Warrings are still well known in the valley.

The last post office heading east out of the valley was Scenega. About two miles east of the present site of Fillmore, was an early day stage stop. Of course that served as the nucleus of a settlement and eventually you could pick up your mail there and kids attended Scenega School. Not too far from the Ealy stage stop was a real cienega near the river. Water came to the top of the ground similar to an artesian well. It was always wet and swampy but the stage stop became known as the Scenega. The Americans could never spell very well so often good Spanish terms got slight changes when they were put into print.

An 1875 Directory for Ventura County shows everyone outside of Santa Paula as being in the Scenega post office delivery district. As settlements grew up around Piru Creek and Sespe Creek, the people got their mail at Scenega. From Rancho Camulos to Scenega was a nice ride, but at least it was a post office for everyone.

To try and locate families in the right area, I checked census records. The 1870 census was enumerated as San Buenaventura. By finding a few names that I know lived around Piru Creek, I can tell others living nearby—they were all listed by the same person, on the same day so were probably neighbors. Rancho Camulos' Ignacio Del Valle family had 15 people listed; nearby was Indian Jose, a saddle maker; farmers Manuel Real and Santiago Dominquez. Indian Jose was the only one listed as being born here; the others were all born in Mexico. Others list occupations as sheep raiser, blacksmith, beekeeper, laborer and stockman and station keepers.

Around Scenega and Sespe Creek, there are more Anglo names listed. Guiberson, Sprague, Lord, Edwards and Stevens are added to Tico, Valdez and Gomez. Many new settlers came by ship to Buenaventura and ventured inland until they found a place that suited them, so nearer the coast we find more Anglo families.

These sources of good water for home and ranch brought settler together. Later David C. Cook bought most of Rancho Temescal that included Piru Canyon, and formally laid out a town he called Piru after the local Indians. The local settlers now had a formal name but they were there long before Cook arrived. The town has never incorporated into a City but their roots go back to Indian days.

The Original Families

When I came to Fillmore to be married in 1947, my first friend was Peggy Gutierrez Hickman. Her husband and my husband had been childhood friends in Oklahoma, so I naturally tried to fit into their threesome while I met more new people in town.

Soon after I met Peggy, she very proudly told me she was a seventh-generation Californian and a descendant of Petra Dominguez. That did not mean much to me since I am a fourth-generation Indian Territory pioneer, but I did put that little fact into the back of my brain to pull out later—much later!

It was about fifty years before, I became very interested in early California history, did a lot of research and reading, and worked as a docent at the Rancho Camulos Museum; and THEN her fact about being a seventh-generation Californian IMPRESSED me! Wow! What a great genealogy to trace.

Now Peggy's great-grandkids can say they are tenth-generation native Californians going back to Petra Dominguez. While Peggy was my first resource about Petra, Michele Ybarra McKenzie and Ernie Morales have recently added to my knowledge.

Petra H. Huanduraga was an Opata Indian from Ures, Sonora, Mexico. She was married in 1840 to Santiego del Carmelo Dominguez, a Yaqui Indian. They came to Rancho Camulos in the 1870s and probably worked as campesinos for the rest of their lives. They were buried in that little rancho cemetery in the early 1900s.

The Dominguez family was the original Indian component to the current Mexican and Spanish families, with some Anglo added for good measure. I am sure the Piru tribe was also involved in this genealogy. Ernie says he is almost certain the following families can trace back to Petra Dominguez: Alamillo, Arredondo, Beltran, Cardonna, Carrillo, Dominguez, Escamilla, Espinoza, Flores, Garcia, Garnica, Gonzalez, Guerrero, Gurrola, Gutierrez, Juarez, Limon, Lopez, Lovato, Medina, Mendez, Morales, Munoz, Olivares, Ortiz, Palacio, Ponce, Ramirez, Reyes, Riesgo, Rios, Rivas, Robles, Romero, Sanchez Sandoval, Siquiedo, Soto, Torres, Vega, Valdivia, Videgain, and Ybarra.

After Rancho Camulos Museum was organized with the docent council, each of us sort of found a place to work and enjoyed helping. Julia Preciado wanted to work on updating the list of burials at the Camulos Cemetery, and she did!

The ranch had a list from long ago, but many family graves were not listed. Julia knew most of the Piru families, and she started tracking down people who knew where their great-grandparents or ancestors were buried. Here is Julia's current list of burials at the Rancho Camulos Cemetery:

> Joseph Ygnacio Aceves, Benigno Acosta, Concepcion Acosta, Elias Acosta, Esteban Acosta, Fred Acosta, Lorenza Acosta, Concepcion G. Aguirre, Jesus Aguirre, Jose Alcocer, Jesus Arellanez, Pedro Avalos, Gianni (John) Basolo, Adriana M. Beltran, Aurelia Beltran, Evarista Beltran, Jose Beltran, Margarito Belteran, Carl Cabelar, Epifanio Carrillo, George A. Case, Maria Antonia Case, Tillie Case, Cecelia Cervantes, Juan de la Cruz, Ygnacio del Valle (disinterred to LA cemetery), Anivar Dominguez, Carmelo Dominguez,

Esteban Dominguez, Francisca Tapia Dominguez, Juan B. Dominguez, Miguel Dominguez, Petra H. Dominguez, Thomas Tapia Dominguez, Manuel Duarte, Ramon Durazo, Gertrudes Encinas, Manuel Encinas, Infant Espinoza, Aurora Espinoza, Jose Espinoza, Miguel Espinoza, Juan Fernandez, Petra H. Dominguez Fulmer, Eulalia Garcia Gaitan, Rita Gaitan, Antonio Garda, Margarita Gutierrez, Isabel Llamas, Ceceilia Dominguez Manriquez, Baby Manriquez, Elvira Martinez Lucia Martinez, Reynaldo Martinez, Carmen Medel, Francisca Medel, Jesus Medel, Lupe Medel, Carmen Nunez, Ramona Nunez, Ysabel M. Nunez, Concepcion Medel Ortega, Maria de Jesus Rodriguez Ortega, Rose Pelayo, Evangelina Perez, Manuel Perez, Spencer Phillips, Magdalena Ramirez, Jose Ynez Real, Joseph Rodriguez, Refugio Rodriguez, Rodrigo Rodriguez, Paz Romero, Angelita Dominguez Ruiz, Guadalupe Ruiz, Francisca Garcia Silva, Adolfo Siqueido, Luciano Siqueido, Maria Amparo Salazar Siqueido (disinterred to Santa Clara Cemetery, del Valle plots), Carmen Rubio Dominguez Smith, Juana Garcia Solis, Maria Souther, Damiana B. Tapia, Alesandro Verdugo, and Refugio O. Verdugo. Julia's own grandmother, Magdalena Ramirez, was the last burial in 1946.

Magdalena was born in 1856 in Mexico and came to the United States in 1920. At the time of her death, she was living with her daughter in Piru. She was eighty-nine years old when she passed February 18, 1946. No other burials have been permitted since then. Orchards are now planted around the cemetery, but often local families still tend the graves. We know the descendants of these families are all among the First Families of our area. Julia continues working on her personal Camulos project.

Juan Fustero

(A 1920 census shows several younger family members living with him, ages fourteen to twenty-two.)

Juan Fustero is called the last Piru Indian. It is believed that Juan was the last full-blooded Tataviam/Chumash Indian in our area. His tribe descended from the Shoshone-speaking people who migrated to Santa Clarita Valley about AD 450. There may be some debate about Juan's title, but we know he was born near Piru and lived in that area all his life. After his death, the family scattered, and we've lost track of them.

In searching old US census records, I got excited when I found *Juan* listed in Piru in 1870. His father was Jose and was shown as a saddlemaker. The census shows them as "Indian" with only first names. Juan was the oldest of the children living at home and was twenty-one at the time. His occupation was shown as "vaquero." The other children ranged in age from one month to thirteen years old. Since the father was a saddlemaker, I am sure this was OUR Juan Fustero.

Juan was born in 1849. According to a detailed article in 1990 by John R. Johnson and David Earle, published by the Journal of California and Great Basin Anthropology, his parents were Jose and Sinforosa. There were several Tataviam rancheria (villages) sites located on Piru Creek. The Tataviam Indians had major rancherias near Castaic Junction and Elizabeth Lake Canyon and Redrock Mountain. Piru Canyon was the western edge of their territory. The coastal Chumash claimed the area up to about Piru Creek, but the two tribes shared overlapping areas. Both were usually peaceful people. Both Tataviam and Chumash probably occupied the rancheria called Kamulas (near Rancho Camulos). It was in Tataviam territory, but the name is Chumash.

Jose and Sinforosa were both Tataviam and raised near Mission San Fernando. Records from there and Mission San Buenaventura show the ancestors for both of them. They were married in 1881. One of Jose's grandparents came from Piru, so perhaps family ties brought Jose and Sinforosa to the Piru Canyon. It was not unusual for Mission Indians to leave the mission and go back home when the opportunity presented itself. It seems pretty certain the couple settled in one of the villages in Piru Canyon, and Juan was born there.

The US census for 1880 lists many names that we still recognize— del Valle, Mutah, Dominguez, Hopper, Salazar, Real, Fernandez, Warring, Guiberson, Fine, Atmore, Grimes, Kellogg, Robertson, and Fustero. In those ten years since the last census, the Americans had arrived in full force. Juan and his family are still shown as "Indian" on the census, but now they have a last name: FUSTERO. The family occupation was making saddles, and the Spanish word for saddlemaker was *fustero*. So now the family had two names just like everyone else. Juan and Rosa married in 1881.

Eventually, the del Valle family bought Rancho Temescal, which contained the original Tataviam village sites. Along the way, most of the Indians had moved or had been assimilated into the population as they found jobs, but Juan Fustero remained in his beloved Piru Canyon. To get rid of him from the del Valle property the family wished to use, they gave him the right to continue living in a northern portion of the canyon, a sizeable herd of horses in payment to make the move, and then left him alone. Fustero married, had several children, and took care of them way up the creek for many years. The kids went to school at Temescal School (now under Piru Lake) and were just regular people.

Recently, I was permitted to make copies of several Fustero family pictures to use in our local history book when it is printed. They show Juan astride a nice horse with his ever-present rifle across his lap and a nice team of horses and buggy taking his women folk to town. An apricot tree was in the background. Everyone was well-dressed and looked happy. The ladies' hats were in the current style and shaded their dark faces above white collars. The younger children looked like any other kids in school pictures. Their home was far enough up the canyon that Juan could hunt, and they seemed to get by. All was right with his world.

When Juan Fustero died in 1921, his grown family scattered. They had no further ties to Piru Creek. Locals placed a marker in the canyon in his memory. It was moved to the top of a hill before the new Piru Lake covered the site in the 1950s.

Women

March is Women's History Month. It is a time when I have often bought special posters and things for the high school library to remind students about women in our past. This week, I have been thinking about local women who were each very special to our community, and I will give you a short sketch about a few of them. I do not guarantee the facts are all accurate, but the memories are! I had other women I wanted to include, but I was unable to get family information about them, so they will have to be saved for another column.

Catherine Cruson Hinckley

Kate Cruson was only two years old when she moved to Bardsdale in 1880. Her father went to work for Union Oil. They had been living in Placerville where her father had been part of the early gold rush. After high school, she married the local dentist, Ira Hinckley. By 1900, they owned a pharmacy as part of his dental office on the SE corner of Ventura and Central.

In 1905, Kate and Ira built a house at 423 First Street on a large lot that was nearly an acre in size. The barn was located behind the house with Bard Street immediately to the north. They had two children, Hattie May and Lawrence.

Hattie May married Chet Hansen, who worked at the Texaco refinery. They had one daughter, Margie, and lived in Fillmore.

Lawrence became well-known as our local artist. He started doing cartoons in high school and progressed to oils. One of his specialties was eucalyptus trees, and many of his canvases hang in Ventura County homes. After they married, Lawrence and Mildred turned the unused barn into a residence, and it was called THE ARTIST BARN. They had one son, Bill. Kate took great pride in Lawrence and his art. She enjoyed her two grandchildren and other young people who lived near her. She was always helpful and interested in their activities.

Kate Hinckley was a widow for many years. When her health deteriorated and she needed daily care, she moved to a retirement care facility in Ventura until her death at age ninety-two. When I visited her there, she complained about being around all those old people.

The original Hinckley home on First Street was badly damaged in the 1994 earthquake. Fillmore Historical Society saved it from demolition and moved it to their new Main Street site near the railroad, where it has been restored and preserved. Repairs were made to the barn, and it is now a bed and breakfast.

Kate Hinckley is remembered as being kind and interested in young people and making the best apple pie in Fillmore.

Dona Ysabel del Valle

Ysabel Vaela was married at the Church of Our Lady of Angeles on December 7, 1851. She was only fifteen but well educated for the time. Her husband, Ygnacio del Valle, provided a house for them on Olivera Plaza in downtown Los Angeles. They lived there for ten years before moving to their Rancho Camulos land grant in Ventura County.

Ysabel was very religious and brought eight orphans with the family when they moved to the ranch. She took care of them with her children until all were grown. Ysabel attended mass almost every day and missed her church when they left Los Angeles. It took five years, but eventually, Ygnacio built her a little chapel near the south veranda of their adobe house. She had prayers there every night and morning. When a mission priest made his monthly trip to say mass at Rancho Camulos, Ysabel had one of the Indian servants take bread and wine and hang it in the sycamore tree near Hall Road, west of Fillmore, for his refreshment on the trail. It was a long walk from either of the missions to Rancho Camulos.

Their ranch was thirty miles from Mission San Fernando and about thirty miles from Mission San Buenaventura, so Ysabel was hostess for every traveler who came down Santa Clara Valley and traveled El Camino Real. The rancho was well-known for its hospitality. After the railroad was completed in 1888, tourists flooded the home site when it made the stop at the Camulos depot. Ysabel was forced to close the ranch to all except local people and their personal friends. Helen Hunt Jackson's book *Ramona* brought unwelcomed notoriety to Rancho Camulos.

Ysabel was not only well educated, but she was also the only person with any medical training in the area. She delivered babies, nursed children with diphtheria, and took care of injured vaqueros when needed. She bore twelve children, but only five lived to be adults. She raised her own medicinal herbs and was always available to attend the ill and injured if her horse and buggy could get her to them.

After Ygnacio died in 1880, she was overseer for the ranch for several years until one of her sons graduated from college and returned to the ranch to take over management. Failing health forced Ysabel to move to her married daughter in Los Angeles in 1900. Her days as Dona del Valle of Rancho Camulos were over. She died in 1905 at Josefa's home. It was truly the end of the early California era.

Inez Kellogg Arundell

Inez Kellogg and Tom Arundell were married in 1881. They left Iowa and homesteaded up Pole Creek in the 1890s. They build a rammed-earth house and a large, quaint six-sided frame barn that stood until a windstorm in the 1950s destroyed it. The Arundells had many hives of bees. They hauled their sage honey by wagon from the ranch to Fillmore and shipped it by rail. In 1911, production was unusually high and prices held, so it was good year for them. Tom was considered the leading beeman in the county for many years. He and Inez acquired more property until they had title to 1,200 acres for cattle and horses, with some dry-land farming in addition to their honey business.

While Inez was busy raising a large family, she still found time to belong to the Women's Alliance of the Fillmore Presbyterian Church in 1903. She enjoyed the company of other members and doing things to help her community. She was mother to Norman, Frank, Elizabeth, Louise, Arthur, Allen, and Ernest. Both Inez and Tom adhered to high principles and standards in every facet of their lives.

My favorite story about Inez was a day she had driven her horse and buggy to town and did not start home until late afternoon. The tiny winding road up Pole Creek passed many large oak and black walnut trees along the way. The big branches often hung over the road and provided nice summer shade when they traveled. On this day, Inez found her gentle mare nervous and hard to control. Just as they went neared a big oak, Inez spotted a mountain lion crouched on a limb and ready to drop down on them. With a wild yell and her buggy whip, the horse quickly lunged under the tree and down the narrow road toward home. Only a true pioneer accepted every situation in stride and took the appropriate action. She arrived home without mishap. What a woman!

Sarah Jane Thompson Shiells

Sarah Thompson was born in England in 1865 and came to the United States in 1892. She married William Shiells the following year. Her Scotsman husband and his brother, Jim, had acquired 1,200 acres in Bardsdale and Guiberson Road adjacent to Fillmore. Montebello Oil Company leased 880 acres and discovered oil there in 1911.

William and Sarah lived in the Somis area for several years before moving to Fillmore. Their first house was near Santa Clara River, but it was moved up the canyon near a large spring of water where it stood until destroyed by brush fires in 2003. William originally developed 175 acres of their holding into citrus and walnuts, and that soon expanded to about 400 acres of orchards. After the discovery of oil on their land, they built the large family home on Guiberson Road, which is still owned by a grandson.

They had four children: Helen, Jim, Lester, and William. Sarah and William moved to Fillmore the day before her third son, William, was born in 1903. She had driven a loaded wagon from her old home in Somis to her new one on Guiberson Road and delivered her baby the next day. Pioneer women were expected to do everything that was needed.

After her husband died in 1922, Sarah had a house built on citrus land they owned in town on the corner of Central Avenue and Second Street, and she lived there until her death in 1952. She gave over an acre of that orchard as the site for the Veterans Memorial Building around 1950.

When the Thomas Bard property was taken over by the navy near Hueneme, his little chapel was moved to Fillmore to become Trinity Episcopal Church in 1933. Mr. Stephens donated the land from his orchard, and Sarah Shiells paid the moving cost to relocate the building on Saratoga Street. It is still used by an active congregation. Sarah was always a lady but also a pioneer and generous to her community.

Sarah Nova King
by Dick Mosbarger

Sarah King was born in 1892 to William and Margaret King in November (hence the middle name) 1892 in Hastings, Nebraska. She lived with her parents and two brothers and a sister in a sod cabin until 1900 when they came to Fillmore by train at the urging of Mr. Arundell, who was a friend of William King. They lived in the adobe cabin up Pole Creek for a time until they moved to property on B Street in Fillmore where William farmed apricots.

Sarah graduated with the first class from Fillmore High School in 1911. She attended normal school in Los Angeles from 1911 to 1913 and became a teacher. She taught elementary school at Mound School in Santa Paula for two years. She became interested in missionary work, having been raised as a Methodist, and enrolled in schooling to become a missionary. Upon completion of her schooling, she was sent to Southern Rhodesia in Africa where she served for thirty-five years. Besides her missionary work, she taught the Rhodesian women and girls

how to sew as well as other types of domestic needs. She also assisted
the men wherever her help could be used. One story that is told is that
Sarah heard a lot of men outside yelling and hollering, and when she
went out to see, they were gathered near a big snake; but no one was
attempting to kill it. So Sarah picked up a hoe that was handy, killed it,
and went back inside. She earned a lot of respect over that act.

She came home for a visit every five or six years, but in 1944, she
returned home because of the war in Africa. She was on a ship heading
for the East Coast of the US when it was torpedoed by a German
submarine. She and most of the passengers and crew were put into
lifeboats and put adrift in the Atlantic. They were in the boats for
twelve to fourteen hours before being rescued by a military ship, and
during that time, one of the women in Sarah's boat had a baby. Sarah
helped care for that baby until they were rescued, and she said the most
surprised person on that ship was the seaman to whom she handed
the newly born baby. They were brought to Newport News, Virginia,
and from there, she returned home to Fillmore. She stayed at home in
Fillmore until 1945. Then she returned to Africa and continued her
mission until 1952 when she returned home.

Back in California, she and her sister Wilma purchased a home in
La Crescenta and lived there until Wilma passed away in 1963. She
then moved to a missionary retirement home in Pasadena until 1976
when she returned to Fillmore and began living with her sister Nettie
and brother-in-law Glen Mosbarger. Glen died in 1978, and Sarah and
Nettie lived together until Sarah passed away in 1985.

EARLY DAY FAMILIES

Lawrence Hinckley

The past week has been a busy one getting things ready at Rancho
Camulos Museum for the SPRING FIESTA on Sunday, May 7. About
three weeks ago, we had an Artists' Day, and forty people came to paint
and draw and make photographs of that lovely old ranch. The history

is enough to make you come, but the gardens will bring you back. Our Spring Fiesta is designed to showcase the artists' work with the addition of old-time art of spinning, weaving, carving, and embroidery. With food, music and dancing, it will be a full day of entertainment and education. I hope you all come out and play with us.

However, that is not the idea behind my column this week, but it did make me think about Lawrence Hinckley—our local favorite artist from the past. Lawrence was born in Fillmore. His grandfather was Fillmore's first resident doctor. His father was our dentist. Lawrence's parents were Ira Hinckley and Kate Cruson Hinckley. Lawrence always loved to draw, and I suspect his cartoons kept him busy in class more often than his math lessons. Everyone in town knew about Lawrence's funnies and enjoyed seeing what Lawrence would do next. In later years, as a member of Rotary Club, he often added his original designs to their programs and newsletters.

As so often happens, Lawrence found the love of his life and married Mildred. They soon turned the old barn at the back of the First Street home property into a dwelling. The old peppertree that had provided shade for the team of horses was soon put to use to provide shade for parties as artists congregated there for many afternoons.

Lawrence did some serious paintings and was well-known in Southern California. While Shiveley painted birds, Lawrence became known for painting eucalyptus trees. Many local homes still have one of his paintings—our personal favorite was a seascape Lawrence did at their Carpinteria beach house. Gene refuses to let me give away HIS Hinckley canvas filled with grays and ocean waves. It is beautiful, and we can smell the ocean just by looking at it. I guess our daughters will have to cut cards to see who inherits it someday.

Fillmore's Central Avenue had a tour bus plowing through town on a regular basis every Wednesday for several years. We all knew it was headed for the Artists' Barn—everyone wanted to see the unique building and the people who lived there.

In the late 1940s, the Hinckleys also sold ceramic items made in the backroom. At one time, a dozen Fillmore ladies worked at casting and hand painting scissors holders, vases, and the original spoon rest—all ideas that Lawrence and Mildred came up to pay the rent. After WWII, the Japanese economy soon recovered, and similar things were sold at a much lower cost; after a few years, another small Fillmore business bit the dust.

The *Fillmore Herald* in 1926 told about Lawrence entering the Eisteddfod Art Exhibit in Oxnard. At that time, he was still a student at the Otis Art Institute in Los Angeles. His oil painting of a Mexican man with a sombrero and serape brought home the second prize; a pastel garnered first place. He was starting to make a name for himself. At the same art exhibit, Teresa Basolo won first place in piano for children under the age of eight. Ah, the way talent gets started. (Does anyone know anything about this art exhibit? I would love more details, so please call me.)

Many in Fillmore still fondly remember Lawrence and Mildred Hinckley. They put Fillmore on the map with Southern California artists in the 1950s. One wall of the old barn is still filled with signatures of well-known people who visited there—the past has so much to tell us.

(A note from Ruth Arrasmith reminded me that Lawrence did a cartoon for Clarence Arrasmith's weekly column "Over the Back Fence" and also did the illustrations for the city annual report.)

George and Hattie King

When we think about early pioneer families, we remember George and Hattie King. These two early Santa Clara Valley residents married in the Piru Methodist Church in 1896. He worked for the Cook enterprises in Piru Canyon.

Hattie was born in the California gold town of El Dorado. Her father had been a Pony Express rider, and her mother came to California in a covered wagon. She came to Fillmore at age twelve and made her home with an aunt, Mrs. S. A. Guiberson.

George started life in Iowa and lived in Kansas before coming to California. Early in the century, he became agent for Thomas Bard, who originally owned all of Bardsdale. Soon the Kings bought their own parcel of land and gradually added to their holdings. George was an early director of Southside Improvement Company, Ciénega Water Company, and Kiroba Water Company. He also served on the board of the Fillmore Citrus Fruit Association.

Hattie was active in the Bardsdale Methodist Church and taught Sunday school for over fifty years. She served as president of the Ventura County Epworth League, Women's Home Missionary Society, and Women's Christian Temperance Union. In 1955, she was named their Mother of California. She truly was a mother to all and furnished a home and financial support to a number of promising young people who made a name for themselves as adults.

When the Fillmore, Sespe, San Cayetano, Bardsdale, Willow Grove, and Ciénega Schools formed the Fillmore Union High School District, George King was elected president of the new board of trustees. He and Hattie financed the first building in which the school opened. It was located on Second Street across from the old Ebell Club. They continued to support the growth of the district as the present school site was bought and the first buildings erected in1911. In 1963, the yearbook was dedicated to Hattie King and Fergus Fairbanks in appreciation of their service to the school.

The Kings enjoyed visiting mission stations all over the world after their two daughters, Agnus and Ona, were grown. George and Hattie were present for the unveiling of a pulpit dedicated to them at a station in India. Their help and influence were appreciated at home and abroad. They were from the old school of pioneers who thought "by their works shall you know them."

The Arundells

Tom Arundell and his wife made the long journey from Iowa, seeking a better life. They brought along their son, Thomas Franklin, who was nine years old. According to the family story, the three came by boat to Panama and crossed the isthmus by horseback and surrey. A side-wheeler took them on to Oregon. Mrs. Arundell died from tuberculosis in 1865. Young Tom and his father made several trips back to Iowa where the older Arundell worked as a stonemason. They returned to California, and the 1870 census lists Tom Arundell as being a forty-nine-year-old farmer with his wife, Jane. They were living near Saticoy, and his property was valued at $3,750 with personal property worth $1,200. The current freeway has a bridge across the Arundell Barranca, which was near their home. Tom continued to work as a stonemason and helped construct the Ayers Hotel in Ventura and several other buildings as the little town grew.

The local census for 1880 shows Tom at age fifty-nine and a wife named Amanda and three small children. He was still working as a stonemason. Tom died in 1882 and was buried in the old Ventura City Cemetery on Main Street (now a city park).

In 1879, at the age of twenty-four, young Tom bought his first colony of bees and took them by wagon to Pole Creek and put them on government land. This was about the time that Thomas More had been killed over water rights to Sespe Creek and the boundaries of the land he bought from Rancho Sespe (that is another story). The following year, Tom took out six tons of honey from his numerous hives. Fillmore was just a few scattered houses and had no post office or railroad, but the surrounding sagebrush was good for honey production. Tom homesteaded up Pole Creek and started acquiring additional property around his home. He eventually accumulated 1,200 acres in and around the canyon.

He married Inez Kellogg in Santa Paula on April 27, 1881, and they lived there for a few years. By 1885, he finished a rammed-earth house in Pole Creek, and the young couple and two sons, Norman and Frank, moved in. His honey business continued, and he was considered the leading beeman in the state of California for many years.

Tom expanded into horses, cattle, and some dry-land farming as his family grew. The last child was born in 1894. His family of seven children was Norman, Frank, Elizabeth, Louise, Arthur, Allen, and Ernest. By 1898, Tom was a trustee of the Fillmore Grammar School and interested in local activities.

My favorite story about Inez was the day she had driven her horse and buggy to Fillmore and got a fright on the way home late in the afternoon. The road up Pole Creek was narrow with many overhanging trees to shade the way. Her horse started acting up, and as she struggled to control it, she spotted a mountain lion on a large branch getting ready to pounce on them. With a quick flip of the reins, they went in a full run along the rocky road and got away without a mishap. So another mountain lion missed an Arundell dinner! I wonder if she told the kids about that while she cooked supper.

As the kids grew and were able to help with some of the chores, Tom had more time and developed an interest in oil on his land and the neighboring properties. During his life, the land never produced oil, but Tom was always interested in the anticlines and inspected every place along the road into his homestead, seeking more knowledge about oil prospects. Big oil companies had holdings all around him, and Tom held out hope.

Thomas Franklin Arundell was not a large man physically, but his general presence made him seem larger than life. He had a mustache and usually was decked out in a full suit and hat when he was not at work. His formal education was almost nil, but he was very literate and self-taught. His knowledge of geology came from books and his own interest in seeking rock outcrops and anticlines. Tom seldom missed a day of going into the post office after it was established in Fillmore. He drove a horse and buggy until he purchased one of the first Model T Fords in town.

High principles and standards were important to Tom Arundell, and he adhered to them. He was well respected and abstained from liquor and tobacco all his life. In his later years, he often leased parts of his land for different ventures and encountered disappointments, but he loved the challenge of new things. He died of pneumonia in 1938 at the home of his daughter Elizabeth Homburg, who lived at the mouth of the canyon. That was probably the line cabin where Rod Leidy now resides. Tom lived a full and fruitful life for eighty-three years, and there are still many of his descendants in Ventura County. Most of this info came from Bob Phillips and E. M. Sheridan. (If any of the family has more stories, please give me a call.)

The Baldens

Julius Balden's mother came from Germany, and his father, from Switzerland. The original family name was Baldeschwieler and was shortened to Balden.

Julius arrived in Fillmore-Bardsdale on October 11, 1891, and went to work shucking corn for twelve cents per half hour. They were living in Bardsdale when their two sons, Harold and Lloyd, were born.

When Julius and Ella moved to town, they bought twenty acres on the south side of Ventura Street between Central and A Streets, with River Street the south property line. The ten acres were already planted to navel oranges and about ten years old. Julius planted the balance in Valencia oranges, and the new little trees were all bare root when they were put into the ground. About 1950, Julius told Gene Wren, an employee, that one year, he cleared enough off his crop to pay the total price of the land and all the improvements of the orchard. Orange prices early in the 1900s were high, and making a living was easier than the present time.

Julius built a rather large three-bedroom house on the NE corner of his property with a forty- or fifty-foot front yard. Water for the orchard irrigation was secured from Sespe Land and Water Company through an open ditch between Ventura Street and the orchard. The Baldens were at the end of the line for water, and often many unnecessary items were floated through to them. It was Harold's job to clean out the screens every two days—he often found dead rats, ground squirrels, and other small animals in the water. The house had a cistern to collect rainwater for home use. The first drilled well was in their backyard (just west of the garage), and at 110 feet, they hit the brownstone formation, so it was probably a long-ago part of Sespe Creek now located far to the west of their house.

Dr. John Hinckley had a large two-story house across Central with a big front yard also (SE corner of Ventura and Central). He was handy when the boys needed attention. One time, Harold cut his hand rather badly at school, and when he went home, Dr. Hinckley just taped it up; but it healed okay. (Harold was getting a cookie at school from one of the kids who had the cookies in a metal can, and Harold ripped his hand on the edge of the can when he took out his hand.)

Harold and his brother, Lloyd, went to school in a two-room building on the corner of Sespe and Mountain View. First to sixth grades were in one room, and seventh to eighth were in the other. Later, the old school was moved to Sespe and Clay (a four-square church site) when the new larger school was built. The first high school was up near the Ebell Club. Later, the high school was relocated to the present site on Central and First Streets. Harold had twenty-one graduates in his class in 1921. His favorite subject was math, and he played basketball and tennis. He attended Davis for one year and then transferred to Chaffee JC, as they had a better citrus program than Davis. He graduated from Chaffee.

Harold and Lloyd usually rode their bikes to school, but on a rainy day, their father would hitch up the buggy and take them to school. The Baldens had a cow, and often when there was extra milk, Harold made deliveries to their neighbors by bike. Their bikes were an important entertainment item for the boys. Often a group of boys would ride to Santa Paula and, without even stopping, come back to Fillmore. Harold took violin lessons and played in the school orchestra, and his mother played piano. Since the boys had to cross the railroad tracks to get to school, it was necessary they be very careful. One day, a cow got on the tracks and was hit by the train and dragged a rather long way before the train could stop, and the boys witnessed it all, so they were cautious crossing the tracks for school or going to town on errands for their parents. Most of their clothing and shoes and food were purchased at the United Mercantile store on the corner of Main and Central Avenue.

Like most boys of this era, Harold and Lloyd worked—they irrigated and hauled fruit with a balky team. When those horses laid back their ears, you knew you were in for trouble. Often they would have to unload the fruit, get the horse going again, and then reload the boxes—it was not a happy time, and the boys and Julius tried suggestions from everyone to CURE those horses. Eventually, one of the men told Harold to rig up a telephone and put the wire under the horse's tail, and when they started to balk to just give it one long ring to get them going. Before Harold got his phone installed, his father sold the team and got rid of the problem.

Fillmore had some apricots that were irrigated, so the pitting shed in summer always needed more help to get the fruit ready for drying. The community had pie suppers and ice cream socials and many fun things to entertain young people. The family attended the Presbyterian Church and then changed for a time to Methodist and then went back to Presbyterian, and every church had special things to keep kids busy. Julius was a good neighbor. He and a friend would give the post office extra money before Christmas to help pay postage for people who brought in packages and did not have enough to pay for the mailing. He was also a faithful 10 percent tither. Julius planted the fan palms along Ventura Street, and some are still growing on the north side of the street. When the highway was changed from Santa Clara Street to Ventura Street down to A Street, Julius had the paving contractor put in a curb on his side of the street so when it needed to be widened, he had a nice curb between the road and his orchard.

Most of the streets were dirt, and a wagon sprinkled them in the summer to help keep down the dust. The only hard-surface streets were a little part of Main and Central Avenue. In later years, when Harold was on the city council, a bid was let to put black top on several more blocks for civic improvement. Some of that black top still remains under the present surface. Julius's first car was an E-M-F 30 touring car. By the time Harold was courting Mary Foster, there was a Model T in the family.

After Harold and Mary married, they lived in a little house on the north side of Ventura Street. Later, they moved to the old McNab place on the NW corner of First and Saratoga. (The huge sycamore tree in this front yard was the location of the apricot-pitting sheds when Harold was a boy. It was cut down in 1996 by new owners.) They both loved to travel and went almost everywhere but China (borders were closed to travelers) and Russia, though they were within fifty miles, but during the Cold War, Americans were not welcomed there either. Their plane landed on three engines during one trip, and they got into a revolution in Portugal, but it was exciting, and they loved it.

Fishing had been a PASSION for Harold since he was a boy. He won a contest, and the prize was a rod and reel—this let him compete with just about anyone on bragging rights for the most fish or the largest. Native steelhead trout filled Sespe Creek and Santa Clara River, and the two large holes near the bridge on the Sespe would yield up a fifty-trout limit most anytime he wanted to go fishin'. Harold loved to eat fried trout or anything else he was able to catch. The fishing trip to June Lake was a summer highlight for his family through the years.

Julius had the usual Fillmore rancher's house on the Rincon so wives could escape the heat in the summer, and the kids had plenty of time to grunion hunting and surf fishing and fry up a mess when they hit it good.

Harold's favorite food was ice cream, and his mother had a very special recipe that was often used for her family. Harold had many BIG bowls till the bottom of the tin can was scraped clean. One day, they were invited to a neighbor's place for ice cream dessert, and they knew Harold's legendary appetite would be there, so he was served the largest bowl. His expectations were dashed when he discovered it was a poor recipe for ice cream, and he was stuck with a huge bowl that was not very good but was expected to clean up—which he did, but he never wanted ice cream at their house again.

When Harold came home from college, he went to work on the ranch. Fruit was hauled by team and wagon to the orange packinghouse on A Street and Sespe with sixty-four field boxes for a load.

Julius belonged to the Woodman Lodge, but Harold joined the Masonic group and was very active in both Masons and Eastern Star with Mary. Both of them held high offices and made contacts and friends all over the United States.

Other Families

In working on the First Families for the fiesta at Rancho Camulos Museum, I found several little things I thought might interest some of you. (Yes, we had fifty-four centennial families who received certificates, and we will continue working on this project and keeping all the information on file at the museum for future use.)

Domingo Hardison was always a question with me. His two names were so different ethnically, and yet they belonged to a well-known local man. There was no problem, but they just didn't go together in my mind. Did you know his father was active in gold mining in Peru, and the family was living there at the Santa Domingo mine when he was born? Yep! Now we know where his name came from.

William and Sarah Shiells lived in Saticoy before they moved to a new homestead on Guiberson Road. The last day of the move, Sarah drove wagon all day and delivered another son, Lester, the next day. Not many of us ladies can top that story! Their land holdings became the largest family citrus ranch in the area in the following years. When oil was found on their hill in the early '20s, they had money to expand the farm operations. The William Shiells Company was a great supporter of community projects and donated land for the Veterans Memorial Building after WWII.

Julius and John Baldeschwieler were born in Illinois. Their father was Swiss, and their mother was German. They migrated to California and settled in Bardsdale in 1891. Both married and had families. All this area was being developed into citrus orchards, and they did the same thing. Julius moved to town and farmed the twenty-three acres that is now the shopping center known as Balden Plaza. (Yes, they shortened their name.) After Gene Wren went to work for Julius, the elderly man told him that one year, he cleared enough to pay for the land and all the improvements on it and still provide for his family. That must have been the heyday for oranges in this valley.

Carlos and Celestina Basolo settled in Illinois when they arrived from Italy. Carlos worked in the coal mines there. They arrived in Ventura County in 1895 and settled into farming. They were parents of ten children. (No wonder we often find someone who is a descendant.)

William C. Brockus was born in Indiana. After the death of his wife and four of his children, he came to Fillmore with his one remaining son. They homesteaded land on Grand Avenue, Sespe. Several of the Brockus kids are still in this part of the county.

The year of 1891 found Ernest Case arriving in Fillmore from Minnesota. His journal notes he is "getting fat and the climate is GREAT." He soon went to work for Union Oil for $2.50 a day and also worked part-time for ranchers. He stayed active with the oil companies and helped form the co-op stores in Fillmore and Piru and the Fillmore Citrus Fruit Association. Ernest was interested in the schools, irrigation companies, and the president of the Rand United Mining Company. He was only forty-eight when he died, but he left his mark on Fillmore.

Soon after the Civil War, Thomas Jefferson Casner came to Julian, California, via wagon from Texas. By 1872, they were in Ventura County. They must have lived east of Fillmore, as a picture of the old Ciénega School shows Tom as one of thirty students. (The story about the trip from Texas will be in my column soon.)

As the railroads were being built, families came West with them. Ignacio and Amanda Avalos Ortega arrived in this area from El Paso in 1904. He worked for Southern Pacific and came to Piru. He worked for Camulos and sharecropped. Later, he leased land from Newhall Ranch and dry-land farmed grain. He sold his crop to Ray Lindenfeld in Fillmore.

Yes, we have a wonderful assortment of people living in Fillmore, and everyone is welcome to join in the fun and be part of our community.

More Pioneer Families

Raymond Holley arrived in this area around 1887 from Michigan via train. He cleared land, planted orchards, and soon was known for great-tasting Sespe and Hopper honey. One year, he shipped forty-two tons.

The parents of Samuel Earl Campbell got to Fillmore a few months before he arrived—he wanted to finish his education at Kansas University and graduate after a successful year as quarterback for their football team, so he was not in a rush to make the move west. The whole family moved to Grand Avenue in 1913, and descendants are still living there.

Missouri folks saw Jacob Michel depart for Bardsdale in 1886. He soon paid Bard $150 an acre for fifteen acres of land to plant prunes, peaches, apples, walnuts, and eventually oranges. His wife had thirty-three acres, and they combined the operations and called it SUMMER ORANGE RANCH.

After Frank Dudley settled in Sespe in 1875, they got bees and, one year, shipped fifty thousand pounds of honey. The blooming sage and orange trees gave local honey a wonderful flavor.

Elijah Fairbanks left Nebraska in 1876 and called Fillmore home in 1907. His son, Fergus, was a charter member of the Fillmore Rotary Club and worked at the Fillmore State Bank before passing the California bar exam in 1919 and becoming a local lawyer.

Frank Erskine was a schoolteacher in commercial subjects in Vermont but pulled up stakes and took a bookkeeping job with a new packinghouse in Whittier in 1908. He accepted the job as manager of the Fillmore Citrus Fruit Association in 1913. By 1926, it was the largest in the state. In 1931, he retired from that job and was part of the founding fathers for Ramona Building and Loan Association and provided funding for many homes in Fillmore.

Adolph Haase came from German around 1884, and after a couple of years, his brother Rudolph arrived and settled in Bardsdale. Rudolph had three dollars in his pocket when he arrived, but he worked hard. In 1892, he claimed his bride and brought her from Posen, Germany, to start his family. In 1893, he bought land near the Bardsdale Church. The couple lived very frugally, and by 1908, he was able to build his growing family a large two-story house on Simi Street. The living room was used by five of the six kids to practice their music most evening, and the Haase family had their own orchestra. Some of his great-grandkids still carry on the music tradition.

William Shank King arrived from Nebraska in 1900, and the family stayed with the Arundells in Pole Creek until he settled into raising apricots and built a house in town on B Street. His son Dale homesteaded up Piru Canyon and son Morris bought a ranch in the same area, and their descendants still live there.

William Sherman Mosbarger came to Fillmore from Bolivar, Missouri, in 1911. He was a teamster hauling hay over the grade to Somis and oil-field equipment up Sespe.

The same year brought John A. Galvin to town. The ink was barely dry on his new University of Michigan law degree, and he was anxious to put it to work. Soon it was time for the hamlet of Fillmore to incorporate, and John got the job of drawing up the papers. He also become the first city attorney for Fillmore and held that job longer than anyone else in the same position in the state. His siblings were soon also residents in Fillmore and active in town.

C. C. Elkins is probably the best-known early resident of Fillmore. He was the first general merchandise storeowner and had a building on Main Street near the depot. He came to Fillmore in 1887 from Indiana after teaching school in Kansas and driving an ox wagon to Colorado and later to California. Yes, he was experienced! As the first justice of the peace, he became Judge Elkins and is still known as such. He set out the first orange orchard on his land where the golf course is now located. He built the first packinghouse to handle and ship the fruit. After setting out an olive grove, he made olive oil and sold it. C. C. Elkins was active in everything in Fillmore. A favorite story is told that he carried his shoes to work from the ranch house and did not put them on until he got to town. While others are laughing about being so frugal, I think he probably just took them off when he got to the river and had to wade across before the Bardsdale Bridge was constructed. No one wants to get good leather shoes wet and then have to wear them all day!

The parents of Harvey S. Patterson came to California from Kansas for health reasons. When they got to Fillmore, Mr. Patterson went to work at the Fillmore co-op and, in 1919, took over as manager for Hickey Brothers Hardware on Central Avenue. When they were ready to close down their store, Harvey bought it from them, and it is still in business. Patterson Hardware is celebrating one hundred years on Central Avenue this year, and no other business in town can make that statement.

William and Rebecca Mayhew left the state of New York for California about 1890, and their grown son, Milton Mayhew, settled in Bardsdale a bit before 1912. The family had orchards and eventually a diary and sold bottled milk to the local households.

Brothers Dietrich and Henry Bartels left Illinois around 1898, and each secured land in Bardsdale and started farming.

C. W. Hawthorn settled in Los Angeles, but by 1915, he thought Fillmore looked like a good place to live, so he moved and went into business here.

New York was the birthplace of Orson Goodenough. He married Zedora Tietsort in Iowa, and they arrived in Fillmore in 1877 after two years in Ventura. The family farm land ran up the east side of Sespe Canyon, and the road now carries his name.

When Frank Atmore arrived from Michigan in 1886, he bought 148 acres of the old Rancho Sespe and set it out in walnuts and citrus.

Illinois waved goodbye to Robert F. and Sarah Robertson when he took an ox wagon and headed toward California. Eventually, they homesteaded near Santa Paula before settling on two hundred acres in Bardsdale. Their son, Thomas, was born there in 1882 and continued farming his father's land, which was planted with walnuts, lemons, and oranges with early day oil wells.

Fillmore-Bardsdale has three unrelated King families. Chalmers King bought land on Guiberson Road around 1913 and moved from the Paso Robles area. His original eighty acres was planted with walnuts and grain.

Siblings Rosie and L. W. Fansler left Nebraska around 1890 for California. Rosie married Ike Cooms and settled in Bardsdale by 1900, and L. W.—with his wife, Dora—arrived in Fillmore two years later.

Charles Barnard came to California from Illinois in 1877 and ranched in Fillmore before expanding his interests to Ventura.

A native of Vermont, Frank H. Padelford bought a tract of land near Buckhorn in 1887 and planted thirty-two acres of oranges.

Alexander Phillips established a truck farm on eighty acres in Bardsdale in 1880. He later became the owner of a grocery store, and the family was active near Rancho Sespe.

Even Canada lost citizens to the California boom. H. E. Peyton left his home country in 1886 and secured thirty-nine acres of the Sespe Ranch to plant to apricots, walnuts, and citrus.

Elijah B. Fairbanks left Nebraska and arrived in Ventura County in 1876 and started building wharves in Hueneme and other locations between Ventura and Santa Barbara.

R. A. Fremlin was a native of England who immigrated to the United States in 1892. Soon he took up roots in Bardsdale with ninety acres of land that he planted with citrus, walnuts, and apricots.

John Guiberson and his brothers left Ohio and headed for California around 1850. His large home and barn were on the south side of the river, and that road became our current Guiberson Road. The barn is still standing.

The Last Great Migration

Even after the turn of the century, California kept calling to the Midwest. In the 1920s, Sam and Zella Myers pulled up their Oklahoma stakes and headed for California with three small children and landed in Fillmore where he found work on a local citrus ranch. After a few years, they had added several more kids to the family, and Sam started his own citrus nursery. Not too long after that, Thad and Nellie Davis settled in Fillmore. Thad quickly found work, and Nellie opened a small maternity home for new mothers. People took advantage of any opportunity that came along.

THE DEPRESSION in the 1930s moved more people around as men sought any possible job to support their families. The Dust Bowl moved many from the Oklahoma and Texas Panhandles, but many others in the Midwest also headed for California with the hope of finding employment. Many of these men had been farmers, so they looked for areas with farm jobs, and Fillmore soon had their share of more new families working at any available packinghouse or ranch job.

Many families rented houses in the unincorporated section of town known as North Fillmore. Like all immigrants, people clustered together near friends or others who understood their circumstances, and all worked together to start a new life in a new state.

From about 1935 to the start of WWII, Fillmore schools grew with the increase of kids from Oklahoma and surrounding states. Dads worked on ranches, moms at the packinghouse, and the kids attended school because their folks preached to them every day to "get your education because no one can take that away from you." Those kids knew about the work ethic and practiced it for the rest of their lives. They were careful with their money and credit, and most were successful. Fillmore kids from Oklahoma became top scholars and good athletes. They were drafted and served their country. Both boys and girls attended college, married, and started families.

I know many of these people (now my age) became useful citizens and stayed active in service clubs to promote the community. Some were elected to the Fillmore school board or city council. We have ranch and packinghouse managers, nurses, bankers, teachers and school administrators, WACS and WAVES (women in the WWII military), career military officers, entomologists, writers, accountants, building contractors, musicians, engineers of all sorts, business owners, oil field workers, preachers, firemen and paramedics, policemen, mayors, and Ventura County sheriff; and one was Oxnard City treasurer for twenty years. And don't forget the gals who stayed at home and became thrifty, hardworking housewives and PTA presidents and Girl Scout leaders. Those kids worked hard and did well!

Here are a few of the men whom I know brought their families to Fillmore during this time:

- James Claudie Taylor arrive in 1936 and went to work for Mr. Gazzaway at his service station.
- George W. Wren and family came in 1941.
- Clifford Butler, Levi Carpenter with brothers Wilbur and Fred.
- Barney Blyth, Malcom and Carl Jackson, and the Ballards settled here about 1937.
- Hendersons, Collins, Breshears, Wallaces, and Hills all came.

This list barely touches the surface.

Many of these families sponsored (encouraged) other friends and families to move west. Often they gave them a place to live and helped them find jobs until the new families were able to be independent and take care of themselves. Like all people with a common heritage, they often lived and worked near each other and shared the good times and the tough times.

After a few years, the new immigrant kids grew up and were marrying the local ranch kids, and now we are mostly just one big happy family. Now you can't tell the difference unless you start checking into genealogy.

No story about the people in Fillmore would be complete without mentioning the Villasenor family. Herky Villasenor was in charge of feeding the camp of braceros during WWII. Many men from Mexico were recruited to work in the United States at that time. They fulfilled a great labor need during the war when so many men were in the military. Housing, food, and medical attention were provided for them; and Herky did the cooking. Several of the braceros married local girls and stayed in Fillmore. Our own dear friends Joe and Isabel Galvan were among them. The Villasenor and Galvan families were active in the community and contributed so much to improving Fillmore. These men were also among the last great migration.

Almost a Hero

Our family almost got to claim Gene Wren as a hero. While our son Steven was serving in Vietnam and earning a Bronze Star for helping rescue a local friend, Louis Villasenor, and getting him to a hospital in the middle of an incident, Gene was accidently almost getting a medal too.

One day, our mail brought a very official envelop from the Carnegie Institute for Bravery with a letter to Gene saying they would be awarding him a medal for bravely rescuing men from a lion's den. It took us a few minutes to sort out their facts and get them into the correct perspective, so here is the real story. Yes, while we were laughing our heads off, we figured it out.

Each year at festival time, the *Fillmore Herald* printed a small extra newspaper that was ALL SPOOFS. The *Pole Creek Bugle* took single local items and made them into a fun-filled event and kidded as many people in Fillmore as possible. Everyone loved reading it to see what Editor Ham Riggs came up with each year. Locals knew it was just for fun with almost no fact in it. Well, the Carnegie Institute did not know it was all spoofs. They thought it was all facts. Fillmore folks knew it was all fun.

Now this is what actually happened. The Lions Club in Fillmore sponsored Scout Troop 406 and used the Scout building as their regular meeting place twice a month. The building was enclosed with chain-link fencing for security, and the scoutmaster left the gate open on meeting nights so the Lions could do their barbecue and have a meeting.

One night during the meeting, kids came by and closed the gate and snapped the open padlock so "everything was secure" while the men were all inside. When the members were ready to leave two hours later, they discovered they were all locked inside the fence and no one had a key. This was before anyone had a cell phone, so they used the inside pay phone to call Scoutmaster Gene Wren to bring a key and open the gate. He arrived shortly, let the men out, and they all went home.

The *Pole Creek Bugle* said Gene had rescued the men from a lion's den and saved them all. It was a major spoof on the club. Somehow the Carnegie Institute read the story in the *Pole Creek Bugle* and thought they had found a local hero. I quickly wrote the Carnegie Institute to explain the whole affair, and our local sheriff, Dick Diaz, wrote them to confirm my story. Gene was off the hook.

Well, I guess Gene did rescue a group of men from the Lions Club den (also called the Scout building) that evening, but it was not worthy of a hero's medal for bravery from the Carnegie Institute. My daughters and I still remember the men in our family who were our heroes. We have tears for one and laughs for the other.

Chapter 13

WWII

WWII Started

As WWII veterans and other folks from that era, we are losing more and more of our stories and history. If you have family members who can repeat some of their memories to you, please write them down. In a few more generations, those stories will be the source of pride and interest in your family.

I don't feel old, but my body keeps reminding me that I am way past my prime in doing things in our community. I can still write (with the aid of a computer) and try to keep life interesting by telling the rest of you stories I know. The class of 2006 probably won't believe many of the things I will tell you this week, but these are FACTS.

When the Japanese attack Pearl Harbor, many rural families still did not have a radio, but word soon spread within every community that we were at WAR. Newspapers were passed around so everyone could read about what was happening. My grandmother said the United States had a war every generation and the time from 1918 and WWI to 1940 just about proved that.

The United States had been self-sufficient forever! If we wanted it, if we needed it, if we thought about it, we did it! That was just the American way. Inventors came up with new ideas; we built factories, and we made it. Our country had the basic raw materials and manpower to do what was necessary. Rubber was about the only thing we had to import, and there was no way we could grow that within our borders. We had just about everything else.

Recruiting for WWII

The Inadomi family was Fillmore's only Japanese residents when WWII started. They were well respected in the community, active, and well-liked. Their son was an Eagle Scout, Mr. Inadomi was active with Rotary, and the family owned a grocery store on Main Street. When the notice came for them to be interned, letters were quickly dispatched asking for their exemption as Fillmore felt sure they were loyal and would not be a problem. These requests were all denied, and the family left Fillmore and never returned. It was truly a loss for our community.

Our country started gearing up immediately. Troops were trained, factories built, and everyone put their shoulder to the wheel and pushed hard! California had blackouts along the coast. Fortifications were installed to repulse an enemy invasion after subs fired on us in Gaviota. A spotter tower was installed behind Fillmore Club in Central Avenue and was manned to watch for enemy aircraft. Almost every home had a Victory garden to grow additional food for home consumption. Gasoline was rationed for cars to three or four gallons a week with a class-A sticker; the speed limit was set at thirty-five miles an hour, and tires were not to be had. Shoes were rationed at one pair a year, and sugar and meat were rationed. People went to work in defense factories and did all they could to keep the war effort on track. Many in Fillmore worked at the base (Port Hueneme).

People left ag to do more essential work, which left the fields and packinghouses around here rather bare. And who filled the gap? High school kids! Yep, the football and basketball and baseball players, and home-ec gals all turned to and went to real jobs. In 1942, school started early each morning. The shortened essential classes were covered for graduation requirements, and at noon, the work started. The packinghouses usually had one or two older men (nondraft age) who pushed, yelled, and shoved those fourteen- to seventeen-year-olds into getting the jobs done. Fruit, mostly oranges and lemons in Fillmore, was picked, packed, loaded onto rail cars, and shipped on time. Sugar beets were topped and harvested for the mill in Oxnard. Jobs continued during the summer, so vacations were short or nonexistent. It was hard to take a vacation since families had little gas or transportation to get out of town. Trains were packed with troops being moved from one base to another. It was a time to all work together.

Every empty tin can from the kitchen was washed, its bottom cut out, and then flattened to be recycled. Chewing gum, cigarettes, and toothpaste were all wrapped in paper with foil. That foil was carefully removed and rolled into a ball and saved. By the time you had a collection about the size of a golf ball, you dropped it into the collection bin at school. When iron was needed to make the steel for tanks and weapons, the schools had collection drives to find every piece of old iron in the county and get it off to war. Barns, backyards, fields, and barrancas were searched for iron of any type. (In Oklahoma, my class got into big trouble when we hauled an old cast iron bathtub out of a field—we won that contest until the farmer demanded his tub back because he used it to water his cattle. Well, we tried.)

The Red Cross ladies knitted socks, hats, and mittens and rolled bandages for field use. Old felt hats were cut up and made into baby shoes to keep little feet warm. Nutrition class taught about meal planning for large groups. (Yes, I worked on all these.) We traded recipes for cooking with less sugar and an old WWI cake recipe was used again. It was a sugarless, milkless, and butterless recipe—but tasted great. (I still use it for making fruitcakes.) Bacon drippings were carefully saved and turned in to help make ammo. I don't know the connection, but grease was a necessary part of the formula.

Schoolteachers were drafted, and I had three different ones for my chemistry class in Oklahoma in 1944. When boys became eighteen, they went into the service even though they were within a couple of months of graduation. Fortunately, most received their diplomas anyway, but they did not know that when they left. These boys knew they would be gone until the war was over. When they were sent out of the country, some had two or three years before they came home for a visit. They could usually only write letters to stay in touch with loved ones. They had no TV, cell phones, computers, or radios. They were lonesome and homesick but tried not to fuss about it.

After physicals, if new recruits did not pass for some reason, they were classified as 4F—not bodily fit for military duty. Several years ago, my new car tag started with 4F, so it was easy for me to remember. When I mentioned that to a younger person, they responded, "What is special about 4F, and what does that mean?" Oh, there is so much the kids these days don't know. Even people on Jeopardy often miss questions that are easy for people who lived during WWII.

For the current elders, it was a "BEEN THERE, DONE THAT" situation. We can't keep from wondering how the United States would fare in the same situation now. We don't even make all the parts that go into an airplane to keep it in the sky—everything is made somewhere else. We have few factories to make cloth, shoes, steel, or essential computer parts—man, looks to me like we would be up the creek without a paddle. I understand free trade, but there's no point in cutting off your nose to spite your face either. Our leaders had better work for PEACE as we can't handle anything else.

Heroes in Fillmore

Recently, I spent the afternoon at the library reading old *Fillmore Heralds* from 1944. That paper published all the weekly Fillmore news. It covered the usual new babies and deaths but also every meeting, party, engagement, and visitor in this area.

I started researching articles about the basketball team from 1943 to 1944. Gene played on that team, and I wanted more memories of his activities and awards. However, I got sidetracked into how things were going during WWII. Here are some of the local happenings:

Pastor William Orr joined the army but the local Presbyterian congregation stayed in touch with him through the Harry Felsenthal family. Marine Corps members Bob Huestis and Don McKendry accidently met each other "some place in the Pacific" (it is a small world). In March 1944, both Roy Hill and Kenneth Mumme got leaves to visit their Fillmore families. William Morage was stationed in the Aleutian Islands. A motorcycle accident kept Bob Gazzaway home longer than his official leave.

The Rotary Club had a speaker, George McCarthy, who was a friend of Mrs. Leland Schmittou's brother in the Philippines. The two families were put into a Japanese internment camp after the fall of Corregidor at the start of the war. The civilians were confined at the University at Manila (named Santo Tomas) and were treated slightly better than the American soldiers. Somehow, Mr. McCarthy was released and returned to the United States and did the program for Rotary. Our own Dick Schmittou remembers this uncle and his return to the United States after the war. His uncle Vernon Thompson weighed a full one hundred pounds when General MacArthur visited the prison and worked on getting the internees back home. The Thompson family, father, mother, and two children all survived the event.

Fillmore boys did Fillmore proud with their flying too. Lt. Robert Spitler was awarded the Distinguished Flying Cross for his work in the Mediterranean Theater. Evidently, Robert took his job as a P-38 fighter seriously. He flew over forty-five combat missions and escorted those Allied bombers as they limped back to England on a wing and a prayer.

GIs in WWII

Lt. Bob Hays received his Distinguished Flying Cross a few months after Robert. He was a pilot of a B-24 Liberator bomber and did over thirty flights over Germany and occupied Europe. He also held the Air Medal with three oak leaf clusters.

One of our local top gun WWII fighter pilots, according to local legend, flew UNDER Bardsdale Bridge. That must have been exciting even with less sand in the riverbed. If any of you know who did that, please give me a call. The story is too good to ignore, and I'd love to have more details.

While we had every available man serving in the military, the women were not to be outdone. Geneva Taylor joined the US Navy

WAVES and was assigned to a large naval shore station until the war was over. Sgt. Inez Haase was a member of the WACS and was attached to an army medical lab in Virginia. (In case you don't remember, these units were separate from the regular military and comprised of all women. They were assigned to noncombat positions, but each of them released an able bodied man for active duty where needed.)

In October 1944, Lt. George Burson was reported missing in action over Czechoslovakia. He was a copilot on a B-17 bomber. Fillmore lost several outstanding grads in all branches of the service. WWII was a long four years for us, but nothing compares to the current ten-year mess. We were taking care of ourselves, doing what was necessary, and soon won the war. Now we are bogged down in taking care of the whole world. Times change!

If you really want to know what the old bombers and fighter planes were like, visit the Commemorative Air Force when it visits the Camarillo Airport. They do an annual exhibit, and you can often go into the planes and see that only a thin sheet of aluminum, held together by rivets, protected our boys from enemy fire. Jerry Schleimer and her sister put in many of those rivets too. There will never be another war like WWII, and maybe that is good.

Wars in Korea, Vietnam, Desert Storm, Iraq, and Afghanistan keep bringing us more heroes—let's don't forget the personal sacrifice made by so many from our little town.

More Info on WWII

Several weeks ago, I spent three days with my teenage grandsons when their mother had to be out of town. This is usually the time when I have a chance to talk with them about lots of different things. Our oldest grandson was so involved with senior activities I scarcely saw him, but the younger one was working on an essay about gun control. One thing led to another after discussing both sides of that question, and we drifted into what it was like to be a teen during World War II.

I am still not sure he believed all the stuff I told him: When I was his age, we saved tinfoil ("What was that?"), toothpaste tubes ("What can you use those for?"), and carefully strained bacon drippings ("Why did you need that?"). We drove thirty-five miles an hour ("Didn't it take you a long time to get anywhere?"), saved our ration of sugar to make cookies to send to our boyfriends in the army ("What is rationing?"), hoped our shoes would last until we got our next stamp for another pair ("Why couldn't you just go buy a pair?"), and stood in line when the grocer got a carton of toilet paper to get one roll. If we were lucky, we hoped someone in the crowd had a car with good enough tires that by pooling our three-gallon gasoline stamps, we could make a trip to the lake to swim ("How far could you drive on just three gallons of gas?"). We applied leg makeup instead of wearing hose and soaked new calico-print material in salt and vinegar to try and set the color so a new dress looked new for a longer time. And, yes, skirts were a bit shorter to save fabric.

Needless to say, it was a trip down memory lane for me and a pretty far-fetched story for my grandson. I have no wish for a war, but I know as grandparents, perhaps it would be good to occasionally relate some of our stories to the kids and hope they understand how it affected our daily lives.

Maybe next time, his grandfather will tell him about going to school from seven to noon, having only intermural sports, and working afternoons till almost dark in the local fields or the packinghouse. Few foremen in a citrus house today could imagine what it was like to have four adults and a crew of kids ages fourteen to seventeen to keep things going. But they got the fruit packed and loaded into railcars for shipping and did the cleaning. The boys knew as soon as they turned eighteen, they would be going into the military. Most parents were employed in a war industry or military base, so the high schoolers did their best to keep things going in the community.

The grandpa in this house topped sugar beets, picked lemons, ran the press, and stacked fruit at the packinghouse. He was once fired for having too much fun while he worked even though he got his job done on time. The high schools did not have annuals that year as the paper had gone to war also. We all learned to make do with a lot less, planted Victory gardens, never wasted any kind of food, shared what we had, and went to church regularly to pray for the safe return of family and friends. Our evenings were spent inside studying, with the radio bringing us the HIT PARADE, or writing V-mail letters of one thin page to our boyfriends and cousins. We had no idea where they were stationed or if they were part of the last battle shown in the Paramount Newsreels at the Saturday matinee. The movie costs us twenty-five cents, but it also had a cartoon and the latest pictures of the war overseas, and it let us see how things were going for the United States and the Allies.

Nah, I guess there is no need in talking about it—the kids would never believe us. (You can see how the last five years have made even this column out-of-date—please explain to the kids the difference between V-mail and e-mail. And don't forget to write down you own memories to pass along.)

WWII: Japan/China

Many of you may have read my column "REMEMBER World War II" and the events leading up to it. I was a teen and as involved as any teenager in the war effort. My memory holds these truths to be self-evident. It was a tough time, but we knew what we were fighting for and who was the enemy and had faith that with hard work, we would win! We did!

During the late '30s and the Depression, the United States bought every item that Japan could produce. We accepted the fact many of the things were not quality products, but they were cheap and would do for us. We had very little money to spend, so cheap was good for most people.

The United States sold Japan every piece of scrap iron available from accumulated heaps in every town junkyard. We were glad to get rid of it. We didn't need it, and Japan was a ready market. The United State supplied Japan with lots of our junk. They were a small country with few resources and needed everything. We had it all, so why not share and get a few dollars for it in the process? We had factories and raw material to build anything we wanted. About the only thing we had to import was rubber.

It wasn't too many years until all that scrap metal came back to us as Japanese planes, ships, and ammo. Without us, they would never have had the resources to start the war. Then when we won, we saw it as our duty to rebuild their country and economy. It is the American way to extend a helping hand. I do not regret the rebuilding. It was the right thing to do.

My generation knew the United States could do anything necessary for the war effort, and we did. Women went to work in factories. Fillmore High School kids went to class in the morning and worked in the fields and orchards in the afternoon until it was too dark to see. Victory gardens at many homes supplemented food supplies. It didn't take six months to build an airplane or ship; it took weeks. The resources of America accomplished the task. Men volunteered or were drafted for the military and knew they would probably be overseas until the job was finished. For many, it was several years until 1945 brought an end to hostilities, and they came home.

It is the present that is unsettling. Our military cannot function without imported computer ware and iron and steel manufactured in other countries. Even the fabric for uniforms is made elsewhere. Shoes are no longer manufactured in the United States. Basic items for the military are made in another country. I think we still provide most of the food, but that is about all. The factories are closed. The steel mills are closed. The shipyards are closed. We still have part of the auto industry working, but without steel from home for parts, the plants in Detroit would soon close down too. Even their tools will not work without computer chips. It looks to me like we will be up the creek without a paddle.

When you go shopping, nine out of ten items you buy are made in China. Our scrap iron, copper, and other raw materials are going to China as fast as it can be put on ships and hauled over. We have lost our ability to gear up for war if we are attacked again. I am old enough that I may not see the next BIG ONE, but a lot of our citizens and the military are going to have a real surprise when we are left holding the bag. We are supposed to learn from history, but I doubt it. It seems to just repeat itself!

The Greatest Generation WWII

After a class reunion for the 1944 and 1945 group, I have been thinking about the greatest generation. As we age and hit the eighty- or ninety-year-old mark, at least a couple of years on either side, I realize how different the times have been during our lives. I suppose many areas of California were similar to the Midwest where I grew up. Perhaps the citrus ranchers around Fillmore fared better than most during the Depression, but their workers felt the brunt of that time from the late 1920s to 1950s.

Most of us were born in the mid-1920s to hardworking parents. The United States was getting back to normal after WWI, and the economy was pretty good after that war. Almost without warning, the bottom dropped out in '29 and the Great Depression was upon us. As companies failed, there were fewer jobs, more unemployment, and agriculture prices hit bottom. As children, we knew things were different because many fathers no longer went to work. In my family, my father and another man shared a job in the New Mexico oil fields so each had a small check at the end of the month. Our mothers learned to cook whatever was available to feed us and planted garden plots with fresh vegetables to supplement. They patched and let out clothes to keep our bodies covered and cherished printed flour and feed sacks as yardage to make shirts, underwear, and dresses since kids still grew. Parents felt fortunate if the rent was paid on time and the family had a roof over their heads. As a ten-year-old, I had a hard time understanding taxes and how you could own a house and still be out on the street if taxes were not paid.

With no welfare of any kind, families moved in together, shared what food and shelter they had, and just managed to exist and keep the kids in school if possible. Many kids dropped out of school by fourteen if they could find any work at all. Often their money was essential for survival of the group and might only be fifty cents for a day's work. Credit was only used to buy food when a family was desperate.

Anything else could wait until there was cash to pay for it. Kids learned they did not ask for things. There was no money.

My mother divorced, and she ended up back with her parents on a small Oklahoma farm. Of course, she took her two kids along. Only men ended up riding the rails looking for jobs across the country. Their families doubled up somewhere. Gene's father had a job from sunup to after sundown, and it was a dollar a day for seven days a week and never any vacation or sick leave. He was fortunate to have work. The job did provide a small three-room house that overflowed when an aunt, uncle, and two small girls moved in with them for several months. A grandfather also lived with them in his final illness before dying.

President Roosevelt pushed to get the WPA organized. It provided jobs and a small wage to unemployed people—they built public buildings, bridges, and improved roads. Rural roads in Oklahoma were widened with better drainage and new fencing installed. Many small bridges still show the date of construction during the 1930s. Some drainage ditches in Bardsdale were lined with rocks and still work fine. Interviews with early day pioneers were written down and later put into print. If you get a chance to read these WPA collections, you will learn a lot from the elders of that period. These stories would have been lost to us if they were not recorded by the WPA. Our little two-room school even had a WPA music teacher who came once or twice a week to Prairie Valley and Deese to teach us singing and piano. The WPA found all kinds of jobs for people. The government gave people jobs, a small check at the end of the month, and hope.

The free public school lunch was started during this period. I am sure that these lunches were the only good meal many kids had each day. Our WPA cook walked seven miles each day to get from his home in town to our rural school to cook beans for us every morning. After work, he walked seven miles to get back home. The menu had nothing but beans and corn bread for that first year. As the government bought surplus food, the next year, he supplemented the beans with fresh apples and California raisins for pies and whatever else the US sent him for commodities. We weren't proud; we'd eat anything he could cook. In the spring, he planted a big garden. During the summer, he harvested and canned the vegetables, so he expanded our menu the following year. He was GOOD. These jobs gave everyone hope. Men had a place to go to every morning and a small paycheck at the end of the month. It was cash for survival.

The CCC was organized for young men to do conservation work. A camp up Sespe made a road and many trails into the backcountry. Shelter, food, and clothing were provided for these men, along with health services. It was similar to being in the army, but most of their paychecks went directly home to mothers. These men were providing for siblings and parents too. They had pride in their work, often learned new skills for the future, and developed pride in themselves. The good food and outdoor experience gave them strong bodies, and they were fit to do anything asked of them.

The Oklahoma Dust Bowl farmers literally starved out. Those poor people went anywhere they could to escape the terrible weather conditions that buried fences with red dirt and smothered the few cows they still tried to pasture. Many headed to California, the fabled land of milk and honey. Eventually, Steinbeck wrote his *THE GRAPES OF WRATH* and made them famous; however, his book did not improve their living conditions as they struggled to find a job in a new place or followed the fruit harvest.

Slowly, slowly the financial situation improved for the whole country. It was a gradual turnaround. Kids got a little older, a few more jobs were developed for fathers, and we got PEARL HARBOR!

That was a major jolt in a lot of ways. WWII brought activity in every form of business and factory and farm in the United States. Our country was a self-contained unit—we had unlimited manpower and raw products to produce everything needed for the war effort. Rubber needed to be imported, but everything else was right at our fingertips. Rationing keep home consumption at a reasonable rate, and everything else went into winning the war.

The early draft filled the needed military requirements. Able men in the CCC were among the first to be called. Women were used to transport planes and fill office and medical needs for the army and navy. Fillmore had several women who joined for duty along with the men. In a mass exit, women started working out of the home. For the first time in the history of the United States, there were jobs outside of teaching and domestic work for women. Aircraft factories were a living museum for Rosie the Riveter. Ladies welcomed wearing pants and tying back their hair in bandanas or snoods for safety. They learned they could do about anything a man could do. The gals moved from the farm and small towns to cities with factories. They had their first taste of real independence while husbands and brothers trained in the military and soon shipped out for duty overseas. The US mail was usually the only way to stay in touch. *Your Hit Parade* played sentimental ballads, and the big band sound was born for dancing in USOs and recreation centers and airplane hangars.

Every town was given a quote for raising money to be used in the war effort, and Fillmore always went over the top. Fillmore schools raised money to help buy the Messie Bessie bomber. Fillmore grad Walter Moreno was a captain in the Eighth AAF. He was the pilot of the Messie Bessie and probably the one who let the Fillmore kids name his Flying Fortress. After many successful flights over Germany, France, and Belgium, he had a hard landing and crashed on their return to an English airfield. Often badly damaged planes were used for spare parts to keep the others in the air, but Captain Moreno insisted the Messie Bessie be repaired and put back into service. He and his crew flew several more missions in her before the war was over. Fillmore High School also raised money to buy a fighter plane. Several P-38s from the Van Nuys air field crashed up the Sespe during training.

Messie Bessie

Virginia LeBard was attending Buckhorn School and won their essay contest. When Buckhorn School won the scrap drive in the county, they were given the honor of christening a new ship, the SS *John Bidwell*. Virginia had the thrill of actually doing the job.

Servicemen from Port Hueneme were invited to send a weekend with families in town and be entertained for a change of pace from their training. People everywhere went out of their way to help boys away from home. One town in Nebraska met every troop train, day or night, with refreshments for the boys.

Kids all did their part by saving foil from cigarette and gum wrappers and toothpaste tubes. Do any of you remember the slogan "Lucky Strike Green has gone to war"? Those cigarettes had a green wrapper. Copper was used in some way for the green color, and it was needed in the war effort, so the packaging was changed to white. Yes, Lucky Strike Green did go to war. Every school had a collection box where you dropped balls of foil and tin cans each day as you went into your first class. Tin cans were carefully washed and flattened for that collection. Bacon grease was strained and put into cans to be sent for manufacture of munitions. Much of the American scrap metal had been sent to Japan before the war started. As the need for metal for making weapons developed, every school across the country had scrap drives. My high school had a contest between classes. (Of course, my class always won any contest they threw at us.) Kids searched every pasture, ditch, and backyard for ten miles to bring in scrap metal. (We did have to return an old cast iron bathtub that a farmer used to water his cow. Drats! And it weighted a ton, but he still wanted it back.) I wonder if some of our Oklahoma bacon fat ended up at Burmite in Newhall to make powder for bullets. As a country, we were united in mind and body. We would win this war!

People never went hungry, but the selection was limited. The lucky ones either lived on a farm and raised their own food (my situation) or had family on a farm so they milked their own cows and churned butter and had chickens, eggs with beef, and pork to slaughter as needed. People living in the cities did not have those luxuries. They had to stretch their ration points and hoped what they wanted would be available. (Oh, the lines when any store received a shipment of toilet paper.)

Some of the new brides tried to follow husbands until they were sent overseas. Ventura County had lots of them who came to be near the men stationed at Port Hueneme and along the coast. In 1943, the County Health Department and the State Department of Public Health combined to provide maternity and medical care of wives of lower-grade service personnel. Any infant under one year was given care for serious illness. Congress provided funds for this purpose.

The USO planned entertainment for the men stationed at the new air base near Ardmore, Oklahoma. The Red Cross instructed women in skills needed to take care of emergencies. I took a class on cooking in large quantities and nutrition. (Scout Troop 406 benefited from that training ten years later when I cooked for summer camp sixteen years.) We tore up old sheets and rolled bandages for field use. Felt hats were cut and made into booties/shoes for European babies. Nothing was wasted.

Gene moved to California with his family and started his junior year at Fillmore High. Classes started about seven every morning, and after lunch all the kids headed to work—usually on the local farms. The packinghouses had a few older men to train/supervise, and the boys and girls learned to sweat and do the job. Local fruit was still picked, packed, and hauled by train to the port for shipment. (A local Fillmore boy got really excited when he saw a box of Fillmore oranges when he was in a Russian port.) Sugar beets were topped and picked and sent to the factory in Oxnard to be made into sugar to be shipped all over the country and used in the war effort. Rationing made the girls learn to make cookies with more honey than sugar, but boyfriends in the military did not complain as they often had more crumbles than cookies when the box arrived. When the girls discovered you could pack with popcorn to keep the cookies whole, the guys ate the packing too. Surprise food boxes were shipped as often as possible, but it was often weeks before they were received. The men fighting in Europe requested warm stockings or boot liners to help with the extreme cold. Letters were often written on V-mail—a very thin sheet of onionskin paper that you put the message on one side, folded along the lines, and addressed on the outside. This system got more mail with less weight to the troops. You worried when mail did not come to you from your favorite fellow overseas. You knew he was either too busy fighting or was unable to write—neither a good omen. If a girl decided to break up with her guy in the service, she wrote "Dear John" and told him. That is how the term *Dear John letter* got started.

An agreement with Mexico brought the bracero program to Fillmore. Most of the men in the Fillmore camp came from Michoacán. Housing dorms and a dining hall for 250 men were built near the packinghouse. Herky Villasenor was put in charge of the food, and it was reported they made about five thousand tortillas a day to feed the men with three meals. Meatless days were observed twice a week as requested for everyone in Fillmore. Herky was paid $1.38 a day per worker for food. This cost was then deducted from the worker's check. On days when it rained and they could not work, the packinghouse paid for their food. A clinic was held twice a week for any illnesses that developed. The pickers signed contracts for either three or six months, and the US provided transportation from their homes in Mexico to the US job site. The pickers earned from five to eight dollars a day and sent most of their money home. The local school kids could not do all the needed work, and the braceros were badly needed.

In June 1945, German prisoners of war from the Saticoy facility were brought to the vicinity of Fillmore to pick fruit. Most of the men were from twenty-eight to thirty-eight years old and noncommissioned officers. Allan Lombard helped give them instructions in German before they started work. There was a short film with German narration to help them. Although Germany had surrendered in May, transfer of prisoners had not been completed.

The *Fillmore Herald* kept news about Fillmore men in a special column on the front page. The weekly report told who had just joined or been drafted, where they were stationed, who was home on leave, and other things of interest to their readers. Often there was a special story sent home by one of our boys about missions accomplished. Most of that news was classified and not repeated until after the war was over. Everyone was careful about ever repeating anything that would help the enemy. Usually, the men never told anything that was a military secret, but the stories you now see in the movies were things that actually happened during the war. Our generation learned responsibility in many ways.

Fillmore had an aircraft spotting tower behind Central Avenue around where the post office is now located. It was manned twenty-four hours a day with people watching for enemy aircraft. They were trained to recognize both foreign and domestic planes by silhouette. Each residential block had wardens to help remind people about blackouts, rationing, and other things to make life run smooth. After the Japanese sub fired on Gaviota, thing tightened up too. The idea of an invasion was always near the surface on the minds around here.

As the tide began to turn with the war, things loosened up a bit. From 1943 to 1944, Gene was a senior, and the kids had a full day in school; sports were back in leagues, and life was returning to seminormal. Gas was still rationed, sugar was in short supply, meat and butter were rationed on the short side, and shoes were still just one pair a year; but people adjusted. Many boys in the class of '44 were drafted as soon as they reached eighteen; a few received their diplomas anyhow, but some had to do more work in later years to get that prized piece of paper to make their mother happy. A local gas station owner filled some gas tanks for the kids without a ration stamp so they had ditch day. Farmers received a larger gas allotment for equipment, so they helped out a little too. Kids managed and still had a good time. (An old annual for Fillmore High in 1945 listed 498 boys from Fillmore in the military service from a population of less than five thousand.)

Travel was limited for civilians. Even with the speed limit at thirty-five miles an hour for cars, a gallon of gas only took you a few miles, so you didn't waste it. Trains were used in moving troops, and it was often almost standing room only for civilians. A few found it necessary to make trips, but it was discouraging to think about the difficulties ahead. If you were brave enough to try it, you needed to take along most of your food as the diner might run out of everything—they too were rationed on food.

When the war was over, it was time to get back to normal again. Men soon started coming home from the military, and each had a good story to tell about his years away from home. Some were so terrible they were never retold, but there were enough good ones a returning serviceman could share with family and friends. Jobs were reclaimed as promised. Factories soon started making kitchen appliances and cars and all the things we had done without for five years. Salaries increased a bit, and soon those paychecks went into buying things for the house—and maybe even buying a house. The GI loans available for veterans enabled many to make their first home purchase. The Depression kids still were careful about accepting credit and paying off loans. As their babies arrived, before any health insurance, pennies took on more meaning; and no one wanted to overextend. Men worked extra jobs to help pay for things they wanted for their families. Women left the factories and married but kept an interest in continuing to work. After learning independence during the war, it was hard to go to being totally dependent upon anyone, even a husband. Many of the women were happy to be staying at home, but many had learned about business and jobs and wanted to continue working in a peacetime job.

After five years without construction materials, the home market was bursting at the seams—all the new families needed a place to live. Newlyweds lived in garages, small apartments, and little granny flats until they got finances worked out. Two or three couples banded together for spaghetti dinners in tiny rooms with barely enough space to sit down, but they had fun, and it was cheap. Movies had been a prime source of entertainment during our lifetime and continued to be after the war. Fillmore Theater was within walking distance for us. That was fortunate since we did not have a car. Many of our new husbands continued to play baseball and basketball in a city league—oh, how much fun those games provided for players and spectators. Cards and jigsaw puzzles on a coffee table made many evenings quickly pass. The fellows were home, we were married, and we were all happy.

The GI bill helped with college costs for many of the returning veterans. There were ag classes at the JC in Ventura. Those helped many vets improve farming techniques and learn how important it was to read and read and read to keep up on the latest methods of farming citrus. Many of the labs during the war were now working on new products for farmers. New fertilizers and pesticides flooded the market, and the fellows needed to know what would be best to use where they worked. It was a changing time.

After years of being separated, couples had figured out what they wanted in life. The boys in the army had either received a Dear John letter or continued to get the daily letter from that girl waiting at home. By the time they married, most had found a life partner. There have been fewer divorces in that group. Few girls were pregnant when they married. Weddings were usually pretty, simple, and inexpensive. Everyone had better things to spend their dollar on than a short extravagant day.

As soon as possible, new families bought their first house and committed to monthly payments and taxes. Finances were taken seriously, and new kitchen appliances had to wait until the savings account had a good down payment accumulated. To pay for babies, a little bit was tucked away each month for doctor and hospital fees before a baby arrived. A hundred twenty-five dollars usually paid for five days in the hospital and the doctor who delivered the child. We were young and seldom needed medical attention, and it was a good thing because health insurance was almost unknown. Children were immunized on schedule; the new wonder drug penicillin was administrated in an emergency, and vitamins were doled out each day. As young families grew, dads advanced in their jobs, and living was slightly easier on everyone. Mothers took extra jobs to pay for dance and piano lessons and cotillion for all the kids. Manners were important. Being polite was insisted upon. Evening dinner was important, and the family sat down together for at least one meal a day. Many mothers continued to sew formals and school dresses. Kids walked to school, went to bed on time, and did their homework. If they got into trouble at school, Dad's first question would be, "And what did you do to cause that problem?" Parents assumed the schoolteacher or principal had a reason for correcting their child.

Communities needed volunteers to keep the PTA, Boy and Girl Scouts, and 4-H Clubs helping the kids. Little League got started. Schools did lots of drama programs and presentations for the town. Everyone—teachers, kids, and parents—worked to give the students experience in doing lots of different things. Art and music were important. Summer camp and brief vacations to see the world outside of Fillmore added to things for the children. Summer fun was an afternoon at the plunge or playing in the Sespe or maybe just being lazy under a backyard tree after chores were done for the day.

It seemed like before we could turn around, Vietnam descended upon us. Sons had grown up and became a part of that war. Daughters found jobs to help pay for college expenses and wanted to take care of themselves. Family funds were split between tuition and house repairs. Often mothers worked more while they worried about the boys in 'Nam and prayed they would return safely. Some returned, and many did not. Fathers who fought in WWII thought we should either win that war or pull out. Eventually, the United States abandoned the whole mess, and our sons came home. Then it was time to try to put their psyches back together. Many of these young men never recovered. Now they grow old carrying that war in their heads and on their bent shoulders.

As grandchildren arrived, we welcomed each one and enjoyed them to the fullest. More of our kids got divorces. More changed jobs frequently. More did things we did not approve of but accepted since we loved them dearly. We tried to raise them properly, but it was a different time. Now when there was a problem, they often thought parents could bail them out, and we often did. When all else failed, they depended upon public funds to keep them afloat, buy food, and often pay their rent. Why worry about working when you didn't have to? We failed to teach them the discipline, pride, and responsibility that we learned in the '40s. We tried to pass our values on to them, but often the lessons did not take.

Our generation still stands with pride and patriotism for the national anthem or when the flag passes in a parade; hats are always removed, and certain songs bring tears to our eyes. We cling to our generation. There will never be another like it in the US—and maybe that is a good thing. Many of us still live frugally and do not fret over having big-ticket items or fancy cars. We wear clothes as long as they do not have big holes in them; our favorite pastimes are TV, naps on lounge chairs, and books. We never want to stop learning. We will volunteer with hospice, civic clubs, meals-on-wheels, and all the kids' thing we worked with for years and years. We enjoy having contact with young people, helping them and advising. We try hard to wait until asked for advice but seldom manage that. Our interests in community affairs continue. As long as we live, we will try to live by the golden rule and make our country a better place for everyone. We are often ashamed of things our country does and disagree with politicians, but we will always support our troops. We never miss a chance to vote. Our ranks are thinning every year, and reunions have fewer attending. We still move, talk, and remember like the elderly but never admit to being old. We may not be the greatest generation, but we are the grittiest!

THE END

FACTS, FUN, FICTION

To my readers: The FACT is, we are taking a short vacation, so I won't be writing for a couple of weeks, and I hope you miss me.

We expect to have lots of FUN along the way, and I may get that stagecoach ride I wanted last year, but things did not work out on the BLM land in New Mexico.

It is FICTION that I have been run out of town. I shall return and be prepared for some new stories!

INDEX

Guiberson, J. A., Jr., 64
Guiberson, John, 308
Guiberson, S. A., 8, 295

H

Haase, Adolph, 305
Haase, Inez, 317
Haase, Paul, 5, 184
Haase, Rudolph, 305
Haase, Ynez, 38
Hagel, Tim, 58
"Bear Howard," 275–77
Haines, Herman, 270
Haley, Gary, 196
Hall, Walter, 190
Hanna, Chuck, 268–69
Hansen, Chet, 288
Hansen, Margie, 261, 288
Hansen, Sarah, 162
Hardison, Domingo, 303
Hardison, L. M., 105–7
Hardison, Wallace, 218
Hardison family, 107
Harmonson, C. A., 8, 64
Harmonson, Tillie, 168, 263
Harmonson family, 8
Harper (hatchery worker), 27
Harrison, Ben, 119
Harthorn, C. W., 307
Harthorn, Stella, 188
Hassheider, John, 86
hatchery, 27–28
Hawthorns, 8
Hays, Bob, 317
Heanan, Ethel, 64
Heilman, John, 271
Heney, Francis, 50
Henley, John George, 64, 266–69
Hiberly (principal), 91
Hickman, Peggy Gutierrez, 283
Highway 126, 38, 154, 278

Hill, Roy, 316
Hillhoit, A. J., 26
Hinckley, Bill, 195
Hinckley, Catherine Cruson, 96, 288–89, 294
Hinckley, Hattie May, 288
Hinckley, Ira, 288, 294
Hinckley, John, 299
Hinckley, J. P., 25, 64, 93, 299
Hinckley, Kate. *See* Hinckley, Catherine Cruson
Hinckley, Lawrence, 288, 293–95
Hinckley, Mildred, 288, 295
Hobson, W. D., 49, 51
Holley, Maud Goodenough, 167
Holley, Minnie, 86
Holley, Raymond, 304
Holley, Sarah, 86
Homburg, Elizabeth, 298
Homeseekers' and Tourists' Guide and Ventura County Directory (Milliken), 63
homesteaders, 4, 39, 82, 112
honey, 9, 33, 64, 85–86, 305
Hooper, Arlie, 207
Hopper, Ari, 36, 54–55, 282
Hopper Creek, 36, 122, 282
Hopper Mountain, 36, 212, 278–79, 282
Horse Thief Trail, 273, 278–79
horse thieves, 273–74
hot springs, 11, 139
Howard, Bear, 275–77
Howard, Frank, 180, 212, 215
Howard, Gerald, 13
Howard, Jeff, 275–76
Howard, Jesse. *See* Howard, Bear
Huanduraga, Petra H., 284
Huddison, J. J., 26
Hueneme, 23, 49
Huestis, Bob, 182, 316

CPSIA information can be obtained
at www.ICGtesting.com
Printed in the USA
BVHW030545070320
574388BV00001B/2